MW01107313

Tyranny of the Minority

Tyranny of the Minority

*The Subconstituency Politics
Theory of Representation*

Benjamin G. Bishin

TEMPLE UNIVERSITY PRESS
Philadelphia

TEMPLE UNIVERSITY PRESS
1601 North Broad Street
Philadelphia PA 19122
www.temple.edu/tempress

Published 2009
Printed in the United States of America

⊗ The paper used in this publication meets the requirements of the American National
Standard for Information Sciences—Permanence of Paper for Printed Library Materials,
ANSI Z39.48-1992

Library of Congress Cataloging-in-Publication Data

Bishin, Benjamin G., 1967–
    Tyranny of the minority : the subconstituency politics theory of representation /
Benjamin G. Bishin.
        p.   cm.
    Includes bibliographical references and index.
    ISBN 978-1-59213-658-2 (hardcover : alk. paper)
    1. Political participation—United States.   2. Minorities—United States—Political
activity.   3. Representative government and representation—United States.
4. Political psychology.   I. Title.

JK1764.B52 2009
320.973—dc22   2008030995

2 4 6 8 9 7 5 3 1

Contents

Preface

Minorities frequently seem to trump majorities in American politics. By and large, not only are theories of representation powerless to explain such outcomes but because so many focus only on representation in the aggregate, we also seem to overlook the fact that such outcomes occur at all. Given these gaps in our understanding, scholars pay too little attention to the questions of who is represented and under what circumstances. One consequence is that published research about legislative representation is much more sanguine about American democracy—in particular, the degree to which popular sovereignty exists—than the evidence seems to justify.

This book is an attempt to address these questions by developing a unifying theory of representation that explains how the different facets of democracy interact. My goal is to apply scholars' insights about citizens and candidates to explain legislators' behavior in Congress and campaigns and the degree to which it reflects citizens' preferences. In so doing, I try to synthesize a series of literatures into a coherent explanation of the American democratic process. To whatever extent I am successful, much of the credit goes to my friends and colleagues.

Ernest Hemingway, in *A Farewell to Arms,* alludes to the utter irrelevance of watching someone else's college play football. The metaphor seems apt. This work has benefited immensely from the generosity of an unusually large number of friends, acquaintances, and colleagues who have shared their thoughts and their time to help improve it. While it would be unfair for them to shoulder much blame for the shortcomings of this work, whatever insights and advances are produced are attributable to their assistance, and so they should share at least some of the credit.

I have been exceptionally fortunate to have a handful of friends and colleagues without whom this project would not have been completed. Chris Dennis is among the most generous people I know and serves as a terrific role model and lunch partner. Feryal Cherif and Matt Lebo each read and commented extensively on multiple drafts of virtually every chapter, and their insights and intellect have made this book much stronger. Their advice, support, and friendship are exceptionally valuable and deeply appreciated. For Matt, this manuscript was some else's football team. For Feryal, this manuscript was someone else's sport.

Jim Adams, Ric Uslaner, and Vince Hutchings, each among the nicest people in the discipline, spent far more time with this manuscript than I had any right to reasonably request. Others provided valuable support through encouragement. My grandfather John Cesario has long been my most vocal advocate. Since my days at the University of California, Los Angeles, Barbara Sinclair has supported this project. I also owe a tremendous intellectual debt to Gary King and Micah Altman. It has been seven years since I was a fellow at the Harvard MIT Data Center, but the intellectual environment they created was unparalleled. I am very grateful for their generosity and the opportunity to work there. Several of the ideas for empirical tests come from conversations about politics with my friend David Karol. Many of the arguments and examples owe directly to conversations with Mike Abrams and Sergio Bendixen, who provide a "realist" perspective about politics. Mike's generously including an assistant professor in his travels through the political swamp of Miami-Dade County was especially valuable for providing the background that underlies much of this project. And Sergio is still the most interesting person I know.

Along the way, a large number of people provided comments and criticism for one or more chapters and helped shape and refine the manuscript. To my benefit (and his students' dismay), Jamie Carson assigned an early version of this book to his graduate seminar at the University of Georgia. He is a first-rate critic and friend. Barry Burden, David Mayhew, Scott Meinke, Mike Harrod, Carl Klarner, Greg Koger, Martin Johnson, and Antoine Yoshinaka all provided helpful comments at various stages of the project. At conferences I received especially helpful and generous comments from Larry Becker, Martin Gilens, Craig Goodman, Jeff Grynaviski, and Robin Kolodney.

The University of Miami diaspora (and a few of those, like Louise Davidson Schmich and Jonathan West, who are still there) read and critiqued a number of versions of various chapters. The intellectual community at Miami cut across subfields, a fact that substantially strengthened the work. I am grateful to Dan Stevens, Jeff Drope, and especially Tony Smith, who continues to read my work and provide valuable advice.

The data collection would not have been possible without the excellent research assistance of a number of undergraduates at the University of Miami, too many of whom we have lost to law school. Michelle Marlin and Eduardo Medina were terrific research assistants. Erika Fisher and Matt Incantalupo (whose work as summer research interns was invaluable) were exceptionally helpful. In an entire career, a teacher is fortunate to come across even a single student as gifted as they. I have found several. We managed to rescue Matt from law school, and, one hopes, his time at Princeton will inoculate him from any pathologies Miami cast on him. If not, he always has poker to fall back on. Erika will fend for herself in law school. At the University of California, Riverside, Tom Hayes and Neil Chaturvedi were nails in finishing up the project under the gun. Tom's work on Chapter 7 is closer to that of a co-author than a research assistant. Anwar Hijaz assisted with editing under tight deadlines, as if trying to catch my many errors was not challenging enough.

I have also been the recipient of financial assistance from groups that have made this book much more manageable. The generous assistance of the Harrison and Ethel Silver Foundation is deeply appreciated and increasingly important, given California's state budget. Similarly, I have benefited from the support of department chairs at the University of Miami and UC Riverside, Fred Frohock and Shaun Bowler.

Soliciting a book manuscript is an incredibly awkward process. Writing one is even stranger. Alex Holzman exemplifies the professionalism one wants from an editor. He is the reason this book is at this press, and I am extremely grateful for both his interest in the project and his assistance. Because of his work (along with that of the anonymous referees), the arguments and evidence are far stronger than they otherwise would have been, and I very much appreciate his support.

My greatest debts, however, are to my mother, Sharlee, who emphasized the importance of hard work, charity, and ambition, and my wife, Laura, who both inspires and sustains me. Her kindness, curiosity, intellect, and eagerness to talk about political science (and entertain friends who love to do the same) not only makes things easy; it makes everything possible. Her actions serve as a daily reminder of how fortunate I am to have found her, and I dedicate this book to her.

1

"¡Quitemos a Castro Ahora!"

I

At first glance, the man selling limes on the busy street corner in Little Havana looked like any other vendor. But something set him apart. Perhaps it was the large bills passers-by stuffed in his pockets while leaving their limes behind. Or maybe it was the reverence with which the buyers treated him. No, this man wasn't just a fruit peddler. This man was a hero. This man was Orlando Bosch.

Bosch took up selling fruit on the corner of Flagler and LeJeune in protest. After violating probation for firing a bazooka from MacArthur Causeway—the busy road linking downtown Miami and Miami Beach—at a Polish freighter, a judge refused to allow him to travel for work while under house arrest.[1] The lime peddler did more than $2,000 worth of sales in just two days and brought traffic to a halt. Clearly, Bosch still had the support of the community, despite a long history of illegal activities designed to overthrow Fidel Castro.[2] Perhaps he was a terrorist, but he was their terrorist.

The passion of the Cuban American community is hard to overstate. For decades, those seen as even mildly accommodating toward Fidel Castro were vilified in Miami's Cuban community, where even innocuous statements invited violence. In 1972, for example, a crowd listening to Julio Iglesias at a nightclub rioted after he commented that he wouldn't mind singing for Cubans. Iglesias left under police escort, and most local radio stations dropped him from their play lists (Mullin 2000). In 1975, Valentin

Hernandez murdered Luciano Nieves, a local writer who advocated dialogue with Castro. Nine years after Hernandez's conviction, Governor Bob Graham received more than 6,000 letters calling for his early release. In 1994, a lawyer named Magda Montiel Davis made the mistake of complimenting Castro as "a great educator" during a pro-dialogue conference. She returned home to death threats and protesters. Her entire office staff quit (Mullin 2000). As recently as 2004, Larry Klaman, a Republican Senate candidate, ran on the slogan "¡Quitemos a Castro Ahora! (Take Castro Out Now!)."

Given these events, politicians are understandably sensitive to the intensity of Cuban Americans. Although Cuban Americans make up just over 5 percent of Florida's population, politicians such as Senator Bill Nelson regularly stop in Miami to seek approval from leaders in the Cuban community before traveling to Cuba (March 2002). And despite most Floridians' indifference on issues pertaining to Castro's Cuba, not a single state official opposes the positions of the Miami hardliners who advocate increased restrictions on travel and trade. Even Democrats like Bob Graham and Bill Nelson, who would seem to have little to gain from courting the votes of the heavily Republican Cuban American community, support the "hardliners'" positions.[3]

Sensitivity to Cuban Americans' preferences extends well beyond Florida. In 2004, most Democratic presidential candidates supported the hardliners' positions, despite the fact that most Americans support the liberalization of ties with Cuba. Studies show that more than 66 percent of Americans and more than 55 percent of Floridians oppose the travel ban (Davies 2001; Rufty 1998).[4] Nationally, public opinion seems to have influenced politicians outside Florida, as separate bills repealing the embargo have passed both the House and Senate in the past few years. John Kerry concisely summarized this apparent contradiction with his admission that foreign policy on Cuba is dictated by "the politics of Florida" (Wallsten 2003).

Given Cuban Americans' intensity, it is not surprising that in the fall of 2002, while national headlines focused on security, terrorism, and the president's march toward war in Iraq, in Miami's newly created 25th congressional district the race focused on Cuba.[5] For the first time since Castro's rise, a major party candidate, Democratic State Representative Annie Betancourt, supported ending the ban on travel to Cuba, a centerpiece of the policies advocated by Miami hardliners. While a broad national movement was growing to repeal the trade embargo to open Cuba as a market for American agriculture, in Miami, Betancourt's stance was heresy.

Betancourt's stand was courageous, but it was also calculated. Her opponent Mario Diaz-Balart, scion of Miami political royalty, is Representative Lincoln Diaz-Balart's brother and the son of Rafael Diaz-Balart, who served as majority leader in the Cuban House of Representatives from 1954 to 1958 (Nielsen 2002). Diaz-Balart was politically connected and well funded. Even more daunting was the fact that Diaz-Balart drew the newly created 25th district for himself. After term limits had forced him out of the state Senate, he took a step down and ran for the state House in order to chair the Redistricting Committee. In so doing, he set himself up as a heavy favorite to win the plurality Republican 25th.

Betancourt was no slouch, though. Previously elected to the state House of Representatives from a district encompassed by the 25th, she had defeated a well-known Latina television personality to win the Democratic primary. Her most valuable asset, however, was her name: Betancourt was the name of a prominent Cuban family and one of Cuba's first presidents. Cubans would recognize her as one of their own. To non-Cubans, particularly those in the western part of the state who might not vote for a Hispanic, the name Betancourt seemed innocuous.

Public opinion was also with Betancourt. For the first time since Castro's ascent, a series of polls showed that a majority (57 percent) of Cuban Americans supported ending restrictions on travel to Cuba (Bendixen 2002). In the 25th district, which is more than 63 percent Hispanic, most of whom are Cuban, Betancourt's move was not just courageous, it was politically astute.[6] With a single announcement, Betancourt set the agenda for the campaign, generated immense free publicity, and temporarily made the race appear competitive.

Ultimately, Diaz-Balart's advantages were insurmountable. Betancourt was trounced. In a district in which Al Gore took about 45 percent of the presidential vote (despite a 43 percent to 35 percent Republican registration advantage over Democrats), Betancourt managed a meager 34 percent (Zollo 2002). While the candidates shared several important characteristics, including their Cuban American heritage, their shared emphasis on Cuban issues was perhaps most surprising. As one editorialist put it, "For a while it seemed like Diaz-Balart's only issue was his claim that Betancourt had only one issue" ("Best Political Miscalculation" 2003). Diaz-Balart emphasized Betancourt's stand on Cuba despite the fact that she propounded the majority's preferred position on the most important issue in the district.[7]

While Betancourt's support for liberalizing ties with Cuba may be viewed as a turning point in the politics of south Florida, it also serves as evidence of a more general political phenomenon. Betancourt lost while espousing the majority view on the most highly salient issue in the election. Perhaps even more curiously, Mario Diaz-Balart, the candidate propounding the minority view, did his best to focus the race on that issue. In so doing, he directly contradicted prevailing theories of representation that suggest Diaz-Balart should have moderated his position on the travel ban to appeal to the largest number of voters.

Precisely because the outcome runs contrary to basic tenets of democratic theory—candidates' supporting the position preferred by the majority of voters should be victorious—the example provided by the race for Florida's 25th district directly challenges the premise underlying what R. Douglas Arnold (1990) calls the most fundamental question facing students of political science: To what degree can citizens in a democracy control their government? Outcomes in which minorities triumph over majorities lead us to question whether citizens can control their government at all.

While Orlando Bosch and the politics of south Florida are unquestionably unique, the counter-democratic example of a candidate's positioning on liberalizing ties with Cuba is not. Considerable evidence suggests that minority-preferred positions often gain elected officials' support. Whether it is Pennsylvania's Senator Rick Santorum supporting the criminalization of homosexual relations ("Gay Issue" 2003),[8] President Bush opposing the importation of prescription drugs from Canada (Nusbaumer 2003), California's Representative Henry Waxman promoting the regulation of vitamins and labeling in direct opposition to a district full of health-conscious consumers (Schwartz 1993), Florida's Democratic senators repeatedly supporting restrictive Cuba policy, or Florida's Governor Jeb Bush sending state police to seize the brain-dead Terri Schiavo to have her feeding tube reinserted,[9] minority positions seem frequently to win when pitted against the will of the majority.

II

Do Legislators Represent?

Democracy is characterized by its emphasis on the values of popular sovereignty, the idea that the majority should rule, liberalism, the idea that all people are equal, and liberty. A system in which minorities prevail over majorities appears inconsistent with these values.

Given the anecdotal evidence that politicians frequently take positions a majority opposes, it is hardly surprising that academics disagree about whether legislators represent their constituents' preferences. On the one hand, dozens of studies suggest that politicians are highly responsive to their constituents' preferences (e.g., Bartels 1991; Bianco 1994; Bianco et al. 1996; Erikson 1978; Erikson et al. 1975; Fenno 1978; Holian et al. 1997; Jackson 1971; Jackson and King 1989; Mayhew 1974; Medoff et al. 1995; Page et al. 1984). These results are counterbalanced, however, by many other studies that find little evidence of representation once alternative explanations are considered (e.g., Bernstein 1989; Bernstein and Anthony 1974; Cohen and Noll 1991; Dennis et al. 1998; Fiorina 1974; Kalt and Zupan 1984; Kau and Rubin 1979, 1993; Lindsay 1990; Page et al. 1984; Peltzman 1984; Poole and Rosenthal 1997; Wilkerson 1990). Of course, many studies find mixed evidence; for a variety of reasons, responsiveness appears large on some issues but nonexistent on others (e.g., Achen 1978; Bond 1983; Elling 1982; Hero and Tolbert 1995b; Hutchings 1998; Key 1963; Kuklinski 1978; Miller and Stokes 1963; Pinney and Serra 1999; Theriault 2005).

Despite the considerable disagreement about whether or not legislators represent, there is much greater consensus about the process through which legislators try to represent. In the paragraphs that follow, I describe the traditional account of representation. I call it the demand model, which is characterized by politicians who consider the views of their entire district when making decisions, and who try to do what constituents either want or are likely to want.[10]

The Representation Process

Perhaps the most common view of how representation works is the "Demand Input Model," which holds that the public demands policy from its elected representatives, who respond (Wahlke 1971).[11] Citizens are linked to their representatives, who, motivated by reelection, produce policy that reflects the majority's preference (Fenno 1978; Mayhew 1974). Citizens evaluate legislators' behavior through elections. Legislators are responsive when their behavior is influenced by constituents' preferences. This basic model describes dynamic representation and behavior over time, as well as behavior across issues in a particular legislature.

One important challenge to the idea that legislators respond to constituents' demands is offered by Robert Bernstein (1989), who suggests that legislators could not behave retrospectively even if they wanted to because citizens lack meaningful preferences on most of the issues legislators confront in Congress. This observation, which is supported by extensive research on public opinion (e.g., Converse 1964; Delli Carpini and Keeter 1996), leads to an important question: How can elected officials represent people who lack meaningful preferences?

A pragmatic answer to this dilemma describes legislators who seek to account not just for the district's opinion on an issue, but for citizens' latent (i.e., Key 1963) or potential preferences, which might be aroused by a challenger or an interest group before the next election (Arnold 1990). In Arnold's view, legislators must account for both current and potential preferences, the latter of which are weighted by the probability that they will be informed and aroused. This explanation accounts for politicians who are either prospective or retrospective, as well as for limitations in the public's knowledge and interest. Jane Mansbridge (2003) describes the prospective process in which legislators seek out constituents rather than simply respond to their expressed preferences retrospectively as anticipatory representation.

While virtually every representation study empirically investigates responsiveness in a manner consistent with the demand input model, as we will see, relatively few suggest that legislators are entirely retrospective. To date, however, only a handful of empirical representation studies account for these differences (e.g., Stimson et al. 1995).[12] While it is difficult to observe cases where citizens' opinions were never aroused because astute incumbents were proactive, evidence suggests that incumbents anticipate threats by looking to the behavior of their most recent challengers and co-opting their issues (Sulkin 2005).

Tracy Sulkin's (2005) observations are especially valuable in that they demonstrate one means by which campaign behavior affects behavior in Congress (e.g., Canes-Wrone et al. 2002; Jacobson 2003), an observation that may help to reconcile differences between retrospective and prospective views of representation.[13] When combined with the iterative nature of the democratic process—the overwhelming majority of incumbents repeatedly stand for and win reelection—one can infer that whether politicians appeal to citizens' expressed or potential preferences, in either Congress or in the campaign, they work hard to satisfy voters. Legislators who anticipate a preference and act on it in Congress can then incorporate that position into their next campaign, both to appeal to voters and to insulate themselves from their challengers' attacks. A legislator's action on the issue in the following Congress amounts to a retrospective appeal to those voters. The repeated process of campaigning and legislating essentially simplifies to a process consistent with the demand input model described by John Wahlke (1971). In the chapters that follow, I refer to studies that assume that candidates and legislators appeal to voters as the demand model, whether the mechanism is retrospective, prospective, or some combination of the two.

In addition to sharing a view about how representation works, the demand model holds that politicians advocate constituents' majority-preferred alternative. Consistent with the notion of popular sovereignty, in a democratic republic responsive politicians are expected to appeal and respond to shifts in the view of the majority. Scholars typically account for this expectation either by imputing a unified preference to constituents (e.g., Theriault 2005) or by averaging districts' characteristics to estimate the majority-preferred alternative.[14] In the latter case, the strength of majority support is often assumed to vary across districts with the proportion who support a position.[15] Large numbers who support one position will pull the district's average toward that position. No matter how it is measured, this majoritarian perspective assumes a perfect liberalism in which all citizens are equal; the views of the legislator's most vociferous critic are given the same weight as those of the staunchest supporter (Achen 1978). Hence, only by considering everyone's views can the majority-preferred position be identified.[16] As we will see, this assumption is highly problematic (e.g., Canon 1999).

Since most of the controversy about representation arises from studies that examine whether legislators represent their constituents' policy preferences, the demand model is applied to questions of policy responsiveness.[17] When we observe typical legislators, whether in committee pursuing allocation responsiveness (e.g., Hall 1996; Shepsle 1978), doing casework pursuing service responsiveness, or at home in the district projecting a sense of "home style" and pursuing

symbolic responsiveness, we find them preoccupied with servicing their constituents (e.g., Fenno 1978, 1996; Mayhew 1974). The controversy about whether
legislators represent does not seem to extend to other aspects of representation.

In many ways, the demand model is quite satisfying. After all, when we
observe legislators closely, they seem to work hard to satisfy their constituents'
demands (e.g., Mayhew 1974). While they may not always be responsive on
policy, they are responsive in other ways (Eulau and Karps 1977), so the system
seems quite responsive overall (e.g., Fenno 1978).[18] Such results imply that pluralist democracy is alive and well. The elected work hard to respond to citizens'
preferences. A cursory glance at the democratic process, however, suggests there
is considerable slippage in the degree to which elected officials respond to the
citizenry.

A Party-Based Theory of Representation?

Party provides a plausible alternative theory of representation that explains
behavior of both voters and elected officials. Party identification serves both as
the single best predictor of individuals' voting decisions (Campbell et al. 1960)
and as a simple heuristic for holding elected officials accountable for their
actions in office by evaluating candidates based on their party's performance
(Arnold 1990). Party leaders also provide legislators with a voting cue, especially
on those votes about which they know little or lack strong preferences (Kingdon
1971).

Party leaders directly influence legislators' decisions as well. One view, called
conditional party government, holds that as the majority party becomes more
homogeneous, party leaders are better able to advance their policy agenda
(Rohde 1991). Alternatively, some hold that legislative parties act as cartels that
both dispense benefits and enforce rules to overcome collective action and coordination problems (Cox and McCubbins 1993, 2004).[19] Through agenda control, the party induces legislators to vote as it wants.

A vibrant literature illustrates the mechanisms and effects of party (e.g., Cox
and McCubbins 1993; Lebo et al. 2006; Lowell 1902; Rohde 1981). The power
of political parties is contested, however, because party members are more likely
to share the same issue preferences and background characteristics. Most nota-
bly, Keith Krehbiel (1993, 1999) questions the power of party and suggests that,
unable to distinguish between the alternative explanations of party and preferences, most studies that document the effects of party are inconclusive.

Despite this, parties play little if any role in most representation theories,
because legislators frequently cast roll-call votes against their parties' positions.
A single national platform inhibits the flexibility candidates need to reflect the
wide variety of interests that constituents have across districts and states. Consequently, because so many violations of party voting occur, representation

studies tend to discount the effects of party as conduits for representation. Instead, scholars disregard the central role of the citizenry and examine party leaders' influence on legislators' decisions in Congress independent of the influence of constituencies.[20]

Subconstituency politics provides an explanation for why politicians take positions contrary to those advocated by their parties. Politicians spurn their parties to exploit the benefits of subconstituency intensity. Moreover, party leaders not only accept but may also encourage such behavior because they recognize that the disproportionate power that accrues to the party is dependent on the party's maintaining its majority status. A party's ability to pressure members is tempered by members' need to be reelected.

Three Puzzles

If, as Harold D. Lasswell (1936) says, politics is the study of "who gets what when and how," then clearly the provision of policy is a central, perhaps even the most important, form of representation. Provision of policy is essential for people to get what they want and need from government. When policy representation occurs, the actions of the elected reflect the preferences of the largest portion of the citizenry.

Given contemporary events, even a casual observer of politics may question whether the majority will prevails. Since policy responsiveness is the most carefully studied aspect of representation, the failure to explain legislators' policy behavior is a major limitation of the demand model. As commonly expressed, the demand model advocates a view that leads to three puzzles, a fact that implies that it poorly explains the democratic process.

Studies that examine the policy link between legislators' behavior and constituents' preferences reach conflicting results that the demand model cannot explain (see Bishin 2000; Fiorina 1974; Krehbiel 1991; Shannon 1968; Uslaner 1999 for reviews). As seen earlier, while some studies find that legislators reflect constituents' policy preferences, numerous others find that legislators are responsive only sometimes or not at all.[21] Post hoc explanations for these conflicting results, such as the Issue Visibility Thesis, which holds that legislators' responsiveness increases as issues become more visible, are untested and, at best, leave us with an incomplete understanding of representation that is unable to explain most of what occurs in Congress, since most issues are of low visibility to the public (e.g., Kuklinski and Elling 1977; McCrone and Kuklinski 1979; Miller and Stokes 1963).

Compounding matters, published studies almost certainly overstate the degree to which legislators are responsive on policy. Consider the process through which political-science research is published. A scholar interested in assessing the influence of constituency on legislators' decisions is likely to have a difficult time getting a manuscript published if the key constituency variable that assesses responsiveness is not statistically significant.[22] Moreover, it is difficult to construct tests that demonstrate that representation does not occur because conventional statistical tests do not allow us to demonstrate the existence of "no relationship." Instead, the researcher is only able to find that we cannot reject the possibility that there is no relationship between constituents' preferences and legislators' behavior. The bias against publishing null findings (e.g., Gerber and Malhotra 2006), taken in combination with the conflicting results observed in published scholarship, suggests that support for the demand model is likely weaker than commonly thought.[23] Finally, the standard for a finding of responsiveness is shockingly low. Scholars typically report a finding of responsiveness any time constituency preferences are significantly related to legislators' behavior. Such a finding, however, indicates only the existence of some, perhaps very small, relationship.

A second puzzle arises from the study of candidates' positioning in campaigns. The logic of the demand model is typically applied to campaigns and holds that candidates should appeal to the average voter in the district through the median voter theorem. The logic holds that candidates who offer policy to the median voter position themselves closest to the largest number of voters. Little evidence exists to validate this prediction, however. In response, a large literature has developed to explain why candidates diverge from this apparently optimal position (e.g., Adams et al. 2004; Burden 2004; Groseclose 2001; Lewis and King 2000; Merrill and Grofman 1999; Rabinowitz and MacDonald 1989).

Many of these studies are theoretical, however, and not easily tested. Contrary to models that suggest that candidates converge to the center of the distribution of voter preferences on the issues salient in their districts (Downs 1957; Enelow and Hinich 1984; Hinich and Munger 1997), evidence suggests that candidates usually take non-centrist positions (e.g., Adams et al. 2004). The directional and discounting models have been offered to explain this finding. The directional model posits that voters evaluate candidates according to the direction and intensity of their proposals, thus giving candidates an incentive to deviate slightly from the median position (Rabinowitz and MacDonald 1989). The discounting model suggests that voters discount what candidates say they will do and instead consider the positions that the legislator is likely to be able to implement (e.g., Lacy and Paolino 1998, 1999; Merrill and Grofman 1999). One major weakness with these explanations is that they do not accurately reflect the level of sophistication of either the voters or the candidates whose behavior they are attempting to predict. As a result, explanations for candidates' taking non-centrist positions predict relatively modest divergences from the median.

Demand models poorly explain candidates' position taking, a crucial aspect of the democratic process. As with the conflicting results in the legislative-representation literature, the lack of voter and candidate convergence implies a misunderstanding of how representation works.

A third puzzle emerges from work that investigates voters' opinion and participation. Perhaps the most widely reported finding in the opinion literature is that the American public is unknowledgeable about and uninterested in politics (Converse 1964; Delli Carpini and Keeter 1996). Citizens' representation and interest is crucial to understanding representation inasmuch as these characteristics raise questions about both citizens' ability to evaluate elected officials' performance and legislators' need to consider citizens' views. While the demand model offers explanations of how civic participation might explain responsiveness by anticipating citizens' potential preferences (e.g., Arnold 1990; Bailey 2001), these alternatives have yet to be empirically examined. Moreover, apathy among citizens is especially problematic, since even if citizens become informed, it is not clear how, why, or under what circumstances they might act. Consequently, while the demand model offers a potential solution to citizens' limitations, as yet it offers little empirical evidence to support its theory. Thus, we have a poor understanding of how citizens' civic capacity affects politicians' behavior in campaigns and in Congress.

These puzzles suggest that prevailing theories of representation as reflected by the demand model inaccurately describe the democratic process. To reconcile them, I offer a new theory—called subconstituency politics theory—in which groups of intense and active citizens, rather than the citizenry as a whole, constrain legislator behavior.

Toward a Unified Theory of Representation

This book develops a unified theory of representation based on subconstituency politics. Subconstituency politics occurs when politicians advocate the preferences of groups of intense citizens over those of the majority in a district. The theory provides an explanation for democratic political behavior that links our understanding of the capabilities and attributes of the citizenry, the role of campaigns and elections in translating the people's views into policy positions, and the behavior in Congress of those who win election. In so doing, it builds on work that seeks to provide macro-democratic theories that describe entire processes rather than focusing only on democracy's component parts (e.g., Sulkin 2005).[24]

Scholars focus a great deal of attention on legislators' behavior in campaigns, in committees, and on roll-call votes but are only beginning to develop theories that simultaneously explain behavior in all of them. As a result, we have learned a great deal about particular aspects of the democratic process, but the ability to generalize our findings is limited. Seldom do theories explain how representation works across the different aspects of the democratic process, examining, for instance, how position taking in campaigns affects roll-call voting in Congress. Only recently have scholars have begun to develop and test theories that explain behavior across democratic venues.

Such theories are rare because they require knowledge of distinct, though complementary, subfields. As Sulkin (2005) points out, the organization of the political-science discipline and, in particular, the division of American politics into the study of behavior and institutions further militates against the development of broad theories that cross subfield boundaries. In the case of subconstituency politics, social psychology explains citizens' opinions and intensity, and the intensity of opinion influences candidates' position taking, which in turn affects legislators' behavior in office.

Despite the scarcity of holistic theories, the idea that subjects central to these subfields affect actors central to others is not especially controversial. Behavior scholars have long recognized that group identity and attachment affect citizens' attitudes (e.g., Campbell et al. 1960). Similarly, students of campaigns note that citizens' opinions affect candidates' campaign positions (e.g., Downs 1957). While under-studied, the notion that candidates' campaign behavior affects their roll-call behavior, and vice versa, is also widely accepted (e.g., Canes-Wrone et al. 2002; Jacobson 1983; Sulkin 2005). Finally, a number of scholars have examined the degree to which aggregate government policies move in tandem with citizens' preferences (Stimson et al. 1995).

While scholars increasingly recognize the importance of subconstituencies such as Cuban Americans, no theory of representation exists that adequately explains why and how politicians appeal to intense minorities rather than to the district as a whole. This book rejects the often unstated, but almost always present, liberal assumption inherent in the demand model, which holds that politicians view all citizens equally. Instead, I develop and test a theory of representation that accounts for the observation that not only do politicians appeal to groups but also the groups to which they appeal may vary across districts and issues. While normatively appealing, treating all citizens equally mischaracterizes the nuanced way that politicians actually see their constituencies (e.g., Fenno 1978) and overlooks the possibility that politicians' view of their constituencies might vary across issues, districts, and elections (e.g., Bishin 2000; Clausen 1973).

A good deal of evidence has accumulated suggesting that politicians appeal to different groups in different districts. Research shows that candidates target their appeals to specific groups within the constituency depending on the nature of the district (Huntington 1950), and that the degree to which a legislator supports particular positions is related to the existence of groups that may act as a source of control (MacRae 1958). Even legislators from the same state and party may represent different groups of constituents who provide them with different benefits (Dexter 1957; Schiller 2000, but see Higgs 1989). Politicians thus see the constituencies to whom they appeal as variable. The particular groups to whom candidates make themselves heard depend on the incidence of costs and benefits to the groups. Arnold (1990) explicitly defines these groups of knowledgeable, informed, and interested citizens as "attentive publics."

This is not to say that scholars entirely overlook the fact that politicians appeal to groups. To be sure, many studies look at the impact of specific groups, most often by accounting for a group's district population and then imputing preferences to all members. To the extent that subgroups have been broadly considered (e.g., Fiorina 1974), they have generally been defined in narrow, usually partisan, terms focused primarily on the idea that politicians appeal only to fellow partisans (e.g., Clinton 2006; Wright 1989), partisans plus independents (Medoff et al. 1995), those who vote (Griffin and Newman 2005), or past supporters (Clausen 1973).[25] Moreover, examples of politicians' appealing to groups in current events, such as Vice President Al Gore's rejecting Clinton administration policy and opposing the deportation of Elian Gonzales during the 2000 presidential campaign, are common. In general, however, groups are considered in a largely idiosyncratic and atheoretical way that fails to account for the fact that the groups that matter vary across issues, districts, and time.[26]

Groups must be considered in a systematic way, because differences in legislators' behavior are related to heterogeneity within districts (Bailey and Brady 1998; Bishin et al. 2006; Goff and Grier 1993). Studies that account for subconstituencies find a more consistent role for constituency as an influence on legislators' behavior (e.g., Bishin 2000; Peltzman 1984; Wright 1989). Moreover, applying several of the various constituency concepts described earlier, Robert Weissberg (1979) shows that differing constructions of constituency lead to very different results about the degree to which legislators represent. Failing to understand when and how politicians appeal to groups means that we fail to understand how and when citizens influence their elected officials.

The purpose of this book is to develop and test a unified theory of representation that overcomes the limitations of past representation research. To do so, I build on past research that recognizes the importance of intense minorities via issue publics (e.g., Converse 1964; Dahl 1950), the role of interest groups (e.g., Berry 1999; Hansen 1991; Olson 1971; Schattschneider 1960; Truman 1951), and social identity theory (e.g., Tajfel and Turner 1986; Turner et al. 1987). Subconstituency politics holds that, owing to the fact that different voters care about different issues with differing levels of intensity, the will of minorities is often represented at the majority's expense.[27] Politicians appeal to the preferences of passionate subconstituencies to build coalitions of intense supporters who are more likely to participate.

Subconstituency politics is grounded in social identity theory (Turner et al. 1987), which explains how and why individuals coalesce into groups. Subconstituency politics provides an explanation for the behavior observed in the everyday actions of politicians including those of Mario Diaz-Balart. It holds that politicians appeal to minority preferences over those of the majority when the benefit of advocating the minority's position outweighs the cost of alienating the less interested majority. The remainder of this chapter is devoted to defining and explaining the subconstituency politics theory and laying out the plan of the book.

The Challenge of Politics

Getting votes from a citizenry that is politically uninterested and unknowledgeable is a difficult challenge, yet candidates' careers depend on their ability to transform passive citizens into active supporters. Appealing to groups of voters called subconstituencies helps solve this problem. Individuals carry multiple and overlapping social identities created through past experiences, which serve to frame the way that they perceive the world. Group identities are activated in large part on the basis of candidates' policy and non-policy (i.e., symbolic) positions. Once an identity is activated, individuals who share it view issues in the context of the group, thereby leading to shared preferences and intensity. Candidates try to develop coalitions of intense groups of individuals who care so strongly about a particular issue that a candidate's advocacy guarantees those individuals' support in the next election. Candidates build a coalition of supporters by developing platforms consisting of positions across multiple issues, each of which appeals to intense groups of constituents. Groups are disproportionately valuable to candidates because their members are not only more likely to vote but also more likely to provide other important resources. Once elected, candidates' behavior reflects the positions of the groups to which they appeal.

In a sense, subconstituency politics merely articulates a phenomenon long described by politicians and observed by journalists, but too frequently overlooked by social scientists—that politicians see constituents not as individuals, but as groups (Hamburger and Wallsten 2006). For many voters, an issue, or small group of related issues, may exist such that a candidate's position will dictate the voter's support. While subconstituency politics theory shares some basic characteristics of the demand model, the different views of constituency generate different implications. A summary of the differences between traditional representation theories and the subconstituency politics theory is seen in Table 1.1.

The main difference between these theories lies in the way the model accounts for constituents' influence. Rather than appealing to the constituency as a whole, politicians appeal to groups of citizens who are likely to be intense on particular issues. Through the course of this book, I show how this crucial distinction serves to explain the puzzles described earlier, comports better with

TABLE 1.1 DIFFERENCES IN CHARACTERISTICS OF REPRESENTATION MODELS

	Subconstituency Model	Demand Model
Politicians' proximate goal	Reelection	Reelection
Primary influence on behavior	Intense groups of citizens	Average citizen
Does responsiveness vary across issues?	No, but the group to whom legislators respond varies	Yes, depending on the visibility of the issue
Amount of knowledge and interest required of the average citizen	Low	High
Other influences on politicians' behavior when citizens lack meaningful preferences	Ideology, party	Ideology, party

the observations of political observers, and overcomes two central observations of research on political behavior: that the average citizen knows and cares little about politics, and that candidates seldom appeal to the median voter.

Methodology

For decades, the unavailability of data has impeded the study of representation. While progress is continually being made, data do not yet exist that, for example, allow for the reliable estimation of citizens' preferences for congressional districts or for small groups within a state or district, or of opinion on a wide variety of less visible issues with which politicians regularly deal. To overcome these limitations, I test the subconstituency politics theory in a wide range of contexts, evaluating as many implications as possible. Specifically, I test the theory's implications in each of the three aspects of the democratic process: public opinion, candidates' behavior in campaigns, and legislators' behavior in Congress.

Doing so requires a mixed-methods approach, employing both case studies and statistical analyses to investigate each of the various aspects of the competing theories of representation. The use of statistical analyses to draw broad generalizations about the nature of representation is often limited by the unavailability of the data necessary to perform such analyses. Two examples stand out. First, reliable estimates of subconstituency opinion are seldom available for congressional districts. Second, data on the opinion of constituents are rarely available on low-visibility issues, which tend to get less news coverage.

To address this limitation, I maximize the generalizability of the results by examining a broad range of policies based on their visibility. Since proponents of the demand model hold that visibility conditions whether or not politicians represent, issues reflecting differing visibility levels are examined. More specifically, I test the implications of the subconstituency politics theory in the context of the Cuban trade embargo (very low visibility), the extension of hate crimes to cover people based on sexual orientation (low visibility), the extension of the ban on assault weapons (high visibility), and abortion policy (very high visibility). Within these particular issues, observations for which particular groups are most likely to exist, and are thus typical of cases where groups exist, are identified to investigate whether politicians respond to such groups. Importantly, because the issues and groups to whom politicians respond vary across issues and districts, as we will see, some observations represent easy tests of subconstituency politics, while others are hard. To the extent that diversity within a district conditions representation, the degree to which an issue constitutes a difficult test can vary dramatically across states and districts.

The incorporation of case studies, a method often overlooked in studies of legislative representation, has ancillary benefits as well. While broad statistical analyses are essential for drawing generalizations about the state of representation, scholars who employ them frequently overlook the substantive impact of representation and cause us to alter the questions we ask about representation. We often speak, for instance, of "responsiveness," a term that describes whether legislators move with their constituents, rather than examine whether legislators are behaving in the manner preferred by, or most consistent with, the views of their constituents. The subtle distinction is important because, as Weissberg (1978) points out, one can observe high levels of responsiveness on issues in which few legislators behave as their constituents would prefer. Examination of candidates' and legislators' positions on specific issues is a simple way to overcome this problem.

A second challenge in investigating the power of subconstituencies is to ensure they are identified in a systematic way and thereby preclude the ad hoc construction of groups for the sole purpose of evaluating the theories. Given the formal definition of groups in the chapter that follows, in any district one is likely to find some configuration of citizens who have common characteristics and fit the data simply by mining public-opinion polls for compatible results after an issue has been resolved. To assuage this concern, the tests that follow rely only on groups identified in previous research. In most cases, I rely on the taxonomy of (largely informal) groups identified by Stanley Greenberg in his book *The Two Americas* (2004). This book defines and describes numerous groups that are identified by their demographic, socioeconomic, and experiential characteristics, all of which relate to socializing experiences that are consistent with the way psychologists view social identities as being formed. Greenberg links these groups to issues they care strongly about, which we can then apply to test the subconstituency politics theory. These groups, which include, for instance, "The Faithful," "F-You Boys,"[28] "Secular Warriors," and "Super-Educated Women," when combined with more widely recognized and well-researched groups such as African Americans, gays, and Cuban Americans, provide independent verification of the existence of formal and informal groups that are active on the policy issues investigated herein and thus allows for a rigorous testing of the subconstituency politics theory.

Despite important differences in institutional design created to influence responsiveness, a general theory of representation should apply to both the House and the Senate. Theories that explain only one chamber or one issue are not very general. Throughout the book, therefore, I test the implications of the theory across chambers. To the extent that these results are consistent across issues and chambers, confidence in the generalizability of the theory and our conclusions increases.

Plan for the Book

The subconstituency politics theory explains citizens' and politicians' behavior in the democratic process. Because subconstituency politics is a psychologically based theory, its implications should be widely generalizable across countries and levels of government. As a first step, this study tests the theory using citizens' knowledge, as well as the behavior of candidates for, and legislators in, the U.S. Congress. Testing subconstituency politics in the context of congressional behavior provides a robust test, since races for and behavior in Congress reflect a diverse set of actors in a wide variety of social and electoral contexts. Moreover, studying Congress offers the potential to contribute greatly to our understanding of representation, since it has been a primary focus of representation research.

The book proceeds in three sections. Chapter 2 completes the first section and articulates the subconstituency politics theory more fully. The second section of the book, Chapters 3–5, focuses on testing the implications of the theory: Citizens' propensity and ability to hold politicians accountable is better explained by subconstituency politics than by the demand model, and the process through which politicians represent constituents is the same for candidates in campaigns and for legislators in Congress. In both cases, politicians appeal to subconstituencies rather than the district as a whole. The third section of the book consists of two chapters that apply the theory to address two unresolved questions of representation. Subconstituency politics suggests an alternative explanation for the puzzling result that politicians from homogeneous states are more responsive than those from heterogeneous ones (Bailey and Brady 1998). Subconstituency politics also directly challenges the issue visibility thesis, which holds that the visibility of issues conditions responsiveness. These applications show that subconstituency politics better explains the interplay between citizens' preferences, candidates' position taking, and legislators' behavior. The book proceeds as follows.

Chapter 2 articulates the logic underlying subconstituency politics. Candidates take non-centrist positions in campaigns to appeal to intense groups of constituents who hold positions that are more extreme than those of the average citizen. Because of these groups' intensity, the benefits obtained from appealing to them frequently outweigh the benefits obtained from appealing to the district's average voter. Moreover, taking extreme positions does not cost candidates the votes of those who disagree, since different people care about different issues. Precisely because the average citizen does not feel intensely about the issue, a candidate's advocacy of the minority position seldom prevents her from obtaining the support of the voter who is opposed to the position but does not feel strongly about the issue. Once elected, legislators work to implement the positions they advocated in the campaign.

Chapter 3 performs a "crucial test" of the implications of subconstituency politics and the demand model for individuals' political knowledge. A common explanation for the conflicting results of representation studies is that politicians are responsive only on visible issues since these are the issues on which citizens are most likely to notice legislators' behavior. This explanation is called the issue visibility thesis, and it explains how the likelihood of citizens' becoming informed drives the conflicting results in the representation literature. Specifically, it holds that enhanced visibility, through media coverage, leads to higher levels of knowledge among citizens. The demand model thus implies that those who are more highly exposed to news media should be more knowledgeable about politics. In contrast, subconstituency politics implies that people are more knowledgeable on issues that relate to an activated group identity and generates the hypothesis that citizens with an activated group identity should exhibit increased political information about issues pertaining to that identity. Consequently, subconstituency politics reconciles the ignorance and apathy commonly ascribed to the citizenry with the democratic requirement that citizens be able to hold the elected accountable.

To test whether subconstituency politics explains behavior within and across democratic venues (i.e., in both campaigns and institutions), Chapters 4 and 5 develop and test its predictions on the issue positions taken during campaigns and on the roll-call votes cast in Congress, respectively.

In Chapter 4, I examine candidates' behavior on two "hard," low-visibility issues: the Cuban trade embargo and the extension of hate-crimes legislation to homosexuals. These are issues about which most citizens lack meaningful opinions and about which responsiveness is expected to be low. I also examine two "easy" issues, partial-birth abortion and banning assault weapons, in which conventional theories are thought to best explain legislative behavior because almost all Americans have meaningful opinions on the issues. More specifically, I test the hypothesis that subconstituency preferences positively influence candidates' campaign positions. Chapter 4 shows that the positions candidates and legislators take appeal not to the average voter, but to subconstituencies.

Chapter 5 demonstrates that the positions legislators take in Congress reflect the preferences of the groups to whom they appeal in their campaigns.

Specifically, I test the theory in the context of legislator behavior in Congress. I test three specific hypotheses: First, subconstituency preferences are positively associated with legislators' roll-call votes; second, once elected, candidates' campaign positions are positively associated with legislators' roll-call votes; and third, legislators from districts with active subconstituencies are more likely to take a leadership role on issues important to the group in the district. In combination, the results of these tests show that legislators' votes in Congress are directly influenced by subconstituency opinion and indirectly influenced through campaign positions that are influenced by subconstituencies. In addition, legislators from districts with active groups are more likely to take leadership roles on the issues that are important to the groups.

Chapter 6 applies the theory to resolve the curious finding that the impact of constituency has been found to vary depending on the degree to which a polity is heterogeneous (e.g., Bailey and Brady 1998). The implication of such research is that the process of representation varies across these states according to diversity. Subconstituency politics instead suggests that, owing to how constituents' preferences are measured, it is easier to detect responsiveness in homogeneous than in diverse states. More specifically, in homogeneous states and districts, the relevant subconstituencies are larger and thus more similar to estimates of mean state opinion. Consequently, the subconstituency politics theory of representation implies that diversity is not associated with increased responsiveness; therefore, legislators from diverse districts should be as representative as those from homogeneous districts. The results show that once we account for subconstituencies, representational differences across states are no longer apparent.

Chapter 7 empirically investigates the demand model's explanation for the conflicting results observed in the literature on roll-call voting that legislators are more responsive on more visible issues. Subconstituency politics holds, in contrast, that legislators should be responsive to groups regardless of levels of issue visibility, since group members are acutely sensitive to issues related to their group identities. Thus, the subconstituency politics theory hypothesizes that legislators will be no more responsive on visible issues than on less visible issues.

Chapter 8 concludes by summarizing the results and discussing the implications of subconstituency politics for democratic theory and for applied politics. The central conclusion is that candidates and legislators are quite responsive but neither in the manner commonly thought nor to the public as a whole. Instead of responding to centrist opinion, they respond to intense subconstituencies. Consequently, subconstituency politics provides a view of representation that is contrary to pluralist principles. In the end, it explains why Mario Diaz-Balart wins even though he advocates minority-preferred positions.

2

The Subconstituency Politics
Theory of Representation

I n the summer of 2000, in the midst of a tight campaign, the Democratic vice presidential candidate Joe Lieberman prepared to do some television interviews. Just before going on the air, an aide suggested that Lieberman "brush the chest hair poking out of his open-necked shirt." Lieberman responded, "Its OK. There's a constituency for chest hair" (Connoly 2000).

While Lieberman's droll response represented a moment of levity, for students of politics it symbolizes something of much greater significance. Lieberman's quip speaks to a world in which candidates and campaigns view voters not as atomistic individuals, but as groups of individuals clustered around shared experiences and common interests.

Subconstituency politics explains why and how politicians appeal to groups. Borrowing from social psychology, the theory explains how one's socializing experiences inform the groups with which one identifies and how candidates exploit individuals' social identities to encourage beneficial political behavior. The chapter explores three general themes, each of which addresses the behavior and motivation of the theory's core actors: groups, individuals, and candidates and legislators. I begin by defining the concept of a group and articulating its political importance. Next, I examine how and why individuals are transformed into groups and why social identities, which provide the mechanism that underlies this process, are so valuable to politicians. Then I explain the role of candidates and legislators who compete to make particular identities salient and thereby strive to activate groups that they think will benefit them. Once elected to Congress, legislators work to service these groups. The final sections develop a typology of candidates' positioning and legislators' behavior and identify the hypotheses implied by the theory. In so doing, I provide the basis for the tests and applications that are the focus of the chapters that follow.

The Definition and Nature of Groups

In studies of politics, the term "group" usually refers to organized interests. In *The Governmental Process* (1951), David Truman outlines the pluralist definition of groups as people who interact, the product of which leads to shared attitudes and beliefs. While people may share opinions or attributes, it is only through physical interaction that an organization of political consequence can be formed. Truman's definition is also consistent with the traditional view of groups from the perspective of social cohesion theory, which stresses group members' interdependence and interaction. Similarly, in *The Logic of Collective Action* (1971), Mancur Olson defines groups as formal organizations that are characterized by a desire to further the interests of their members.

While these definitions seem appropriate for the study of organized interests, they overlook the fact that some groups are not formally organized (e.g., Schattschneider 1960).[1] Individuals who have neither met nor formally joined an organization may share identities and, hence, attitudes stemming from shared experiences and interests. Consequently, studies of group behavior overlook an important aspect of political participation: that groups need not be organized to be influential.

The subconstituency politics theory holds that politicians overcome the problem of lack of interest among citizens by exploiting the fact that people coalesce through common experiences, outlooks, and interests. In the political context, politicians do this by making appeals that activate identities that relate to these experiences and thereby energize groups around issues. This view of how representation works relies heavily on the self-categorization theory of social identity (e.g., Turner et al. 1987) which holds that, to varying degrees, individuals categorize themselves as either unique or as group members depending on circumstances and context.[2]

Instead of requiring interaction or interdependence, groups consist of individuals who share some activated social identity that is the antecedent of the group.[3] Social identities form in response to one's social environment and thus are largely a product of life experiences. Jan Stets and Peter Burke (2000, 225) summarize the group as "a set of individuals who hold a common social identification or view themselves as members of the same social category." Group membership serves as a source of esteem and causes people to "think, feel and behave and define themselves in terms of group norms rather than unique properties of the self" (Terry et al. 1999, 284). Moreover, "self categorization leads to psychological group formation—subjects demonstrate collective behavior in the form of shared responses" (Turner et al. 1987). Importantly, because individuals see some identities as more central to their esteem and identity (i.e., who they are), issues that tap these identities provoke highly passionate responses. A group forms when an issue that activates an identity in large numbers of people becomes salient. The activation process is a form of social priming.

These characteristics have important implications for politics. First, they allow the concept of the group to be determined beyond the reach or discretion of the individual. Social circumstances, rather than an individual's decision, often serve to highlight particular events that may activate a specific identity. The absence of individual control increases the chance that commonalities can be exploited by outsiders, such as a candidate, to evoke a shared response. Skilled candidates can thus overcome the problem of individual lack of interest by activating the group identities they think will benefit them.

Subconstituency politics theory thus defines a group as *a constellation of people, either organized or not, who share a social identity owing to a common experience that leads to shared concerns and preferences.* This definition reflects the fact that two individuals can identify as part of the same group even though they have never met. Despite having never met or joined an organization, African Americans from Oregon and Florida, for instance, may hold identical and intense preferences on civil-rights issues owing to a shared experience of racism. Importantly, this definition does not exclude those who belong to well-organized groups, as long as members meet these criteria. On many issues, groups consist of those who are members of a formal organization, as well as those who hold similar attitudes based on shared experiences but who have neither joined a group nor interacted with others.

By this definition, the existence of a group necessarily means that there is a shared social identity. However, that identity may not always result in shared views that are *politically* useful. For instance, veterans share a general experience of having served in the armed forces of the United States. And they seem to share preferences on a wide variety of topics. Recent work shows, however, that they do not seem to have shared political preferences (Bishin and Incantalupo 2008). For political purposes, veterans are often latent. Ultimately, the degree to which groups share views on an issue is an empirical question.

Latency

Research shows that individuals' identities are dynamic (e.g., Huddy 2001; Turner et al. 1987). At any given time, some of an individual's identities are active (or salient), while the others are latent, or inactive. Members of latent groups may exhibit the behavioral characteristics of those who are unaffiliated with groups (i.e., individuals) in terms of the resources and effort required for a politician to activate them. More specifically, if an identity is not active, individuals may revert to a more "natural state," taking an interest in politics only when they see it as relevant to an active identity (e.g., Abrams 1999; Katz 1960). Individuals act based on their active, often apolitical, identities which are usually primed by non-political actors and events.

Important aspects of the social-identity perspective are categorization and depersonalization, in which an individual seeks to classify another person as similar or different based on an ideal example, called the prototype, of one's own salient social group (Hogg 2006). In this process, the individual who is the object of classification is depersonalized in the sense that he is evaluated based on the degree to which his group-related attributes conform to those of the prototype. This process produces favorable impressions if the object's attributes are similar to those of the prototype and negative impressions if the attributes are different (Hogg 2006).

The political implications of ingroup and outgroup categorization lie in the fact that intense reactions can be evoked by stigmatizing someone as different from one's group identity. Thus, one effective strategy for politicians who seek to appeal to groups is to classify their opponents as different from the groups to whom they are trying to appeal.

Politicians try to make beneficial identities salient. By recognizing that skilled politicians can activate latent identities by raising relevant issues to create or activate new groups, this definition of group goes beyond the specific cases of issue publics and interest groups, which refer to active and generally long-standing associations, to provide a more general explanation of why groups are so powerful. Moreover, it is useful to note that skillful politicians raise issues designed to highlight what people have in common.

While it shares some similarities, this definition of the group differs substantially from the concept of issue publics (Converse 1964).[4] Unlike V. O. Key's (1963) inattentive groups, Phillip Converse's issue publics do not include those with latent identities that are not yet activated. The concept of issue publics also overlooks the tie between interest in an issue and an individual's experiences that link similar socializing processes to shared views. This link is important for subconstituency politics because it is the socialization that leads to intensity on the issue. Moreover, issue publics refer to all persons with an interest in a particular issue, not just those with a particular view on the issue. In marked contrast to the perspective offered here, on contentious issues, issue publics include groups that both support and oppose a given issue position.

The definition of groups employed by subconstituency politics also allows for recognition of the fact that the role and meaning of the concept of the group has different implications for individuals than for candidates. For the individual, the importance of the group lies in the benefits that accrue from membership according to the social-identity perspective. These need not be tangible, as identification with a group has been shown to enhance esteem, to reduce uncertainty in making evaluations, and to help to balance between the desires of sameness and uniqueness (Hogg 2006). On some issues, group membership, such as party identification, may thus provide a heuristic shortcut.[5]

The example of party identification nicely exemplifies several of the points made in this section. Even the earliest studies of party identification saw partisanship as an affective attachment to a political party that stems from one's personal socializing experiences (Campbell et al. 1960). More recently, scholars have shown that party is more than an affiliation; it is a social identity that appears to be constructed through these experiences, a fact that explains its stability over time (Green et al. 2002). Party is an especially valuable exemplar of subconstituency politics, as candidates regularly make explicitly partisan appeals at least partly to exploit identifiers reliance on party as a heuristic. Moreover, it illustrates the point that one may have a social identification without being a member of a formal group, as when political scientists find that independents who reject formal membership often behave more like partisans than do self-identified party members (e.g., Keith et al. 1992; Petrocik 1974). This point further illustrates the distinction between the individual and the conception of the group. As noted earlier, one may develop an outgroup identity (indicating distinctiveness from the group) that may serve to motivate behavior that contrasts with the defined group's preferences.

For candidates, the importance of the group emanates from the implications that stem from individuals' shared perceptions, which offers ambitious politicians an opportunity to gain group members' support. For example, among Cubans who immigrated after 1980, the experience of the Mariel boat lift and, for many, internment at Guantanamo Bay, shapes their outlook on issues relating to Cuba. These shared experiences give candidates an opportunity to develop policies, such as relaxing travel restrictions for those with relatives in Cuba, that exploit the social identities that stem from the shared experiences and, as in our example, thereby activate the support of these immigrants.

Social Identity and Social Context: The Role of the Individual

A particularly important aspect of social identity is that individuals have multiple group identities that stem from their categorizations, roles, and experiences. As Stets and Burke (2000, 225) put it, "Each person, . . . over the course of his or her personal history, is a member of a unique combination of social categories; therefore the set of social identities making up that person's self-concept is unique." The strength of these identities varies, and many are often latent, with their existence occasionally going unrecognized (Turner et al. 1987).

The political relevance of these associations varies depending on both the social context and the strength of an individual's group identification. The degree to which an individual's "deck" of identities is reshuffled likely depends on how important the identity is to one's ego. Alternatively, lacking a relevant context, many identities never become salient. Consequently, it is not surprising that social psychologists find that the link between attitudes and behavior are strengthened when the relevant group membership and norms are salient (Terry et al. 1999, 287).

The importance of particular identities to an individual varies depending on social context (e.g., Turner et al. 1987). Events may lead individuals to subordinate the importance of one issue and raise the prominence of another in the face of events that activate another identity. In this way, an exogenous shock may temporarily supplant primary issues and lead to a change in active identities. After the terrorist acts of September 11, 2001, for instance, the major political parties put aside their issue differences, as a nationalist American identity was activated (Huddy et al. 2002).[6] Individual associations with different groups vary but are activated based on the social context. Absent other attacks, the salience of September 11 will either diminish with time or be superseded if events occur that activate alternative identities, such as economic hardship, for instance, that at least temporarily supersede the previously active identity.

For candidates, two implications pertaining to individual behavior are especially important. First, as noted, individuals may share attitudes or predispositions on the basis of some common characteristic or shared experience, despite the absence of formal group organization, personal interaction, or interpersonal dependence or attraction (Turner et al. 1987). Neither a membership card nor an organizational hierarchy is needed for individuals with common identities to become politically active in response to visible issues. Reagan Democrats and soccer moms are two examples of groups that lack formal organization, membership, and interaction, but their shared socializing experiences lead to shared attitudes.[7]

A second implication is that group membership may go unrecognized by the individual until activated by the candidate or external events. Summarizing decades of cognitive psychology research, Turner and colleagues (1987, 29) conclude that "groups can be formed because people are categorized from the outside." This point is crucial, because it implies that candidates may be able to impose categorizations or identities and make them salient based on their perceived electoral value. Specifically, they try to take positions that will appeal to existing group identities or activate latent ones, in which case the individual may not even recognize that he is a member.

The idea that individuals have multiple social identities, some of which are latent, raises an important question about the limits of group membership. The boundaries of a group are delineated by the absence of shared self-identification

Citizens

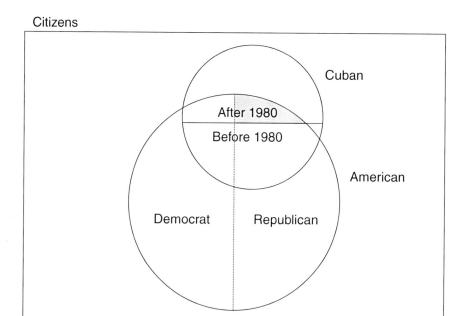

FIGURE 2.1   A stylized mapping of group identities.

or self-perception. For instance, while two Cuban immigrants may share a Cuban group identity, different socializing experiences pertaining to when they immigrated and their experience with the Castro regime leads to association with different groups when issues that expose this distinction become salient.

The manner through which group association maps from identity to political preferences can be illustrated through a hypothetical example. Since group associations are a function of personal identity, even the politically uninterested have latent group associations. If the social context does not make the identity salient, however, an individual may not think of an association for long periods of time, if ever (Turner et al. 1987). A stylized mapping of group associations illustrating these distinctions appears in Figure 2.1.

The shaded area in the figure reflects the overlapping associations of a Cuban American Republican man who immigrated in the Mariel boat lift.[8] The degree to which these various group associations are politically relevant depends on the degree to which he identifies with each group and the degree to which a particular identity is made salient to him. The events of September 11, 2001, for instance, may have shifted one's active identity from a Cuban American to an "American" concerned about national security. A particular identity is activated when something occurs that leads a person to rely on it when interpreting or evaluating events.[9] Such an event might include, for instance, a current event, a well-designed advertisement (political or not), a news story, a personal tragedy, or a public speech. Since both the identity activated and the strength of the activated identity may vary, association with a particular identity related to a group is highly variable. The intensity of group associations based on these identifications depends in large part on the degree to which the individual sees the issue as important or relevant (e.g., Sherif and Cantril 1947). As one's intensity increases, one is increasingly likely to participate on the issue.

The importance of active and intense group associations can be seen in the race for Florida's 25th district House seat described in the previous chapter. Here, differences in group identity led to widely divergent opinions among a population that is often assumed to be monolithic. Recall that Annie Betancourt attempted to capitalize on a shift in Cuban American opinion fostered by an increase in recent immigrants who hold more liberal opinions about Cuban policy. By 2004, 35 percent of Cuban Americans who had immigrated prior to 1970 supported repealing the embargo, while 61 percent of those who immigrated after 1990, an approximately equally large population, supported the same position.[10] Similar cleavages are seen across a variety of issues, including the ability to remit money to Cuba, opening dialogue with Castro, and the travel ban.[11]

Differences across these immigrant groups also underscore the differences in intensity between active and inactive group associations. Recall that members of the first wave of Cuban immigrants were political refugees; for many, Castro seized their assets and imprisoned or executed their relatives. The second wave consists largely of economic refugees. One indicator of the relative intensity of these groups is seen in their rates of political participation. Among those who are eligible, about 86 percent of the older group (pre-1970) is registered to vote, while only 22 percent of the newer group (post-1990) is registered. Hence, differences in group identity have broad political implications even among people who have a great deal in common. They may well explain Mario Diaz-Balart's landslide victory in the 2002 election.

How Voters Behave

The role and motivation of the individual in subconstituency politics theory relies on several assumptions that are supported by extensive research in psychology and voter behavior. First, and perhaps most important, individuals are more knowledgeable on issues about which they are intense and active than on issues in general (e.g., Converse 1964; Key 1963). Second, individuals' attitudes and voting behavior are seldom motivated solely by self-interest (e.g., Kinder and Kiewiet 1979). Third, research finds that candidates' positions galvanize group identities, even for informal groups, and lead them to vote as a group (Schaffner 2005). Finally, individuals may vote based on group identities activated by shared symbolic (i.e., non-policy) preferences such as traits (e.g., Hayes 2005), as well as issue preferences or stereotypes (Petrocik 1996).

Research demonstrating that citizens are more knowledgeable on issues that are important to them provides an important mechanism underlying the theory (e.g., Campbell et al. 1960; Hutchings 2003; Lavine et al. 1996). Recall that the basic framework of the demand model requires knowledgeable, or potentially knowledgeable, citizens who act as principals and thereby condition their legislator's behavior. Clearly, a citizenry that demonstrates interest in an issue—or, at least, a willingness to become interested and active—is a citizenry with which candidates must reckon. Studies show, however, that few citizens have levels of political knowledge or interest high enough to constrain the elected (Converse 1964; Delli Carpini and Keeter 1994).[12] These results imply that the traditional conceptualization of the demand model is untenable. Vincent Hutchings's (2003) work, for example, shows that citizens have knowledge levels sufficient to control legislators on those issues that are most important to them; issues that research shows are related to their group identity (e.g., Schaffner 2005). Candidates must pay attention to these groups because, unlike the district as a whole, even if the groups are not watching, they are more easily mobilized if the candidates misstep (Arnold 1990, 1993).[13]

An explanation for individual behavior called the theory of symbolic politics is consistent with an appeal to group identities. A wide range of research shows that people seldom vote on the basis of narrow self-interest (see Sears and Lau 1983 for an overview).[14] Without using self-interest as a cue, the process of issue positioning is made tremendously more difficult for candidates, since it is harder for them to determine the basis of the voting decision. An important alternative to self-interest, called symbolic politics, suggests that people acquire "predispositions in early life which influence their adult perceptions and attitudes" (Sears et al. 1979, 371). Candidates who make symbolic attitudes salient can evoke underlying political predispositions.

While subconstituency politics holds that identities continue to be formed as one ages, the process underlying the symbolic politics thesis is consistent with subconstituency politics. Consider that the development of self-interest comes from experiences that may well contribute to the creation of social identities. Irrespective of the cause, the rejection of self-interest as a motive for a wide range of behavior provides additional, albeit indirect, evidence for the subconstituency politics theory.

As we have seen, subconstituency politics holds that candidates who are best able to activate intense groups are the most likely to be successful. The greatest opportunity to activate latent groups occurs in the campaign, and the challenger is the most obvious instigator. Candidates' effectiveness depends on their ability to identify and activate key groups, especially informal ones. Informal groups provide a difficult test for subconstituency politics because, while we can easily see how issue appeals to highly organized groups such as unions could be translated into votes, it is less clear whether and how politicians activate and mobilize informal groups.

Brian Schaffner's (2005) work both explains and validates this process. Studying the women's vote, Schaffner shows that politicians recognize the important strategic benefit of appealing to women and target them by publicizing issue stands that women view as important. Women respond to such appeals and vote in higher numbers for the candidates who make them. This work demonstrates the individual voting behavior on which the efficacy of subconstituency politics rests. Groups of voters respond to politicians' appeals on positions central to the group.

Research suggests that politicians can use issues, as well as symbolic positions, such as traits, to activate social identities that benefit them. Viewed from the perspective of subconstituency politics, theories of issue ownership (Petrocik 1996) and trait ownership (Hayes 2005) imply that elections are essentially battles between candidates to activate identities that advantage one candidate over the other rather than attempts to educate voters or change their minds. In particular, these theories suggest that parties and candidates own (or lease) particular issues and traits, and that by having the election become a referendum on their preferred issues, voters are asked to make a decision while the advantageous identity is active.

In combination, these findings suggest that voters' behavior comports well with the depiction of the electoral process described by the subconstituency politics theory. Intense groups of voters either have or are more likely to obtain the knowledge necessary to hold candidates responsible for their behavior. Voters respond to candidates' cues on issues of importance to them, and candidates attempt to frame the voting decision in terms that evoke identities that provide an advantage.

The Cost of Citizens' Ignorance and Apathy

The civic shortcomings of the American voter are central to the logic of why candidates appeal to groups. Most citizens know little about politics and are unable to explain which issues go with ideological concepts; nor can they identify even the most visible political figures and their stances (e.g., Converse 1964; Delli Carpini and Keeter 1996). Citizens' lack of political knowledge is costly for candidates because informing citizens to garner their support can be expensive and ineffective.

Apathy further increases these costs. Even knowledgeable citizens may not act. The proportion of those eligible to vote but unregistered suggests that most citizens do not participate in the electoral process (Rosenstone and Hansen 2003).

Social psychologists explain such apathy as rational, because few see the direct relevance of politics in their daily lives (e.g., Katz 1960). Most of the issues citizens care about are sparked not by candidates but by external events that directly affect them, such as an act of terrorism or a plunge in the stock market.

Ignorance and apathy also make it costly for candidates to become known. Studies show that challengers require more resources than do incumbents to overcome a lack of name recognition (Jacobson 1983). Moreover, appeals to uninterested citizens waste campaign resources. If reaching these potential voters is costly, influencing their behavior may be impossible. As a consequence, it is difficult to figure out how to motivate or activate such voters. Given these conditions, candidates strive to identify those individuals who care strongly enough about one or more issues and may therefore, even unknowingly, have a stake in the system.

Candidates and Legislators: The Economy of Appealing to Groups

Appealing to groups provides politicians with many benefits. Group members are more likely to be interested, active, and knowledgeable about issues that pertain to their shared beliefs or attitudes. These commonalities offer increased potential for mobilization. Members of organized groups distinguish themselves as receptive to political entreaties through their behavior, opinions, or associations and thereby overcome the greatest barrier to participation: lack of interest. In so doing, group members make it clear that they intend to be active and thus signal politicians that their support is more likely to pay off at the ballot box and through the provision of other resources. Since individuals are not unique, appealing to groups has additional benefits because one appeal reaches many voters.

Within any constituency, groups of voters coalesce around particular policy or symbolic issues. Social psychologists and sociologists report that groups form in response to their environment on the basis of shared attitudes, experiences, or outlook (Sherif and Cantril 1947; Turner et al. 1987; Whyte 1956). Members of these groups share beliefs and attitudes about which issues matter, which positions to advocate, and how intense they feel (e.g., Rice 1928; Terry et al. 1999).

Groups provide resources to politicians. They are easier to activate than individuals and provide disproportionate benefits. In addition to voting, they may provide money, time, contacts, prestige, and information that aids candidates in their drive to get elected. In addition, they are often geographically concentrated, and this amplifies their relevance. For instance, racial and ethnic minority groups tend to be concentrated in urban areas, while farmers and religious conservatives tend to reside in rural ones. People also segregate by class. Concentration may further reduce the cost of appealing to potential voters and facilitate communication among group members about issues that affect their interests.[15] Tapping into these networks facilitates candidates' ability to disseminate political messages.

Appealing to groups is economical because groups are more easily activated politically than are collections of individuals. Because issue attitudes are related to group association, campaigns that activate such associations can use them to encourage the desired behavior—whether casting a vote or writing a check. Politicians expend fewer resources to activate these potential voters. Even when attitudes are not pre-existing, these group members are not likely to need as much convincing, only an impetus to act. While activating a shared identity may not dictate an individual's behavior, it should serve to reduce the cost to candidates who are trying to tap that identity, especially when compared with the costs of attempting to motivate the behavior of a typical, apathetic individual.

Less obviously, the social context of the group also has important political implications for candidates. First, formal groups pressure members to conform in order to reduce dissonance (Sherif and Hovland 1961; Terry et al. 1999; Turner et al. 1987). This pressure may lead to a shift in opinion or to increased apathy among group members who hold minority views. Individuals who develop such feelings may withdraw from the group or reduce the intensity and frequency of their participation (e.g., Berger 1960; Finifter 1974). Indeed, Truman (1951) finds that members of groups who have heterogeneous preferences tend to withdraw from group activity. Even when they do participate, their preferences are less intense. It seems possible that this general process may even occur, though likely to a lesser degree, among members of informal groups. The benefit to candidates is an increased homogeneity of group members.

Second, communications can be transmitted more easily and more credibly, both formally and informally, via social issue networks. Statements made by fellow group members are more likely to be perceived as valid, while those made by members of opposing groups or outgroups are not and are immediately discounted (van Knippenberg 1999). Because group members share experiences and values, information transmitted through social issue networks may be viewed by the receiver as more reliable. Research shows that people are more open to information that comes from a reliable source (e.g., Iyengar and Valentino 2000). Thus, accessing a group allows politicians not only to reach members who care about the issue but also to disseminate their message via a highly trusted source. This gives added weight to the message—an impact that is not available through mass approaches to individuals. In combination, then, group dynamics serve to provide credible and "pure" cues to members.

The appeal to groups also has practical benefits for the campaign. Groups help reduce problems of issue timing. To secure resources and become credible, candidates must adopt issue positions before the formal campaign begins and before most voters have thought much about the election. This asymmetry between candidates' and voters' positioning increases the uncertainty candidates have about the appropriate issue position to take. Candidates also need to consider the extent to which opinion or group preferences in the district evolve over time.

Focusing on groups helps overcome this problem in two ways. First, the issue positions required to appeal to groups are often obvious well in advance of the campaign. Second, the inventory of groups—a virtual census of all latent and active groups that might be activated in a state or district—may largely be known in advance of the campaign. Consequently, group appeals can be incorporated into the campaign platform and exploited to lock up early support. By adopting an intense group's preferred position, candidates can activate group identities, gain the group's support, and achieve the benefits described earlier. The characteristics of groups, and the manner in which they help candidates overcome the limitations inherent in appealing to individuals, influences how candidates build coalitions.

The Strategy of Coalition Building

With election as the proximate goal, candidates strive to obtain more votes than their opponents. The probability that a candidate will win is largely a function of the degree to which supportive district groups exist in sufficient strength and numbers. Candidates create a coalition of groups of intense supporters by developing a platform of positions across issues. The political geography of the district—specifically, the nature of the group associations—affects the positions a candidate takes, the probability that a candidate will win, and the policies the candidate will pursue once in office.

A candidate's personal political beliefs, public statements, and affiliations, as well as the groups to which he appeals, restrict the groups from which he can seek support. Groups can be seen as favorable, neutral, or opposed to the legislator's predispositions, agenda, background, or other supporters. Candidates build coalitions from among the groups that are either neutral or positively predisposed to the candidate's stated position or intention on the group's key issue or issues. Further, since American elections are characterized by single-member districts, building a coalition might be thought of as a zero-sum process. Garnering the support of one group reduces the size and number of groups available to an opponent. Keep in mind, however, that because group associations stem from social identities, an individual whose group association might favor a candidate when one identity is active may well favor a different candidate when another identity is active.

The Context in Which Positions Are Taken

Candidates need name recognition, resources, and, most important, votes to win.[16] Their behavior reflects the desire to acquire these resources. Candidates acquire these political assets in three ways. Perhaps most obviously, they advocate issue positions that are popular in the district. Candidates also acquire support through non-policy, or symbolic, positioning. By engaging in behavior that resonates with groups of voters, candidates might build reputations or images in non-policy terms. A candidate may try to develop a reputation as a religious person, for example, by publicizing church attendance to appeal to those with strong religious identities. Marisa Abrajano (2005) finds that receptivity to non-policy cues increases as education levels decrease.

A third way that candidates acquire these resources is "pre-political" (Fenno 1996). Descriptive characteristics such as race, gender, age, personal experiences or relationships, or fame from previous careers all help garner name recognition, support, and resources. Arnold Schwarzenegger's fame, for example, gave him unparalleled name recognition as a gubernatorial candidate. Such cues can provide a shortcut to voters. Support might also result from a candidate's personal life experiences, such as being a veteran or a fraternity member. In the 2004 election, the escape of Florida's Senator Mel Martinez from Cuban tyranny in Operation Pedro Pan spoke not just to Cuban Americans but to Florida's large immigrant population more broadly. In each of these cases, candidates implicitly appeal to voters who identify with a group. As each candidate's descriptive and experiential characteristics are limited and inflexible, however, so too are the groups to whom the candidate can appeal.

Examples of the importance of personal experience and descriptive characteristics on people's voting proclivities abound. Senator Edward Kennedy's well-publicized car crash off a Chappaquiddick bridge limits his support. New Hampshire Senator Robert Smith's defection from, and later return to, the GOP clearly angered staunch partisans, who removed him in the 2002 primary election. The benefit of descriptive characteristics such as race (e.g., Lublin 1997) and gender (e.g., McDermott 1997) can also be seen in selected races. Each of these factors provides cues to groups and voters that may be related only indirectly to issue positioning. In some cases, these characteristics may inoculate a candidate or give them greater freedom in the range of issues they can propound. For some voters, issue positions work indirectly and help to create stereotypes or reputations about candidates' personal characteristics on which the voting decision is based (Hayes 2005). More specifically, groups may be mobilized by symbolic or valence characteristics.

The inflexibility of these attributes implies that in most cases, issues are likely to be important either directly, because the group cares strongly about the position, or indirectly, because the issue position plays to a broader stereotype to which the group is sympathetic.[17] Issue positioning often dictates which groups can be included in a support coalition. Gun-control advocates should not expect National Rifle Association members' support any more than should candidates who have changed positions expect the support of those looking for a "strong leader." The context in which issues are taken and groups are mobilized is a product of constituencies' preferences, candidates' past group associations, candidates' individual preferences, and a function of timing.

Constituency constraints are limits that result from the nature of the state or district and stem from voter geography and the political preferences of district groups. For years, no south Florida candidate of either party would, or could, either take a stand against the Cuban trade embargo or support easing travel restrictions to Cuba. To do so would ensure defeat. In North Carolina, for instance, neither party nor ideology matter at all. Only a fool opposes the federal tobacco buyout.

The ideological predisposition of the organized groups in a constituency also conditions candidates. Candidates running in districts with large, well-organized groups must account for these preferences if they have any hope of gaining or maintaining office. When the groups are powerful, they can force politicians to respond. The case of hardline Cuban Americans in Florida is again instructive. By 2003, many hardliners were disappointed by the Bush administration's failure to take strong action against Castro and tighten Cuba policy. The dissatisfaction was ultimately embodied in a letter to President Bush signed by thirteen prominent Hispanic Republican state legislators who implied that failure to take action would lead to the loss of Cuban American support. Immediately upon receipt, the administration promised the legislators that action would be taken, and a commission was quickly appointed to study the policy. By July 2004, the administration had implemented new regulations tightening restrictions on Cuba (Corral 2003). The number, intensity, and political predisposition of the groups must be favorable—or, at least, neutral—toward a candidate for that candidate to generate the resources necessary to win.

Candidates' personal reputations and group affiliations also constrain their position taking and the groups to which they can appeal. Political party is a primary association that provides a well-organized, intense group of individuals with shared identity who work to get their candidates elected (Green et al. 2002). Party affiliation constrains candidates to varying degrees. Once elected, the party may pressure the candidate to support state- and national-level platforms, parts of which may not be consistent with constituents' preferences. A worst-case scenario is seen in the case of Representative Marjorie Margolies Mezvinsky (R-Penn.), who cast the decisive vote on President Bill Clinton's first budget and paid for it with defeat.[18] Other affiliations may have similar effects. Advocating a group's positions influences the attractiveness of the candidate to the voters outside the group—those that make up the remainder of the constituency. Further, membership in, or association with, particular groups may preclude garnering the support of other, opposing groups.

Candidates' personal preferences also limit the positions they take. One widely recognized goal is the production of good policy (e.g., Fenno 1978). Those with firm moral, ideological, or religious beliefs may reduce the set of acceptable issue positions around which coalitions can be built.

Candidates' past positions constrain their current ones because position change can be costly (e.g., Burden 2004). Legislators may switch positions when the resources gained outweigh the potential costs of alienating the group that supported the position, and the costs that stem from appearing to pander owing to the concomitant loss in perceived leadership ability. Position change seems most likely to occur when the relative importance of the groups within the candidate's constituency changes.

Dynamic Positioning

While candidates seek to activate beneficial group identities, they can also use symbolic or policy positions to activate identities that disadvantage their opponents. A candidate's pre-political advantages might be diminished by their opponent's shrewd issue positioning. One candidate's advantage in appealing to the single group in a district might be offset if both candidates take the same position on the favored issue. Alternatively, an opponent may take positions designed to deactivate groups that would otherwise support a candidate. In the 2004 senatorial race in Colorado, for example, the conservative Democrat Ken Salazar highlighted Republican Pete Coors's support of a gay film festival in his work as president of the Coors Brewing Company (Florio 2004) to undermine social conservatives' support for Coors.

A Typology of Position Taking

Expectations about candidates' positioning and legislators' behavior are guided by three observations. First, a typology should explain a politician's behavior both in campaigns and in Congress. Second, legislators and constituents do not take positions on all issues, since the distribution of constituent groups and constituents' interests in issues varies both within and across districts. Third, politicians are not free agents who can act without regard to past behavior, since past positions are costly to change. In sum, a typology of issue positioning must address the circumstances under which candidates adopt groups' positions and legislators work to implement them.

On most issues, politicians' first recorded stands are taken during or immediately preceding the campaign. Issues raised in campaigns seem more likely than congressional roll-call votes to focus on issues relevant to the district. Research suggests that even incumbents adopt new positions through the campaign process (Sulkin 2005).

TABLE 2.1   A TYPOLOGY OF CONSTITUENT CONSTELLATIONS AND CANDIDATES' POSITIONS

Scenario	A Group Exists?	An Opposing Group Exists?	Politicians' Action
1	Yes	Yes	Candidates take opposing positions closest to traditional (often partisan) supporters
2	Yes	No	Both candidates take the active group's position
3	No	No	Opinion in district does not exist or is not meaningful; other cues (e.g., party, ideology) used if position is taken at all

Subconstituency politics holds that candidates appeal to and activate groups of intense citizens to gain electoral advantage. Behavior in Congress is an attempt to serve those groups or to expand the legislative coalition. Expectations about candidates' positioning must account for the fact that individual districts vary in their preferences across issues and that the relevance of issues varies across districts. In some districts, no meaningful opinion exists on many issues, but on other issues, opinion is intense. Other districts are characterized by high levels of opinion diversity on some issues and perfect homogeneity on others.

The expectations for candidates' behavior under the varying constellations of groups are depicted in Table 2.1. Candidates' positions are forecast using the answers to the following questions: Does an active group exist on the issue? Does an opposing group exist on the issue?

In the first scenario, groups in the district disagree. Opposing candidates advocate the opposing groups' positions on the issue by selecting the position closest to their respective ideological or partisan preference. In the second scenario, when groups in the district have the same opinion on the issue, only one active group exists. Under these circumstances, both candidates adopt the position of that group. In the third scenario, groups do not exist on the issue, so candidates must rely on cues other than constituency. In particular, they take positions that more closely align with their personal preferences, ideology, or party if these cues are tied to the issue. Such issues are especially likely to go unmentioned in campaigns. Once elected, however, they may be forced to vote on such issues.[19]

An example of how groups can unintentionally coalesce around some issues despite fiercely opposing one another on others is seen in the controversies in South Carolina over gay marriage and whether the Confederate battle flag should fly over the state capital.

In South Carolina, two groups were activated on the flag issue. African Americans, who constitute about 30 percent of the state's population, were strongly opposed to the flag (Firestone 2000). Older, white, male South Carolinians, akin to Stanley Greenberg's (2004) uneducated white men, strongly advocated that it remain flying. These conflicting groups' preferences are reflected in the positions candidates took in two Senate races. The more recent of these saw the Republican primary dominated by the flag issue as Jim DeMint excoriated his opponent, former Governor David Beasley, for changing his position on the flag and agreeing to have it removed from the capital (Sheinn 2004). While the Republican Senate candidates during that period (Lindsay Graham and Jim DeMint) supported flying the flag, the Democrats (Alex Sanders and Inez Tenenbaum) opposed it.[20]

In contrast, while the same groups are active on gay marriage, both African Americans and white males oppose it (Langer 2004; Ly and Harris 2004). Not too surprisingly, then, DeMint and Tenenbaum held the same position opposing gay marriage when the issue became salient in 2004.

While this typology is concise, it is not comprehensive. In particular, the typology provides a snapshot of candidates' positioning at a given time and therefore provides little guidance when the constellation of district groups changes over time. In this case, an incumbent politician who advocates the position preferred by a long-established single group may be cross-pressured if a new group develops that is more closely aligned with the politicians' party. The reputational cost of changing positions, and the likelihood that the legislator has a good deal of credibility on the issue, suggests that politicians faced with the emergence of a second group should maintain their long-held position.[21]

Micro-targeting

Expecting candidates to recognize the power of social identity that underlies group membership may be unrealistic. Politicians clearly recognize the benefits of appealing to groups of voters, however, even if they do not understand why such appeals are effective. While the average candidate may not know that appealing to more recent Cuban immigrants is effective because of their shared experience at Mariel, for instance, they are likely to recognize that taking positions to appeal to these groups of later migrating Cuban voters may be advantageous because they feel intensely about the issue.

Appealing to subconstituencies is a tactic widely employed by politicians and marketers to exploit the advantages of groups articulated herein. While there is a long historical legacy of politicians and parties targeting groups based on demographic or socioeconomic characteristics, technology has enhanced the precision with which candidates can make narrowly targeted appeals. Strategists used to target groups to turn out based on very broad indicators: "Democrats would target Black areas while Republicans would focus on the suburbs"

(Hamburger and Wallsten 2006). As early as 1990, however, strategists recognized the importance of peeling off subconstituencies within broader demographic groups, such as the benefits to Republicans in targeting socially conservative blacks (Keyes 1989).

Modern technology allows for much greater precision. Today, both major parties employ political campaigns that engage in micro-targeting—the identification of small subconstituencies and the development of appeals designed to woo them—to make narrowly tailored political appeals to members of groups that share a characteristic the campaigns view as exploitable. These appeals do not necessarily rely on activating identities through adroit issue or symbolic positioning; they more often make affective appeals using methods such as pre-recorded phone calls from leading figures in the party (Von Drehle 2004). More often, candidates identify some interest that binds a group together. In 2006, Michigan Republicans sought to oust Senator Debbie Stabenow by appealing to snowmobilers on the basis of her support for environmental legislation that limited the development and use of trails. In many cases, candidates attempt to play on group identities either explicitly or implicitly. In the 2008 presidential primary, Hillary Clinton frequently highlighted her struggles as a woman in an explicit attempt to attract female voters, a strategy that was widely credited with giving her a come-from-behind victory in the New Hampshire primary.

News accounts give Republicans a substantial edge in the ability to target groups of voters because their database, dubbed "Voter Vault," is larger and contains more specific information about voters' preferences (Reynolds and McManus 2004; Von Drehle 2000). One reporter described the sophistication of the Republican strategy: "Republican strategists can quickly pull up information not only about voting histories, age, address and marital status, but also consumer habits, vehicle ownership, magazine subscriptions, church membership, hobbies, major purchases—even whether a household prefers bourbon over gin. (Bourbon drinkers tend to be Republican; gin is more often a Democrat's drink)" (Hamburger and Wallsten 2006). The Republican targeting program was so effective that by 2005, Democrats had commissioned a study to determine how to catch up. Despite launching a $9 million project in 2006, Democrats were still thought to be far behind (Hamburger and Wallsten 2006).

Micro-targeting provides sophisticated candidates the ability to reach individual voters on the basis of their background experiences and to make group-based appeals in a nuanced way. The relevant group characteristics of different family members, for example, can be identified, and each member can be targeted individually, along with other group members who share similar characteristics and concerns. The next step for these strategists would seem to be to improve their understanding of which cues are most likely effective in motivating both turnout and vote choice.

Predicting Voters' Behavior, Candidates' Position Taking, and Legislators' Behavior

The subconstituency politics theory borrows heavily from notions of social identity to explain why and how groups of individuals can be brought together to advance the interests of strategic politicians. Candidates raise issues designed to activate group identities, which helps to transform otherwise apathetic individuals into excited participants. Once activated, citizens become more knowledgeable on the issues related to their group identity and are thus better able to hold politicians accountable on issues that relate to their group association. Candidates work to exploit and activate identities that benefit them in the campaign, often through the positions they emphasize and take. Once elected, legislators not only support the positions they propounded in the campaign by casting roll-call votes but also actively work to promote the groups' preferences behind the scenes.

The motivation behind the theory has important implications for how citizens and politicians behave. If citizens' ignorance and lack of interest is overcome by appealing to them on issues they view as important, then they should know more about issues that relate to their active identities. In contrast, if, as the demand model suggests, citizens only become knowledgeable as the visibility of issues increases, then those who are most exposed to news and politics should be most knowledgeable about politics. Similarly, if politicians appeal to groups, then the positions taken in the campaign, the roll-call votes cast, and the bills worked on behind the scenes in Congress should reflect those groups' preferences. If, however, politicians appeal to the average voter in the district, as the demand model suggests of legislators and the median voter model suggests for candidates, then we should observe candidates taking positions designed to appeal to the average voter in both campaigns and in Congress. Each element of the theory is examined in greater detail in the chapters that follow. The chapters can be seen as opportunities to test the hypotheses implied by the theory that serve to organize the rest of the book. In particular, I begin by testing the implications of the theory and applying the theory to test the following hypotheses:

1. *Group knowledge:* Citizens with an activated group identity should exhibit increased political information about issues pertaining to that identity.
2. *Candidates' positioning:* Subconstituency preferences positively influence candidates' campaign positions.
3. *Legislators' responsiveness:* Subconstituencies' preferences are positively associated with legislators' roll-call votes.
4. *Legislators' consistency:* Once candidates are elected, their campaign positions are positively associated with their roll-call votes.

5. *Legislators' activity:* Legislators from districts with active subconstituencies are more likely to take a leadership role on issues important to the group in the district.

6. *Diversity:* Legislators from diverse districts should be as representative as those from homogeneous districts.

7. *Issue visibility:* Legislators will be no more responsive on visible issues than on less visible issues.

Summary

The preceding discussion illustrates how and why politicians appeal to groups. While Lieberman's joke about chest hair would seem to be an appeal unlikely to resonate with many voters, it is indicative of a much broader phenomenon. While the average citizen is uninformed about and uninterested in politics, the average group member is not. Consequently, group members' support is disproportionately valuable.

Individuals have multiple, overlapping social identities that are developed in response to their life experiences. These identities are activated in response to external stimuli encountered in everyday life. Different identities are activated depending on particular social circumstances or contexts. These identities provide individuals with shortcuts for dealing with social situations.

In the context of the campaign, politicians attempt to prime individual identities that they believe carry electoral benefits. By raising particular issues or advocating particular non-policy stands, they attempt to simultaneously prime large numbers of citizens and galvanize social groups that are more likely to participate in a beneficial way.

3

Overcoming Ignorance and Apathy

Testing Individual-Level Implications of Representation Theories

> *Systematic differences in political knowledge have serious implications for the ability of some groups to perceive and act on their self-interest or their notion of the public interest. If Jefferson is right that the people themselves are the best protectors of their own interests, then many groups are hindered in this effort by their relative lack of information.*
> —Michael X. Delli Carpini and Scott Keeter,
> *What Americans Know about Politics and Why It Matters*

The uncertain role played by citizens in becoming informed consumers of political information is among the most serious challenges to explanations of how the representation process works. Extant theories of representation, summarized in the demand model, require levels of knowledge and interest far beyond citizens' apparent capacity. Citizens' failure to exhibit levels of knowledge or interest sufficient to constrain politicians' behavior raises questions about the degree to which citizens have the ability to hold politicians accountable for their behavior and whether politicians, upon recognizing this fact, exploit it. Citizens' ignorance leads us to question both the validity of explanations of American representation and citizens' ability to govern themselves.

Students of representation seek to describe, explain, and link the preferences of the people with those of the elected. Just as different theories of representation lead to differing expectations about legislators' behavior, they also rely on different explanations for how citizens evaluate their leaders. Consequently, the capacity of the citizenry to hold its leaders accountable is an important aspect of representation that is all too often overlooked. Seldom do scholars investigate the degree to which citizens behave in a manner consistent with their theories.

This chapter examines whether the demand model or the subconstituency politics theory better explains what people know about politics.[1] Citizens' knowledge about politics is important for understanding how representation works, because knowledge is essential to hold elected officials accountable for their behavior. I begin by describing the processes by which the two theories explain how and when citizens are best able to hold politicians accountable. To evaluate these competing explanations, I examine whether media exposure or being a member of an activated group better explains political knowledge. The results suggest that individuals most exposed to media are no more knowledgeable than is the public as a whole, contrary to the implications of the demand model, while individuals with an activated group identity show dramatic increases in knowledge.

What Representation Theories Require of Citizens

The conventional wisdom of representation is articulated in the demand model and holds that legislators try to account for citizens' preferences by supporting or creating specific policies. Citizens evaluate politicians' behavior through elections, which serve to legitimize legislators' behavior (Wahlke 1971). Though often implicit, this basic process underlies explanations of representation that examine legislative responsiveness across districts within a Congress (e.g., Arnold 1990; Bernstein 1989) or over time (e.g., Wlezien 1995, 1996).[2]

The observation that citizens lack political knowledge (and interest) raises basic questions, however: How is it that unknowledgeable citizens are able to hold legislators responsible? Why would elected officials respond to such citizens?

Recall the two perspectives linking legislators and citizens. One view holds that citizens must be knowledgeable on a wide variety of issues and must record legislators' behavior on those issues to compare it with what they wanted the legislators to do (e.g., Bernstein 1989). Alternatively, if legislators anticipate that citizens may come to care about an issue because it is publicized by an instigator, citizens need to become knowledgeable about and interested in those issues. Even explanations suggesting that citizens need not be knowledgeable at the time of a particular event, therefore, would seem to require levels of attentiveness and interest beyond that demonstrated by the average citizen. Studies show that citizens who rely on heuristic shortcuts make mistakes in their evaluations of their leaders' positions (e.g., Kuklinski 2007).

One example of these processes is illustrated using the case of the Armenian Genocide Resolution in the 110th House and the Turkish government's threat to expel U.S. military forces if the House passes the resolution. While few citizens are aware of the legislation, legislators fear that those who care about the safety of the soldiers waging the wars in Afghanistan and Iraq would be angered if Turkey makes good on its threat and endangers American soldiers. For legislators to be held accountable for supporting the resolution, however, citizens who care strongly about the soldiers' safety must somehow become knowledgeable enough about the issue to tie their opinion to their legislators' missteps on the issue.

All theories of representation require that citizens need to be knowledgeable enough to hold legislators accountable on at least some occasions or legislators will be free to do as they wish. Research that examines how citizens hold legislators responsible suggests that issue knowledge is essential to ensure responsiveness as citizens' use of shortcuts is inefficient and leads to mistakes (e.g., Wolpert and Gimpel 1997). Moreover, relying on instigators such as challengers or interest groups to publicize legislators' misdeeds does not solve the problem of citizens' ignorance; it simply changes when citizens have to become knowledgeable. While Richard Lau and David Redlawsk (2006) find that most citizens are educable, the practice seems so costly as to be impractical. Educating citizens seems to require well-funded candidates and groups with interests that coincide with those that are under-represented by their legislators in order to make such issues visible. Moreover, these instigators must link incumbents to the unpopular position and challengers to the popular position. Given the infrequency of high-quality challengers in American politics, this standard seldom seems to be met and thus casts doubt on both prospective and retrospective examinations of responsiveness. Absent interest and knowledge, one must doubt citizens' ability to use elections to hold legislators responsible.[3] The requirement that citizens must be knowledgeable and attentive raises questions about the feasibility of the demand model, since evidence conclusively demonstrates that citizens lack the knowledge and interest required to hold legislators accountable (e.g., Converse 1964; Delli Carpini and Keeter 1996; Wahlke 1971; Wolpert and Gimpel 1997).

The issue visibility thesis attempts to reconcile the inconsistency between what we know about citizens' capacities and the requirements of the demand model and has gradually developed to explain why legislators appear responsive on some issues but not on others (e.g., Bianco 1994; Bianco et al. 1996; Froman 1963; Hurley and Hill 2003; Hutchings 1998, 2001; Hutchings et al. 2004; Key 1963; Kingdon 1971; Kuklinski and Elling 1977; McCrone and Kuklinski 1979; Miller and Stokes 1963; Page and Shapiro 1993; Theriault 2005). The issue visibility thesis holds that legislators' behavior becomes increasingly visible as an issue is increasingly publicized. Owing to this enhanced visibility, citizens are better able to compare their legislators' behavior to their own personal preferences.

Research on media politics, for example, suggests that only on the most important and visible issues is news coverage of legislators' behavior sufficient either to inform the citizenry about the complexity of the issues or to identify how the legislator behaved on the issue (Iyengar and Simon 2000).[4] Variation in issue visibility is thought to explain issue responsiveness.

The issue visibility thesis holds that as the visibility of an issue increases, citizens' information levels, as well as the visibility of legislators' issue stands, increase in response. Increased visibility gives citizens the opportunity to become knowledgeable on an issue. Moreover, even if citizens do not become knowledgeable, legislators must account for the increased probability that citizens *may* become knowledgeable on visible issues. It may be easier for a challenger to bring misdeeds to the public's attention on more visible issues. Consequently, visibility should be associated with increased responsiveness.

While both theories hold that citizens monitor legislators' behavior and compare these actions to their own preferences, they differ in their description of how this occurs. The subconstituency politics theory avers that people hold their legislators responsible on those issues that relate to their activated social identities. Since social identities originate from conceptions of the self, issues that relate to them are seen as very important to each individual. Research shows that citizens exhibit higher levels of knowledge on issues they view as important (Lavine et al. 1996). The increased intensity about these issues gives group members incentives to overcome their limited knowledge of and interest in politics. Legislators are held accountable by subconstituencies that consist of intense group members who are knowledgeable about issues related to their activated group identities.

Individual-Level Implications of Issue Visibility and Subconstituency Politics

The issue visibility thesis holds that responsiveness increases with issue visibility. Subconstituency politics, in contrast, suggests that members of an activated group are more sensitive to, and more likely to seek, information. They are thus more knowledgeable about issues pertaining to the activated social identity. While candidates appeal to latent groups and try to activate them, the benefits of doing so occur once the identity becomes active. The competing explanations of how issue visibility affects representation lead to testable implications about individual behavior.

In the case of the issue visibility thesis, awareness and knowledge increase with visibility. The ease with which a citizen becomes aware, however, depends on his exposure to the media. The hermit who totally ignores the media seems unlikely to become knowledgeable about an issue simply because it is better covered. The average citizen becomes more knowledgeable and aware when an issue receives increased media coverage. One expectation is that those who regularly read papers or watch television should be more likely to become knowledgeable about an issue. These highly exposed individuals receive levels of information consistent with the effect of increased visibility and should therefore be more knowledgeable. Consequently, the issue visibility thesis implies that people exposed to high levels of media will know more at any level of issue visibility.

Subconstituency politics suggests that once a particular social identity is activated, an individual will be more sensitive to information and hence more knowledgeable about issues relating to it. In a sense, the argument can be seen

TABLE 3.1   INDIVIDUAL KNOWLEDGE PREDICTIONS OF
ISSUE VISIBILITY AND SUBCONSTITUENCY POLITICS

Do Active Groups Exist?	Issue Visibility	
	High	Low
Yes	High, high	Low, high
No	High, low	Low, low

as a more general version of selective attentiveness, which holds that context interacts with visibility to make group members aware about relevant issues (Iyengar and Simon 2000, Hutchings 2003). Visibility in the abstract is not directly relevant.[5] Group members are likely to be more knowledgeable even about low-profile issues that may not be overly visible. Consequently, activated groups should show high levels of knowledge about relevant issues and lower levels of knowledge about issues that are not relevant to their activated identity. The competing expectations are summarized in Table 3.1, which shows the knowledge predictions for each model across levels of issue visibility and group activation.

The subconstituency politics theory predicts high levels of knowledge among group members on any issue for which a group is activated and low levels on issues when a group identity is not active. Issue visibility predicts high levels of knowledge on issues of high visibility and lower levels of knowledge on less visible issues. Examples of the types of issues that fall into each cell are shown in Table 3.2.

The examples of the issues included in each category are illustrative rather than exhaustive. We can certainly imagine similar issues in different cells. The Armenian Genocide Resolution of 2007 began as a low-visibility issue on which groups existed, but it became highly visible when the Turkish government withdrew its ambassador to the United States. The typology provides only a rough guideline as to how citizens' knowledge might be expected to vary across different types of issues. Major policy issues tend to be visible and contentious owing to group conflict, and it is here that both theories suggest people should be most

TABLE 3.2   EXAMPLES OF ISSUES THAT FALL INTO EACH CATEGORY

Do Active Groups Exist?	Issue Visibility	
	High	Low
Yes	Major, contentious legislation (e.g., NAFTA, flag burning)	Ethnic political issues (e.g., apology to comfort women)
No	Technical legislation (e.g., increased mortgage limits, bankruptcy reform)	Most private bills (e.g., commemorations)

knowledgeable. Many questions of ethnic politics, such as the resolution to ask Japan to apologize for the enslavement of the sex workers known as "comfort women" during World War II, are indicative of less visible issues on which groups are active.

While particular group identities often become active and then recede, it is more difficult to identify issues on which no groups are active, since raising issues is costly and requires someone to care strongly. Nonetheless, most private-legislation seems unlikely to galvanize citizens into an active group. These bills are seldom controversial and are of exceptionally low visibility. It is also hard to identify highly visible issues on which activated groups do not exist, although highly technical legislation supported by narrow special interests, such as increasing the size of mortgages that are considered conforming loans or bankruptcy reform, in some circumstances may either not be relevant to groups or may relate to latent identities. These issues seem likely to be rare.

To determine whether the theories correctly explain how people behave, I first identify an issue on which groups have activated identities. Next, I develop a measure of news exposure to examine how visibility affects group members' levels of political knowledge on those issues. Then I examine whether members of activated groups are more knowledgeable about issues relevant to the group identity.[6] Finally, I directly compare the degree to which visibility and group identity explain issue knowledge.

The Clarence Thomas Nomination

One of the few issues for which data are available to evaluate the competing implications of these rival theories is the Senate vote on Clarence Thomas's nomination by President George H. W. Bush to replace Thurgood Marshall, the first African American to serve on the Supreme Court. To be confirmed Thomas needed approval from the Democratically controlled Senate. While Thomas shared Marshall's skin color, the two men's political and judicial philosophy could not have been more different. As a consequence, Thomas's nomination provided something of a wedge issue among Democrats, who liked the idea of supporting an African American but opposed the confirmation of a conservative. Indeed, while the average African American supported Thomas, black elites were divided in their support for him (Alston 1991). Further charging the atmosphere, numerous lurid accusations were made against Thomas during his confirmation hearings. The most salient of these was the charge of sexual harassment by Anita Hill, a law professor at the University of Oklahoma. The fantastic and salacious nature of the hearings led to full television coverage of the Senate Judiciary Committee's proceedings. The hearings included graphic descriptions of the pornography and crude humor to which Anita Hill testified she was exposed, as well as Thomas's claim that the confirmation process had become a "high-tech" lynching. Ultimately, the committee voted to report Thomas's confirmation to the floor, and the Senate confirmed him 52–48 on October 16, 1991.

The politics underlying Thomas's confirmation suggests that several groups may have become activated by the charged hearings. African Americans were clearly energized and strongly supported his confirmation. Women might also have been activated in response to both the sexual-harassment charges and Thomas's conservative judicial philosophy. In particular, college-educated women who tend to be more progressive and feel especially strongly about social issues such as abortion, a group akin to Stanley Greenberg's concept of Super-Educated Women, seem especially likely to have been activated (Greenberg 2004). This group seems likely to have been activated by Thomas's conservatism and Hill's allegations of harassment. In contrast, the combination of Thomas's conservative views and his standing up to charges of sexual harassment may have served to activate less-well-educated, married white men, a group that generally corresponds with what Greenberg (2004) calls the F-You Boys.

As a high-visibility issue on which groups were active, the Thomas nomination provides an opportunity to evaluate the theories' predictions. The case is especially interesting, as the groups active on the issue are among the least likely to follow politics: the F-You Boys and African Americans tend to exhibit low levels of socioeconomic status.[7] In the case of the Thomas nomination, the groups that the subconstituency politics theory suggests should be most knowledgeable are opposite those that students of voting behavior might expect, thereby providing a very difficult but useful test. Finally, Robin Wolpert and James Gimpel (1997) show that the Thomas nomination also serves as a case for studying accountability both because citizens' opinions were lasting and because several challengers later publicized the incumbents' vote on the issue (Wolpert and Gimpel 1997).

Identifying Groups

The first step toward investigating whether the subconstituency politics theory or the demand model is more consistent with citizens' civic capacity is to identify activated groups on some issue about which a measure of citizens' knowledge related to legislators' behavior is available. To test these hypotheses, I employ the American National Election Study: Pooled Senate Election Study (PSES) of 1988–1992, which surveyed citizens about their senators' positions on the Thomas nomination in November 1992.

As defined in Chapter 2, subconstituency politics defines groups as people with shared experiences that lead to similar attitudes and opinions. While "groupness" can be based on ethnic, religious, or socioeconomic experiences, group membership can also arise from any profound experiential element that

TABLE 3.3   VARIANCE OF OPINION ON THE
CLARENCE THOMAS NOMINATION

Group	Variance
African Americans	.22
F-You Boys	.22
Super-Educated Women	.25
Deep South	.24
Privileged men	.23
Cosmopolitan states	.25
Union families	.25
Entire sample	.25

shapes or frames the interpretation of political events. One implication is that on issues relevant to the group, activated individuals should show less diversity of opinion than the public as a whole. While increased homogeneity of opinion is a necessary trait for identifying active groups, it is insufficient for defining them, since random collections of individuals or latent homogeneous groups could show similar homogeneity of opinion. That is, shared opinions are insufficient to identify the group.

Identifying members of active groups can be difficult because surveys seldom ask questions designed to elicit information about one's social identification and its relationship to a given issue. Ideally, we would like information about one's issue intensity, opinion preferences, and social-background characteristics. Absent these data, researchers must infer which people are likely to have activated identities. Specifically, active groups should have an identity that relates to the issue and have opinion preferences that are more homogeneous than those of the general public. Groups that meet these criteria are most likely to be activated.

We can examine whether attitudes and opinions are more homogeneous within the relevant groups by examining opinion variance.[8] Table 3.3 shows the variance of public opinion for various groups Greenberg identifies on the confirmation of Clarence Thomas.[9] In addition to presenting the variance for the groups we expect to be active, I also present the variance of the next two largest groups Greenberg identifies in each party's sphere of influence.[10]

The results in Table 3.3 describe the homogeneity of groups on the issue. Opinion among African Americans and F-You Boys is more homogeneous than is opinion within any other group.[11] While not conclusive, these results are consistent with the idea that African Americans and F-You Boys were activated on the Thomas nomination. In contrast, the variance of Super-Educated Women's opinion is slightly larger than that of the public as a whole, a finding that is inconsistent with the group-identification criteria articulated earlier. These empirical results imply the existence of two active groups.[12]

Explaining Political Knowledge

The knowledgeability of particular groups provides an excellent opportunity to test the mechanism underlying individual behavior described in the competing theories by testing hypotheses about the groups that should be knowledgeable about the Thomas nomination.

To determine the degree to which individuals are knowledgeable, I examine the proportion of group members who were able to correctly identify the way their senators voted on the Thomas nomination. This task requires citizens tie a specific roll-call vote or legislative position to a specific legislator. While the task is a difficult one given citizens' lack of knowledge about their legislators (e.g., Delli Carpini and Keeter 1996), it is consistent with the knowledge required both to force legislators to consider constituents' views and for citizens to hold legislators accountable.

The theories imply unique predictions concerning citizens' knowledge. To test the claim that active group members are more knowledgeable, I examine the degree to which African Americans and F-You Boys correctly identified their senators' votes. In contrast, the claim that responsiveness increases on more visible issues as citizens are more likely to become aware of legislators' behavior on such issues implies that those who are most exposed to the news should be most knowledgeable about an issue.

To test this, I examine the knowledge of the people getting the most exposure—those who score above the median (6 or more) in number of days per week watching television and reading the newspaper. We can directly compare the subconstituency politics theory's explanation (activated identity) for increased knowledge with that of the issue visibility thesis (exposure) by using these measures and comparing them with the knowledge level in the entire sample. The results in Table 3.4 show the proportion of each group able to correctly identify how both senators voted on the Thomas nomination.

The results in Table 3.4 are consistent with the idea that African Americans and F-You Boys were activated on the Thomas nomination, as both groups were better able to identify their senators' votes than were either the highly exposed group or the public as a whole.[13] Both of these groups were statistically significantly better able to identify both senators' votes than was the average respondent.[14] Interestingly, those most frequently exposed to media are slightly less well able to recount their senators' votes than is the average citizen, a result that is inconsistent with the issue visibility thesis.

All of the results presented here hold individually for newspapers and television. The finding regarding papers is especially important, since papers have an explicit news component that general television viewing may lack. I combine television coverage with reading the newspaper because research shows

TABLE 3.4   PROPORTION OF ALL RESPONDENTS
WHO IDENTIFIED BOTH SENATORS' VOTES

Group	Thomas Nomination (%)
African Americans	38.2*
F-You Boys	38.9†
High exposure	27.9
Super-Educated Women	24.2
Deep South	31.2
Privileged men	33.5
Cosmopolitan states	21.0
Union families	24.1
Entire sample	28.4

Note: One-tailed significance test of the difference between the group and the population.
* $p < .05$.
† $p < .01$.

that most Americans get their information on current events from "soft" news (Baum 2002).

Comparing general knowledge levels with knowledge of a specific issue allows for another test. Specifically, members of activated groups should know more about relevant issues than they do about those irrelevant to the activated identity. Moreover, the increase in knowledge across issues should be higher for activated groups than for the non-active groups, and those most exposed to media should show higher levels of knowledge than the public as a whole. In addition, those exposed to high levels of media should exhibit little change in their knowledge levels relative to the population as whole.

One way to examine whether shifts in knowledge are driven by group identities or media exposure is by comparing group members with the general public across knowledge indicators (i.e., different issues). Dividing by the proportion of the public able to complete the task allows us to norm the results relative to the difficulty of the questions and allows us to assess whether knowledge patterns are consistent with identity activation or media exposure. Norming the results lets us compare differences in the ability of particular of groups relative to the public as a whole to facilitate comparison across issues. Unfortunately, data on comparable issues are unavailable. We can employ a general measure of political knowledge, however. To do this, we compare group members' ability to recall senators' votes on the Thomas nomination relative to the population with group members' general level of political knowledge relative to the population. The general knowledge baseline serves as the first issue and reflects the proportion of respondents in each group who were able to correctly name the positions held by two of four prominent political figures.[15]

TABLE 3.5   RATIO OF ISSUE KNOWLEDGE BETWEEN EACH GROUP AND THE
POPULATION FOR THE BASELINE AND THE CLARENCE THOMAS NOMINATION

Group	Knowledge Baseline	Thomas Nomination	Difference
African Americans	.76	1.35	.59*
F-You Boys	1.08	1.29	.21
High exposure	1.33	.98	−.35*
Super-Educated Women	.82	.85	.03
Deep South	1.17	1.10	−.17
Privileged men	1.25	1.18	−.07
Cosmopolitan states	.72	.74	.02
Union families	.94	.85	−.09

Note: One-tailed significance test of the difference in knowledge across indicators.

$*p < .01$.

The political-knowledge ratio is created by dividing the proportion of each group that correctly identified at least two (of four) prominent figures by the proportion of the population that was able to complete the same task. The Thomas nomination ratio is created by calculating the proportion of each group who correctly identified how both of their senators voted on the Thomas nomination by the proportion of the population who correctly identified their senators' votes. The political-knowledge ratios can be interpreted in the following way: A group with a knowledge ratio of 1 is exactly as knowledgeable as the general public. Those with political knowledge ratios above 1 are more knowledgeable than the public, while those with ratios of less than 1 are less knowledgeable.

Subconstituency politics suggests that political-knowledge ratios for activated groups should be larger than ratios for inactive groups on issues related to the activated group identity. The issue visibility thesis predicts that the high-exposure group should also be higher than average across indicators, since those exposed to more news should be especially sensitive to increased news coverage on the visible issue. These hypotheses are tested in Table 3.5.

The general political-knowledge ratio for F-You Boys (1.08) is about the same as for the public as a whole, while African Americans show substantially lower knowledge levels (.76), indicating that they are about 25 percent less likely to correctly identify two of four prominent leaders than is the general public. For both African Americans and F-You Boys, the specific political-knowledge ratio was much greater for the Thomas nomination than it was for the public as a whole. These groups show the highest ratios of issue knowledge on the Thomas vote, but not on the baseline or general measure. While the results are in the expected direction and appear large relative to the scores across most other groups, they are statistically significant only for African Americans (probability $[p] < .07$) but not for F-You Boys ($p = .31$). The results for African Americans are particularly striking, showing the second lowest general political-knowledge ratio but the highest knowledge of how their senators voted on the Thomas nomination. In contrast, the highly exposed group shows a surprisingly massive and statistically significant ($p < .01$) *decrease* in knowledge, contrary to the issue visibility theory's expectation of no difference. Simply put, those most exposed to media are less able to identify their senators' votes.[16]

While the analyses presented here are illustrative and generally consistent with the implications of the subconstituency politics theory, they do not allow us to directly compare the competing explanations of enhanced political knowledge. We can use a regression framework to directly test these competing theses while controlling for alternative explanations, however. In particular, we can examine whether activated group identity or media exposure better explains political knowledge.

To do this, we employ a dependent variable that reflects the number of legislators whose votes citizens could correctly identify. Higher scores correspond to increased knowledge, as the scale ranges from 0 (unable to identify how either senator voted) to 2 (correctly described how both of their senators voted).

The active group's variables are binary and are scored "1" if the respondent is a group member and "0" if otherwise. The F-You Boys are married, white men under 50 who lack a college degree. *African Americans* are respondents who identify themselves as African American or black. Each of these variables should be positively signed. The issue visibility thesis suggests that knowledge should be positively associated with exposure (a sum of the number of days in the past week that the respondent watched television or read the newspaper).[17] The scale ranges from 0 to 14. This variable should be positively signed. People who are interested in politics should know more about how their legislators voted. A variable called *Interest* accounts for this by summing up correct responses to questions that ask them to identify famous political figures. Respondents were asked to identify the offices held by Dan Quayle, William Rehnquist, Tom Foley, and Al Gore. Scores range from 0 to 4 and should be positively signed. Knowledge of a legislator's vote should also be positively related to one's *Income,* which is scored using seven categories.[18]

Binomial probit is used to estimate the model because the dependent variable is the number of correct responses out of the two questions posed. As with the previous analyses, the survey weights are employed.[19] The results are in Table 3.6.

These results provide substantial evidence for the subconstituency politics theory and suggest that the issue visibility thesis fails to perform as promised. Both *African Americans* and *F-You Boys* are statistically significant and signed correctly. Moreover, contrary to the demand model, *Exposure* does not approach statistical significance. These results are extremely robust to alternative specifications: Regardless of the alternative explanations considered, these same basic results are supported.[20]

TABLE 3.6   BINOMIAL PROBIT OF KNOWLEDGE
ON EXPOSURE AND ACTIVATED GROUPS

Group	Thomas Nomination	
Interest	.09†	(.04)
Exposure	−.014	(.02)
Income	.012	(.021)
F-You Boys	.187*	(.086)
African American	.295†	(.13)
Constant	−.23*	(.12)
Pseudo log likelihood	−23,748.55	
Observations	1,878	

Note: One-tailed tests. Standard errors are in parentheses.
* $p < .05$.
† $p < .01$.

The results also call into question the process underlying the demand model. Issue visibility is thought to enhance legislative responsiveness by increasing the likelihood that citizens will notice their legislators' misdeeds. Media exposure appears unrelated to knowledge of a senator's vote, however, suggesting either that this link does not exist or that both scholars and legislators are mistaken in their understanding of how citizens obtain information. Taken in combination with Wolpert and Gimpel's (1997) finding that citizens are not especially knowledgeable even when alerted to legislators' missteps, the results are equally problematic, regardless of whether one subscribes to a prospective or retrospective view of representation. Both require visibility as a prerequisite to awareness.[21] Simply put, visibility does not seem to ensure knowledge levels high enough for retribution.

The results are consistent with the mechanism underlying subconstituency politics. Membership in activated groups is associated with increased knowledge on issues that are relevant to the group identity, because group members are more sensitive to and seek out knowledge pertaining to these activated identities, even when political knowledge, education, and income levels are low, as is the case with African Americans.

Conclusion

This chapter addresses a fundamental, and too often overlooked, question about representation: How well do competing theories fit with the cognitive capacities of the citizens whose behavior they seek to explain? This chapter develops and tests expectations about how people acquire political knowledge according to the leading theory of representation, the demand model, and compares the results to the predictions of the subconstituency politics theory.

TABLE 3.7   SUMMARY OF RESULTS FOR TESTS OF INDIVIDUAL-LEVEL
IMPLICATIONS OF REPRESENTATION THEORIES

Test	Demand Model	Subconstituency Politics Theory
Homogeneity of group opinion		+
Increased group knowledge		+
Shifts in group knowledge	−	+
Variation in issue knowledge	−	+

Note: Blank spaces indicate that the models make no predictions in a context.

As summarized in Table 3.7, the results presented in this chapter strongly support the subconstituency politics theory and provide evidence against the issue visibility thesis. Members of active groups exhibit greater homogeneity of opinion than do non-active groups; increased knowledge levels on issues relevant to their activated identity; and a pattern of knowledge increases on specific issues that is consistent with group activation. Perhaps most important, in a direct test in which subconstituency politics and the demand model generate different predictions, being a member of an activated group is a significant predictor of increased issue knowledge.

In contrast, the implications of the issue visibility thesis hold that citizen knowledgeability is a function of political-issue visibility. If true, then those most exposed to media should be among the most knowledgeable. Contrary to expectations, however, people who are highly exposed to news appear no more knowledgeable about the votes of their senators on the Thomas nomination than is the general public. Moreover, increased exposure to news sources has no discernable impact on knowledge of how their senators voted on the Thomas nomination.

While the results of these tests are far from conclusive, at every step they are consistent with the results we would expect to see if the theory of subconstituency politics is correct. Nonetheless, the limitations of these findings are strong. Owing to data limitations, we have examined implications of these theories on only one issue, the Clarence Thomas nomination.[22] Having demonstrated that subconstituency politics provides an explanation more consistent with data concerning individuals' capacity to hold their legislators responsible for their actions, I will next turn to examine the link between citizens' preferences and legislators' behavior in campaigns.

4

Subconstituencies in Campaigns

In the fall of 1994, Senator Chuck Robb of Virginia faced a tight reelection contest against Oliver North. Robb, who was stumping for votes at a factory, stopped to take questions from the press when the following exchange with *Washington Post* reporter Don Baker occurred:

SENATOR ROBB: At least give honest and realistic responses to the tough questions, because otherwise we are going to continue to up the national debt and the budget deficit is going to be almost impossible to solve.

DON BAKER: Senator, in the spirit of your desire to talk about these things, we're outside a unionized plant here. Tell us what your position is on striker replacement.

SENATOR ROBB: It has not changed.

DON BAKER: Well, what is it?

SENATOR ROBB: You've . . . you've heard it.

DON BAKER: I've never heard you give it. Maybe I've missed it. Are you for it or against it?

SENATOR ROBB: I've said that I've not taken a position on the merits. I did vote for cloture. My position on the basic underlying issue has not changed, and I take that position. On Virginia being a right to work state, I've not changed my position on that.

DON BAKER: So you're opposed to striker replacement?

SENATOR ROBB: No, I did not say that.

DON BAKER: You're in favor of striker replacement?

DON BAKER: You don't have a position on striker replacement?

SENATOR ROBB: I told you, I take the position that it's more important in my judgment to work on labor–management cooperation, and that is a divisive issue that is not coming to the fore. Period.

DON BAKER (turning to a Robb campaign official): Will you give us a translation of that statement?[1]

Robb's response to the question about striker replacement is problematic for scholars who seek to understand candidates' campaign positions, because extant theories poorly explain such answers. Contrary to Robb's answer, theories of candidates' position taking suggest that they have little incentive to equivocate on major issues of policy. Instead, they tend to hold that candidates should be decisive either by appealing to the median or average voter, an appeal that indirectly reflects the desire to appeal to majorities (e.g., Downs 1957), or through more extreme, expressive position taking (e.g., Boatright 2004) often propounded by candidates with virtually no chance of winning.

Setting aside the possibility that the response was just a gaffe, Robb was an incumbent who repeatedly refused to take a position on the issue, even in televised debates. One possibility is that Robb saw no way to gain votes on the issue of striker replacement. An alternative explanation, however, might lie with subconstituency politics. If no groups held intense preferences on the issue, then equivocation would leave him free to act as he wanted later, perhaps to logroll on some other issue.

This chapter investigates the conditions under which candidates target different constituencies through their position taking. In particular, I evaluate whether politicians tend to respond more closely to the will of the majority, as typically assessed using average district preferences, or to intense subconstituencies. Employing case studies and quantitative analyses of candidates' positioning on the Cuban trade embargo, extension of hate-crimes protections to cover sexual orientation, extension of the assault-weapons ban, and abortion, I test the hypothesis articulated in Chapter 1 that subconstituency preferences positively influence candidates' campaign positions.[2]

Group Influence and Issue Positioning

Surprisingly little is known about how candidates decide which district groups to pursue and how to appeal to them. Most studies of campaign positioning assume issues away and examine behavior in the abstract terms of ideological placement and distance (e.g., Downs 1957). While ideological impressions almost certainly matter, most campaigns are fought with, and over, issues.[3]

One explanation of how legislators take positions on issues to appeal to different combinations of district groups is given by Morris Fiorina (1974).[4] In consensual districts, legislators appeal to the one active group. In diverse districts, however, a legislator's position depends on the strength of the groups. Under these conditions, they cannot gain support; legislators are forced to choose from among the positions that cost them the least. Consequently, Fiorina recognizes that some conditions exist in which legislators can profitably vote with a smaller group if the group cares more intensely about the issue. While these predictions have not yet been empirically validated, related research supports these claims.[5]

While Fiorina's predictions are intuitively appealing, they rely on several simplifying assumptions that limit their applicability for the study of positioning more generally. One limitation is that these predictions apply solely to roll-call voting decisions. If we think about the representation process as one in which elections and the legislative process are linked, then accounting for campaign positioning seems quite important. As the context in which campaign positions are taken differs substantially from the legislative context, explanations that overlook the conditioning effect of campaigns appear limited.

Campaigns, Elections, and Democracy

Elections and the campaigns that precede them are central to democratic theory and republican governance. Taken together, they serve to educate the public and to provide a mechanism that allows the people the opportunity to hold their elected officials accountable. Candidates present the positions and platforms on which they stand on the central issues of the day. In contrast to roll-call votes, the issues most likely to be addressed are tailored to the concerns of the district's citizenry. Such issue positions are likely to be first adopted during the campaign.

Campaigns also play an important role in explaining how citizens hold legislators responsible. Campaigns provide information, since voters must be knowledgeable about candidates' positions to choose whom to support. Campaigns also help to provide accountability. Voters can evaluate whether the elected officials have fulfilled their past promises or support voters' current wishes.

The study of campaigns also speaks to questions of representation in that campaign position taking is more likely to reflect the issues important to the district than is other types of behavior, such as roll-call votes. Since candidates choose which issues to speak about, the study of candidate positioning seems especially valuable for learning about how and why candidates adopt the positions they do.

Given the widely recognized importance of political campaigns, one might expect students of representation to routinely test theories in this laboratory.

While studies of candidate positioning are common, however, candidates' positions are seldom used to evaluate responsiveness.

Toward a Typology of Position Taking

Clearly, development of a unified representation theory requires accounting for the influences on candidates' issue positioning. Recall from Chapter 2 that subconstituency politics holds that the position candidates will take depends on the constellation of groups in a district. When only one group cares about an issue, both candidates will advocate its position. When two or more groups have conflicting preferences, candidates will take divergent positions closest to their traditional ideological or partisan positions. The exception to this rule occurs when a district changes over time from a one-group to a two-group district. In such cases, the cost of changing positions may lead the politician to continue to appeal to the previously dominant group, as the politician likely has much greater credibility on the issue owing to her longstanding position.[6]

To test the subconstituency politics theory, we need to identify issues on which both activated constituent groups exist and for which there is sufficient media coverage to ascertain candidates' positions. To identify such issues, we can perform a thought experiment in which we imagine a continuum that ranks issues according to the likelihood that legislators will respond to constituents. At one end is a high-visibility domestic-policy issue on which citizens have well-formed preferences. At the other is a low-visibility issue about which citizens have little knowledge. Capturing issues that cover a range of visibility levels allows us to evaluate whether the positions the candidates take are more consistent with subconstituency politics or the demand model.

In this chapter, I examine four issues that reflect the range of variation on this continuum. Abortion politics and the assault-weapons ban are indicative of highly visible issues with intense groups advocating competing positions. Low-visibility issues are the Cuban trade embargo and the extension of federal hate-crimes legislation to protect people based on their sexual orientation. As we will see, abortion and the Cuban trade embargo are typical of issues on the ends of this scale.

One concern about selecting these cases is that some issues inherently involve well-organized groups whose positions and preferences seem obvious and thus constitute an easy test of the subconstituency politics theory. It is important to recognize, however, that on any issue, groups and preferences vary across districts. An issue that is an easy test in one district may provide a very difficult test in another. While the Cuban trade embargo, for example, appears to be an "easy" case, we will see shortly that it provides a very difficult test in cases where the theory predicts that farm-state Republicans will buck their party leaders to support rolling back the embargo, or in cases where Democrats buck

TABLE 4.1   ISSUE VISIBILITY BY NEWS MENTIONS IN THE YEAR PRECEDING
CONSIDERATION

Topic	Time Period Covered	Number of News Articles
Cuban trade embargo	July 25, 2000–July 24, 2001	18
Extension of hate-crimes legislation	September 27, 2006–September 26, 2007	704
Assault-weapons ban	March 2, 2003–March 1, 2004	2,207
Partial-birth–abortion ban	March 12, 2003–March 11, 2004	3,482

their liberal districts (and party leaders) to support the hardline positions advocated by mostly Republican "old Cubans," those whose families immigrated before 1980.

These four issues also provide difficult tests for subconstituency politics because the central actors are primarily unorganized groups like "new Cubans" (those whose families immigrated after 1980), F-You Boys, The Faithful, and Secular Warriors. Past research suggests no reason to expect these unorganized subconstituencies to have any influence when facing off against groups like old Cubans that either are well organized or are closely affiliated with well-organized groups.

To get a sense of the visibility of these issues at the time legislators had to make decisions on them, Table 4.1 shows the number of stories on each issue that appeared in the year before the issues were considered in Congress. We can clearly see that the Cuban trade embargo was least well covered; extending hate-crimes legislation to cover sexual orientation was slightly better covered; and the renewal of the assault-weapons ban was much better covered but received substantially less coverage than did partial-birth abortion.

I begin by examining the cases of the Cuban trade embargo and the extension of hate-crimes protections to homosexuals, which, owing to their relatively low visibility levels, constitute hard cases for representation theories to explain.

Testing the Subconstituency Politics Theory: The Cuban Trade Embargo

The Cuban trade embargo was implemented in 1963, as an attempt to pressure Fidel Castro by isolating the Cuban government in the international economy. The hope was that sanctions would hasten the transition to democracy. The Trade Sanctions and Export Enhancement Act of 2000 slightly reduced sanctions by authorizing the export of medical supplies and agricultural commodities to Cuba for humanitarian purposes. The law requires, however, that sales must be paid for in cash, and it prohibits the extension of credit either by the sellers or by American banks. This last provision substantially restricts trade, as Cuba is a cash-poor country (Pianan and DeYoung 2000).

The politics underlying the embargo bear directly on the interests and preferences of at least three groups. Most supportive of the embargo are Cubans who fled in the late 1950s, during the period around the revolution until about 1980 (Bendixen 2002). Residing primarily in south Florida, and to a lesser extent in New Jersey and New York, these immigrants were the elite of Cuban society. With Castro's rise, many of these political refugees had relatives imprisoned, tortured, or killed and saw their assets seized by the state. Given their experience, it is not surprising that they actively support the embargo. For years, this was the only vocal group on the issue of Cuba.

Over the past decade, however, other groups with identities tied to Cuba have emerged. Chapter 2 described the schism in the Cuban American community that is based largely on time of immigration. Newer immigrants, especially those who migrated after 1990, oppose the embargo and travel ban (Veiga 2000). These Cubans tend to be economic refugees, many of whom have relatives who still live on the island. Because shortages are so common, the embargo adversely affects their relatives' quality of life by denying them full access to American foodstuffs. It also limits the amount of money they can send to their relatives and the frequency with which they can visit.[7]

Following the passage of the 2000 Trade Sanction and Export Enhancement Act, farmers began to see Cuba as a valuable and largely unexploited market. Cuba does not produce enough to feed its people and must rely on imports to augment domestic agricultural production. Owing to its geographic proximity, the United States is a natural trading partner. Not surprisingly, then, farmers have increasingly come to either oppose the embargo or support rolling it back to facilitate the sale of agricultural products.

To evaluate the competing theories, we need to identify districts that fit each of the constellations of constituent groups. The single-group case, described in the first scenario, occurs where there is a large concentration either of only old Cubans or of farmers.[8] The multiple-group case, described in the second scenario, requires a district in which two or more conflicting groups exist. New Cubans tend to live alongside old Cubans in cities, while farmers are concentrated in rural areas that lack Cubans almost entirely. The case studies that follow begin by identifying appropriate cases fitting each scenario and examining candidates' positions in each of these districts.[9]

The Single-Group Case

The subconstituency politics theory predicts that candidates in districts with only one group will advocate that group's position. With the exception of New Jersey's 13th district and Florida's 11th, 17th, 20th, and 22nd districts, which have only old Cubans, single-group districts are farming districts.[10] Single-group cases are identified via a ranking of each state's population that is employed in agriculture, forestry, and hunting using data from the 2003 American Community Study. From this list of states, I examined candidates' positions in the five states with the largest number of farmers.[11] Among these states, I further selected the three districts with the highest proportions of farmers. Few Cubans live in these districts. A second type of single-group district has only old Cubans. Along with the four Florida districts noted earlier, New Jersey's 13th district contains Union City, which is known colloquially as "Havana on the Hudson" and is among the oldest Cuban American enclaves.[12]

The positions taken on the embargo in twenty-four one-group cases, including the ten Senate races from the five states and the House races for Idaho's 1st and 2nd districts; Iowa's 4th and 5th districts; Nebraska's 3rd district; North Dakota's and Montana's at-large districts; New Jersey's 13th district; and Florida's 11th, 17th, 20th and 22nd districts, are summarized in Tables 4.2 and 4.3.

Overall, these results are highly consistent with the subconstituency politics theory. In total, 90 percent of candidates (26 of 29) supported the predicted position, a highly significant result ($p < .001$). In agricultural districts, only two candidates took positions contrary to the predictions, while in the old Cuban districts, every candidate but one, Carol Roberts, took the expected pro-embargo position. Perhaps most impressive, as seen in Table 4.2, more than half of the incumbents in the farming districts were Republicans and thus were cross-pressured on the issue because their announced position ran contrary to that of their party. Despite this, seven of the eight Republican incumbents (from the farm states) took a position opposing the embargo. Similarly, as shown in Table 4.3, four of the five Democrats in the old Cuban districts also bucked their party by supporting the embargo.

Perhaps the most interesting case is that of Republican Senator Conrad Burns. While we are unable to find any public statement of support or opposition to the Cuban trade embargo, Burns has supported the sanctions in past Congresses. He voted to maintain sanctions in 1996 (H.R. 927). By October 2000, however, the Washington Post reported, Burns had become conflicted about the issue. In negotiations with the House leadership, he advocated reducing trade restrictions. Once it was made clear that such a provision would not pass, however, he voted to support the embargo (Pianan and Morgan 2000).

How can we explain Burns's position on the embargo? Several reasons for his equivocation seem compelling. First, his position on the embargo was adopted, at the latest, in the mid-1990s, well before anyone seems to have had any idea that the issue would become relevant to farmers. Recall that the agricultural exception did not become law until October 2000. At that time it may not have been clear that Cuba would be interested in buying such products from the United States, even if sales were allowed.[13] Second, Burns had not faced election since farmers became activated on the issue. Finally, it appears that prior to facing election in 2006, he attempted to change his position on the issue. Consequently, there seems to be a good reason why he has not spoken publicly about the issue.

TABLE 4.2   POSITIONS ON THE EMBARGO OF CANDIDATES FROM SINGLE-GROUP AGRICULTURAL DISTRICTS

Year	State	District	Candidate	Position
2004	Idaho	Senate	Scott McClure (D)	Favored
			Michael Crapo (R)	Opposed
2002		1st	Butch Otter (R)	Opposed
			Naomi Preston (D)	Opposed
		2nd	Mike Simpson (R)	Opposed*
			Lin Whitworth (D)	Opposed
		Senate	Larry Craig (R)	Opposed
			Alan Blinken (D)	•
2004	Iowa	Senate	Charles Grassley (R)	Opposed
			Arthur Small (D)	•
		4th	Tom Latham (R)	Opposed
			Paul W. Johnson (D)	Opposed
		5th	Steve King (R)	Favored
			E. Joyce Schulte (D)	•
2002		Senate	Tom Harkin (D)	Opposed
			Greg Ganske (R)	Opposed
2004	Montana	1st	Dennis Rehberg (R)	Opposed*
			Tracy Velazquez (D)	•
2002		Senate	Max Baucus (D)	Opposed†
			Mike Taylor (R)	•
2000		Senate	Conrad Burns (R)	•†
			Brian Schweitzer (D)	Opposed‡
2004	Nebraska	3rd	Tom Osborne (R)	Opposed
			Donna J. Anderson (D)	•
2002		Senate	Chuck Hagel (R)	Opposed
			Charlie Matulka (D)	•
2000		Senate	Ben Nelson (D)	•
			Don Stenberg (R)	•
2004	North Dakota	Senate	Byron Dorgan (D)	Opposed
			Mike Liffrig (R)	•
		House	Earl Pomeroy (D)	Opposed
			Duane Sand (R)	•
2000		Senate	Kent Conrad (D)	Opposed
			Duane Sand (R)	•

Note: D, Democratic Party; R, Republican Party. The predicted position in the New Jersey case is to support the embargo. A bullet indicates no position announced. Roll-call votes are not considered.

* Favored repealing trade aspects of embargo, but not travel restrictions.

† Baucus and Burns both voted to strengthen the embargo in 1996. Burns recently equivocated, however.

‡ Position not formally announced, but traveled to Cuba in 2004 to negotiate the sale of dry beans.

TABLE 4.3   POSITIONS ON THE EMBARGO OF CANDIDATES FROM SINGLE-GROUP
OLD CUBAN DISTRICTS

Year	State	District	Candidate	Position
2004	New Jersey	13th	Robert Menendez (D)	Favored
			Richard Piatkowski (R)	Favored
2004	Florida	11th	Jim Davis (D)	Opposed
			Robert Johnson (L)	•
		17th	Kendrick Meek (D)	•
		20th	Debbie Wasserman Schultz (D)	Favored
			Margaret Hostetter (R)	•
2002			Peter Deutsch (D)	Favored
2004		22nd	Clay Shaw (R)	Favored
			Robin Rorapaugh (D)	•
2002			Clay Shaw (R)	Favored
			Carol Roberts (D)	Opposed

Note: D, Democratic Party; R, Republican Party; L, Libertarian Party. A bullet indicates no position announced.

The Multiple-Group Case

Nationally, Cuban Americans are most heavily concentrated in four congressional districts: Florida's 18th, 21st, and 25th, and New Jersey's 13th. Cuban Americans are so highly concentrated in south Florida that the population in each of these districts is higher than the population of Cubans in any other *state* except New York.[14] Moreover, only in these Florida districts do both old and new Cubans reside side by side.

In contrast to the south Florida districts, anecdotal evidence suggests that the Cuban population in New Jersey's 13th district consists predominantly of old Cubans.[15] Florida's proximity to Cuba and its massive Cuban community provide an attractive destination for largely poor recent immigrants searching for economic opportunity. Moreover, extensive polling in south Florida documents the existence of both groups of Cubans and their diverging political preferences (Rufty 1998; Veiga 2000). Consequently, the three Florida districts seem to be the logical place to examine the impact of conflicting groups on candidates' positions.

We can evaluate the first condition by examining the positions taken by the candidates in Florida's 18th, 21st, and 25th districts and the 2000 and 2004 Florida Senate races to see whether or not candidates took opposing positions. Recall that subconstituency politics predicts that when active groups with conflicting preferences exist in a district, candidates will take opposing positions, with each adopting positions closest to her traditional supporters. In contrast, the demand model suggests that both candidates will take the position held by the average voter in the district.

These five observations also allow us to examine positioning in a variety of electoral contexts. Each of the three House districts is represented by a Cuban American Republican, so old Cubans' policy preferences are consistent with their party's established pro-embargo, anticommunist position. Thus, we would expect the incumbents in each of these races to support the embargo, while the challengers should oppose it. In contrast, the 2004 Senate race was for an open seat. We would expect Republican candidate Mel Martinez to advocate the embargo while Democratic candidate Betty Castor should oppose it. Finally, in 2000, Democratic candidate Bill Nelson faced Republican candidate Bill McCollum. At first glance, the theory predicts that Nelson will oppose and McCollum will support the embargo. Table 4.4 summarizes these candidates' positions.

Table 4.4 shows that in 2004, Illeana Ros-Lehtinen and Lincoln Diaz-Balart maintained their long support of the embargo, while their opponents, Sam Sheldon and the Libertarian Party candidate Frank Gonzalez, favored loosening the embargo. In his last contested race (in 2002), Mario Diaz-Balart strongly supported the embargo while his opponent, Annie Betancourt, opposed it. In the 2004 Senate race, Betty Castor opposed the embargo while Mel Martinez strongly supported it. In these four cases, the Republican candidates supported the embargo while their main opponents opposed it, as the subconstituency politics theory predicts.

One observation is inconsistent with the subconstituency politics theory, however: In 2000, Democratic Senator Bill Nelson strongly supported the embargo, as did his opponent, Bill McCollum. Nelson's position is inconsistent with the theory, which suggests that when conflicting groups exist, candidates will take opposing positions. In sum, a statistically significant 90 percent (9 of 10) of candidates in multiple-group districts took the position that subconstituency politics predicts ($p < .01$).[16] Moreover, a close inspection of the nature of

TABLE 4.4   POSITIONS ON THE EMBARGO OF CANDIDATES FROM FLORIDA'S MULTIPLE-GROUP DISTRICTS

Year	District	Candidate	Position
2004	18th	Ileana Ros-Lehtinen (R)	Favored
		Sam M. Sheldon (D)	Opposed
	21st	Lincoln R. Diaz-Balart (R)	Favored
		Frank Gonzalez (L)	Opposed
	Senate	Mel Martinez (R)	Favored
		Betty Castor (D)	Opposed
2002	25th	Mario Diaz-Balart (R)	Favored
		Annie Betancourt (D)	Opposed
2000	Senate	Bill Nelson (D)	Favored
		Bill McCollum (R)	Favored

Note: R, Republican Party; D, Democratic Party; L, Libertarian Party.

the constituent groups provides an explanation for Nelson's position that is consistent with subconstituency politics.

Bill Nelson has supported the embargo since he was first elected to Congress in 1978. At the time he took his position, Florida had only one active constituency on the embargo. Recall that the second constituency consists of Cubans who immigrated to America between 1980 and 2000. The existence of this group has only been recognized since the spring of 2002, however, almost two years after Nelson's last campaign began (Oppenheimer 2002). Given these facts, and the potential cost of changing positions, it would make little sense to support a group that did not exist.[17] Moreover, his actions are consistent with subconstituency politics' prediction that, for legislators with long-held positions, the cost of position change might outweigh the benefits of such change.

Overall, the results are also inconsistent with predictions of the demand model. Recall that the demand model predicts that candidates will take the same position in each race—the position consistent with majority opinion. In four of the five races, the candidates took differing positions, a result that is inconsistent with the demand model. However, the case in which the two candidates agreed was Bill Nelson's Senate race. As noted in Chapter 1, since measures of statewide opinion on the embargo in Florida are available, we know that while both candidates agreed, in doing so they supported the *minority*-preferred position. While the candidates agreed, they did so in a way that is inconsistent with the expectations of the demand model.

Taken together, these results are statistically significant and highly consistent with the predictions articulated in Table 2.1. Despite examining cases with legislators who were cross-pressured because of their party affiliation, almost every candidate from an agricultural district opposed the trade embargo, and almost every candidate from an old Cuban district supported it.

Evaluation

Overall, these significant results are consistent with the predictions of the subconstituency politics theory. About 90 percent of those from single- and multiple-group districts took the predicted position on the Cuban trade embargo. Only the Republican Steve King, who attributes his position to visiting Cuba and seeing totalitarianism firsthand; Idaho Senate challenger Scott McClure; and Democratic long-shot Carol Roberts backed positions inconsistent with the theory. In another curious case, an otherwise highly visible senator, Conrad Burns, appears to be changing his position and has avoided speaking publicly about the issue—even though he has supported the embargo in the past. Burns's position also appears to have been taken well before the issue became relevant to the group.

In the districts with two conflicting groups, candidates running in the three south Florida districts took positions contrary to those offered by the incumbent Republicans. This finding is consistent with the subconstituency politics theory but inconsistent with the demand model, which suggests that candidates should take the same position. In contrast, only two of the thirty-six candidates from single-group districts failed to take the predicted position.

Finally, the difference between Tables 4.2–4.3 and Table 4.4 is also interesting. Where every candidate took a position in the multiple-group districts, in the single-group districts, many did not. While some rural districts may receive less coverage (but see Arnold 2004), it is also possible that coverage of an issue may be reduced when candidates agree. More specifically, the invisibility of positions on the embargo may be a function of the fact that candidates are unable to distinguish themselves from their opponents by playing up such issues, and newspaper reporters may be less interested in covering issues on which the candidates agree.[18]

Testing the Subconstituency Politics Theory: Hate Crimes

The extension of hate-crimes protections to individuals based on sexual orientation became a prominent issue following the murder of Matthew Shepard, who in early October 1998 was beaten, robbed, tortured, and left to die tied to fence posts in rural Laramie, Wyoming (Brooke 1998). The brutality of the incident generated tremendous publicity and controversy (Kenworthy 1998).[19] Anti-gay church members picketed Shepard's funeral, while gay-rights organizations and others pushed for federal hate-crimes legislation designed to extend protections to gay men and lesbians, as well as transgendered people.[20]

Extending hate-crimes legislation to protect people based on their sexual orientation was first considered in Congress in 1999, when it passed both chambers but was killed in conference. Since then, hate-crimes legislation has been considered in every Senate. It passed in 1999; its backers failed to end a filibuster that killed it in 2002, only to see it pass again in 2004. In the 110th Congress, the Matthew Shepard Act (H.R. 1592) passed the House of Representatives in a 237–180 vote on May 3, 2007. Moreover, a filibuster designed to kill the bill was defeated by cloture vote on September 27, 2007. The bill passed by voice vote immediately thereafter. As of this writing, President George Bush has promised to veto the legislation ("A Chance to Fight Hate" 2007).

The politics surrounding the bill are extremely contentious. While a fairly large political coalition has been brought together to support the legislation by extending protections to gender and the disabled, substantial opposition to the bill has come from religious conservatives. According to news accounts, opponents of the legislation consist mostly of those who are evangelical or born-again Christians. The coalition of supporters is marked primarily by gay-rights supporters and liberals in Congress.

As occurs with many low-visibility issues, methodological obstacles inhibit our ability to study issues pertaining to gay rights. As a group subject to discrimination, gay populations are difficult to identify, and opinion on extending hate-crimes protections to gays does not exist (as it does for more visible issues, such as same-sex marriage). Religious groups can also be difficult to identify, as the U.S. Census does not ask questions about religious adherence. To overcome these limits, I employ case-study methods and identify appropriate cases using 2005 estimates of the gay population produced by the Williams Institute at the University of California, Los Angeles, Law School (Gates 2006). Born-again Christians are identified using the 2004 National Annenberg Election Study.

An additional difficulty in examining issues of interest to gays and the religious right results from their uneven dispersion across districts. Employing the same 5 percent criterion used in the case study of the Cuban trade embargo, we are left with only one district in which only a gay group exists.[21] Even in California's 8th district, which has by far the largest gay population (16.8 percent) in the country, 5 percent of the population identifies as born-again. Nationally, the self-identified born-again population, averaging 27.1 percent, dramatically outpaces the number of gays, which averages only 4.1 percent. This asymmetry biases the tests against a finding for subconstituency politics and in favor of the demand model, because in many of the districts in which gay groups exist, they are dramatically outnumbered by born-again Christians.

Subconstituency politics holds that in one-group districts, both candidates will advocate the position of the dominant group, while in two-group districts, candidates will diverge to positions nearest their party. If so, then Democrats should support extending hate-crimes legislation to gays, while Republicans should oppose it. Cases to test the one-group hypothesis were selected by ranking states by group population from largest to smallest and selecting the first three districts (or states) on the list that did not have an opposing group (i.e., the gay population was less than 5 percent). The two-group cases were identified by taking the first three districts (of eleven that exist) and the only state in which more than 5 percent of the population identified as gay and the population of those who identified as born-again was above the mean (27 percent).

The expectation in the one-group cases is that all candidates from the religious districts should oppose the hate-crimes legislation. The 1st districts in Kentucky and Tennessee and the 6th district in Alabama are predominantly rural and Southern and are all held by very safe Republicans. In contrast, both candidates from the nation's only "gay" district, California's 9th, should support

TABLE 4.5   POSITIONS ON THE EXTENSION OF HATE-CRIMES LEGISLATION OF
CANDIDATES FROM SINGLE-GROUP DISTRICTS

Year	State	District	Candidate	Position
2004	Kentucky	1st	Ed Whitfield (R)	•
			Billy Cartwright (D)	Opposed
2006	Tennessee	1st	David Davis (R)	Opposed
			Rick Trent (D)	Supported
2004			Bill Jenkins (R)	Opposed
			Graham Leonard (D)	•
2004	Alabama	6th	Spencer Bachus (R)	•
			J. Holden McAllister (L)	•
2006	California	9th	Barbara Lee (D)	Supported
			John Den Dulk (R)	Opposed

Note: R, Republican Party; D, Democratic Party; L, Libertarian Party. A bullet indicates no position announced.

the hate-crimes legislation. This district is centered in Berkeley and is an extremely safe seat held by Barbara Lee. The results of the candidates' positions are shown in Table 4.5.

Of the six candidates for whom positions could be ascertained, four (67 percent) took the position predicted by the subconstituency politics theory. Both exceptions were challengers, as all incumbents voted consistently with expectations. These results provide only modest support for subconstituency politics, as they do slightly better than one would predict from chance alone ($p < .24$).

One explanation for these results might lie in the absence of competition in these races. Both of the candidates who took the position inconsistent with subconstituency politics were extreme long shots. Rick Trent's election, for example, would have marked the first victory by a Democrat in Tennessee's 1st district since the nineteenth century. Similarly, in California's 9th district, incumbent Barbara Lee routinely secures 80 percent of the vote; her challenger, John Den Dulk, seemed to recognize his fate, stating, "I'm not running to win, I'm running to witness" (Gizzy 2006).[22]

While these results are generally consistent with subconstituency politics, they do not provide an especially powerful test of either theory, since both hold that candidates should share positions in these districts. Fortunately, the two-group case provides a more powerful test.

In contrast to the demand model, subconstituency politics holds that candidates will advocate opposing positions in two-group districts and states. Every one of the ten candidates depicted in Table 4.6 took the position subconstituency politics predicts. Particularly noteworthy are the cases of the Texas Democrats from largely rural districts who supported extending hate-crimes

**TABLE 4.6 POSITIONS ON THE EXTENSION OF HATE-CRIMES LEGISLATION OF
CANDIDATES FROM MULTIPLE-GROUP DISTRICTS**

Year	State	District	Candidate	Position
2006	Texas	26th	Michael Burgess (R)	Opposed
			Tim Barnwell (D)	Supported
		31st	John Carter (R)	Opposed
			Mary Beth Harrell (D)	Supported
	Michigan	2nd	Pete Hoekstra (R)	Opposed
			Kimon Kotos (D)	•
	Washington	Senate	Maria Cantwell (D)	Supported
			Mike McGavick (R)	Opposed
2004			Patty Murray (D)	Supported
			George Nethercutt (R)	•
2000			Maria Cantwell (D)	Supported
			Slade Gorton (R)	Opposed

Note: R, Republican Party; D, Democratic Party. Positions for candidates in House races (except for the incumbents) are unavailable before 2006. A bullet indicates no position announced.

legislation to gays, a result that is inconsistent with what the demand model would likely predict for districts in which more than 40 percent of residents describe themselves as born-again. While we cannot identify the district's majority-preferred position, subconstituency politics theory necessarily contradicts the demand model in two-group districts because it holds that both candidates should take the same, majority-preferred position. The subconstituency politics model perfectly predicted all positions, while the demand model correctly predicted only five of ten—exactly what one would predict due to chance. These results may also speak to the findings that gays are a victim of electoral capture (e.g., Smith 2007).[23]

Overall, these results seem to provide strong, albeit uneven, support for subconstituency politics, as 87.5 percent (14 of 16) of candidates took the positions the theory predicts—results far beyond what one would expect due to chance alone ($p < .002$). The results are also inconsistent with the demand model, as the two-group cases show that legislators from diverse districts advocate conflicting positions. Unfortunately, we cannot clearly evaluate the demand model in one-group districts because we lack opinion data about this issue and have but three challenger positions.

The results are even more impressive when one considers that the hate-crimes bill was of very low visibility, a fact thought to give politicians more latitude to do as they wish. Moreover, the case of extending hate-crimes protections to gays is difficult because of the disparate size of the two activated constituencies. In each case, candidates who advocated on behalf of the gay subconstituency backed a group that was about 20 percent the size of the born-again subconstituency.

Testing the Subconstituency Politics Theory: Assault-Weapons Ban

Gun control is among the most popular public policies in the United States. Surveys show that roughly 60 percent of citizens favor increased gun regulation.[24] Despite this popularity, efforts to regulate guns have been largely unsuccessful over the past decade, a fact often attributed to the power of special interests such as the National Rifle Association. Gun control appears to be an issue on which the minority's will rides roughshod over that of the majority.

Owing to its popularity, gun regulation would seem an unlikely issue for minority groups to defeat the majority. Powerful special interests exist on both sides of the issue, and debate about gun control tends to be quite visible. According to the demand model, such conditions should lead to higher responsiveness. Moreover, gun control provides a difficult test for subconstituency politics because the groups that favor gun control are larger than those that oppose it.[25] To successfully thwart such policies, a smaller but more intense subconstituency opposing gun control must overcome a much larger but less intense opponent. If it becomes increasingly difficult to prevent a policy from passing as its popularity increases, then a stringent test of subconstituency politics theory is the assault-weapons ban, which routinely garners two-thirds of the public's support.[26]

The Federal Assault Weapons Ban was a provision in the Violent Crime Control and Law Enforcement Act of 1994 that banned many semiautomatic weapons for a ten-year period. Attempts to extend the ban in 2004 passed in the Senate but were defeated in the Republican House. The expiration of the ban became highly visible in the presidential campaign as the Democratic nominee, John Kerry, campaigned on the importance of renewing the bill and President Bush failed to push for its passage, despite his statement of support for the measure.

With the Democrats' recapture of the House in 2007, the assault-weapons ban again became viable and was introduced in both the House as a standalone bill and in the Senate as part of the Violent Crime Control and Law Enforcement Act of 2007. While the bills have not received as much coverage as they did in 1994, the issue was highly visible and thus provides a case for further examining the explanatory power of the subconstituency politics theory.

While support for the assault-weapons ban is widespread, its opposition is deep. Led by the National Rifle Association, gun-control opponents have been disproportionately effective in thwarting gun restrictions. The primary opponents of gun control tend to be white men with characteristics that correspond roughly to Stanley Greenberg's F-You Boys (Greenberg 2004). Among the most ardent supporters of gun control are voters whom Greenberg refers to as Secular Warriors.[27]

Because of the relatively high visibility of the issue, candidates' positions on the assault-weapons ban tend to be more widely available than for the lower-visibility issues, although as we will see, many candidates' positions on the issue are difficult to ascertain precisely. Increased availability of data allows the use of statistical models to test theories for Senate candidates. Unfortunately, opinion data at the House district level do not allow for reliable inference of constituents' preferences. Taken together, the results of these analyses reinforce the conclusions.

Subconstituency politics holds that candidates from two-group districts should take divergent positions, while those from one-group districts should take the position of the dominant district group. The demand model holds that both candidates should take the same position—that preferred by the majority of the citizenry. As in the previous case studies, a subconstituency exists when its members constitute 5 percent or more of a district's population. Owing to the disparate sizes of the F-You Boys and Secular Warriors groups, no districts exist that have only F-You Boys. Consequently, all one-group districts are those with only Secular Warriors.[28]

By identifying cases in which the disparity between the Secular Warriors and F-You Boys is largest, such that F-You Boys are dramatically outnumbered in the districts, two-group cases were selected to create the most difficult test for the subconstituency politics theory. Selecting such cases provided a difficult test of subconstituency politics because majoritarian models, such as the demand model, predict that candidates will take the majority-preferred position. For each district, the most recent contested race is depicted in the tables that follow. The results for one-group districts are seen below.

Regardless of the candidate's party, Table 4.7 shows, all of the positions obtained (6 of 6) were consistent with the expectations of both subconstituency politics and, presumably, the demand model, since the ban is widely popular, and these districts lack substantial numbers of the most intense opponents, F-You Boys.[29] These results are exceptionally unlikely to be the product of chance ($p < .02$).

While the preceding results are consistent with subconstituency politics, they are also consistent with the demand model. The positions taken on the assault-weapons ban among candidates running in two-group districts provides a more informative test. As Democrats are seen as more supportive of gun restrictions and Republicans are more strongly opposed, we would, given the existence of the two groups in the districts, expect candidates from the different parties to take positions that reflect these traditional stances. Recall, however, that these cases were selected to make the most difficult test possible for subconstituency politics because districts and states were selected that were most lopsidedly in favor of the Secular Warriors' pro-ban position. Candidates should be most tempted to advocate the position of the overwhelmingly dominant group in such districts.[30]

TABLE 4.7   POSITION ON THE EXTENSION OF THE ASSAULT-WEAPONS BAN OF
CANDIDATES FROM SINGLE-GROUP DISTRICTS

Year	State	District	Candidate	Position
2006	New York	14th	Carolyn Maloney (D)	Supported
			Danniel Maio (R)	•
		11th	Yvette Clark (D)	•
			Stephen Finger (R)	•
2006	California	12th	Tom Lantos (D)	•
			Mike Maloney (R)	•
2006	Georgia	4th	Hank Johnson (D)	•
			Catherine Davis (R)	•
2004	Florida	20th	Debbie Wasserman Schultz (D)	Supported
			Margaret Hostetter (R)	•
2006	Connecticut	Senate	Joe Lieberman (ID)	Supported
			Ned Lamont (D)	Supported
2004		Senate	Chris Dodd (D)	Supported
			Jack Orchulli (R)	Supported

Note: D, Democratic Party; R, Republican Party; ID, Independent Democrat. Single-group districts with Secular Warriors only; no single-group districts with only F-You Boys exist. A bullet indicates no position announced.

The significant results seen in Table 4.8 are highly consistent with subconstituency politics ($p < .01$), as candidates took the positions of their dominant subconstituencies in every case (10 of 10). These results also militate against the demand model in that in both of the cases where positions for Republican candidates could be ascertained, they advocated the preferences of their subconstituency rather than the position that was most likely preferred by the majority.

Statistical Analysis

While the results presented to this point are consistent with the subconstituency politics theory, they are largely illustrative. It is possible, after all, that alternative explanations better explain candidates' position taking, or that the conclusions change when behavior is examined simultaneously across different types of districts. Employing a statistical framework allows us to better account for these possibilities.[31] Unlike for the lower-visibility issues, sufficient numbers of candidates' positions for the assault-weapons ban are available, thus allowing statistical analysis.

The analysis examines forty-eight U.S. Senate candidates' positions on the assault-weapons ban between 2002 and 2006, obtained primarily through newspaper accounts or interest groups' reports on candidates' responses to their surveys (see Table 4.9).[32] This period covers the time during which the assault-weapons ban was discussed in campaigns. The relatively small number of

TABLE 4.8   POSITIONS ON THE EXTENSION OF THE ASSAULT-WEAPONS BAN OF CANDIDATES FROM MULTIPLE-GROUP DISTRICTS

Year	State	District	Candidate	Position
2004	Massachusetts	3rd	Jim McGovern (D)	Supported
			Rod Crews (R)	•
2004	New York	22nd	Maurice Hinchey (D)	•
			William Brenner (R)	•
2006	Maine	1st	Tom Allen (D)	Supported
			Darlene Curley (R)	•
2006	New Hampshire	2nd	Paul Hodes (D)	Supported
			Charlie Bass (R)	Opposed
2004	Nevada	3rd	Jon Porter (R)	•
			Tom Gallagher (D)	Supported
2006	Vermont	Senate	Bernie Sanders (S)	•
			Rich Tarrant (R)	•
2004			Patrick Leahy (D)	Supported
			Jack McMullen (R)	•
2004	Oregon	Senate	Ron Wyden (D)	•
			Al King (R)	•
2002			Gordon Smith (R)	•
			Bill Bradbury (D)	Supported
2004	Colorado	Senate	Ken Salazar (D)	Supported
			Pete Coors (R)	Opposed
2002			Wayne Allard (R)	•
			Tom Strickland (D)	Supported

Note: D, Democratic Party; R, Republican Party; S, Socialist Party. Positions for candidates in the House races (except for incumbents) are unavailable before 2006. A bullet indicates no position announced.

positions stems from the specificity of the issue and the infrequency with which candidates addressed it in the 2002 campaigns.[33]

The dependent variable is whether a candidate supported extending the assault-weapons ban. Candidates who supported the ban were coded "1," while those who opposed it were coded "0." The key independent variables are the measures of public opinion on the assault-weapons ban.[34] *Average Opinion* reflects the implications of the demand model, which holds that candidates respond to majority opinion. *Subconstituency Opinion* reflects the opinion among the subconstituency to whom candidates are expected to appeal in a state. In states with only one group, this measure reflects the opinion of Secular Warriors, as there are no states that contain only F-You Boys. For Republican candidates, the measure reflects the opinion of F-You Boys in two-group states, while for Democrats, it reflects the opinion of Secular Warriors.

The implications of the subconstituency-opinion measure are illustrated using Democratic candidate Bill Nelson's 2000 race against Republican Bill

TABLE 4.9   HECKMAN PROBIT OF CONSTITUENCIES' INFLUENCE ON
CANDIDATES' POSITIONS ON THE ASSAULT-WEAPONS BAN, 2002–2006

	Assault-Weapons Ban		Did Candidate Take a Position?	
Constant	2.40	(6.81)	−3.19†	(1.02)
Average opinion	5.62	(9.41)		
Subconstituency opinion	8.21†	(2.51)		
Population	−.02	(.05)		
Education	−2.75	(2.27)		
Partisanship	−.04	(.05)		
South	−.55	(.79)		
Competitiveness			.37†	(.10)
Secular Warrior			3.86*	(2.19)
F-You Boys			12.74	(8.70)
Lexis-Nexis sources			−.04	(.03)
Newspapers			.02*	(.01)
Incumbent			.40†	(.22)
2002 election			−.56*	(.24)
Rho	−.31	(.62)		
Observations	48		187	

Note: Standard errors are in parentheses.

* $p < .05$.

† $p < .01$.

McCollum in Florida, a two-group state. The subconstituency politics theory holds that Nelson should appeal to Secular Warriors, while McCollum should appeal to the F-You Boys. McCollum's subconstituency opinion score is measured using the average of opinion among Florida's F-You Boys, while Nelson's score is the average opinion of Florida's Secular Warriors.

Candidates may take positions for reasons other than a desire to reflect citizens' preferences. *Population* accounts for state size and the notion that candidates in more populous states may be more amenable to restrictions on firearms. *Partisanship* reflects the net advantage the Republican Party holds in a state and should be negatively associated with support for the ban. Southern states tend to be more conservative and more permissive on gun issues, and the variable *South* should be negatively signed. *Education* accounts for the average number of years of formal education.

One complication in examining candidates' positions is that whether we observe a position may be influenced by strategic factors. Research suggests that candidates in close races are more likely to gain news coverage and that candidates in safe seats are less likely to take positions. So, *Competitiveness* may affect the likelihood that we observe a position (Kahn and Kenney 1999). The proportion of a state's population that consists of intense groups would seem to increase the likelihood that the candidate will publicly address the issue, so

Secular Warriors and *F-You Boys* reflect the percentage of a state's population consisting of these groups. The degree of media coverage in a state also affects the likelihood that a position will be reported, and so the number of *Newspapers* in the America's Newspapers electronic database and the number of *Lexis-Nexis Sources* account for the media coverage of these races (see Appendix 4A). Finally, as the ban had not yet come up for renewal, candidates in the *2002 Election* (Senate races) were less likely to take a position on the ban.

To account for whether a candidate supported the assault-weapons ban, contingent on whether we could ascertain her position, I employ a Heckman selection probit estimator. The measurement of all variables is in Appendix 4B.

Several factors in Table 4.9 systematically influence whether a candidate took a position. Candidates in close races were more likely to have their positions reported, as were those who resided in states with more newspaper coverage. We cannot tell, however, whether competitiveness matters because candidates in close races were more likely to take a position or because the media is more likely to cover such races. Strategic forces seem to matter as well. Candidates were sensitive to the proportion of a state's population consisting of Secular Warriors, and while the estimate of F-You Boys' influence is not significant, it is fairly large and correctly signed. Incumbents were also more likely to take a position, or have one reported, and as expected, candidates who ran in the 2002 election were less likely to have a position reported.[35]

The results provide no evidence to support the demand model, as average opinion is insignificant. In contrast, subconstituency opinion is highly significant and correctly signed. Despite simultaneously controlling for alternative explanations of candidates' positioning, once again we find strong support for subconstituency politics and no evidence to support the demand model.

As a visible issue supported by a strong majority of the public, the assault-weapons ban provides a test of representation theories in a context that should favor the demand model. Such conditions are precisely where majoritarian theories should be most successful. Despite this, however, the demand model poorly explains candidates' behavior.

Testing the Subconstituency Politics Theory: Abortion

Almost every political discussion about abortion addresses whether the Supreme Court's decision in *Roe v. Wade* in 1973 should stand. In *Roe*, the court ruled that the state's interest increases as the fetus develops and that, consequently, while women have a right to an abortion in the first trimester of a pregnancy, and to have one under slightly more restricted circumstances in the second trimester, they have no right to third-trimester abortions.

Contemporary political debate concerns the conditions under which abortions should be allowed. Most recently, attention has focused on whether a method of abortion called "intact dilation and extraction" should be legal. This rare procedure (it covers fewer than 1 percent of cases) was termed "partial-birth abortion" by pro-life legislators to help frame the national abortion debate in favorable terms.[36] Framing the issue in this manner also served to provide a wedge among Democrats, whose constituents were less unified on the question of partial-birth abortion than they were on *Roe*.

Abortion is a highly visible and controversial issue appropriate for testing the subconstituency politics theory, as almost all Americans have an opinion (Jelen and Wilcox 2003), active groups exist in every state, and most candidates tend to take a position on the issue. The availability of state-level data on abortion allows for use of multiple methods to evaluate the competing theories' predictions. In addition, because groups that care about abortion exist in virtually every district, many cases are available for analysis, which facilitates accounting for alternative explanations of candidates' positioning. Finally, since the public has well-formed preferences, and the issue is highly visible, abortion should provide a much easier test for the demand model.

While highly organized groups have well-articulated positions on the issue, many of those with the strongest attitudes are members of informal groups. Two of the groups with the strongest views are The Faithful, who consist of white Protestant Evangelicals who attend church weekly, and Super-Educated Women, who are women with at least a college degree (e.g., Greenberg 2004). Research shows that church attendance and religious affiliation are among the best predictors of attitudes on abortion (Singh and Leahy 1978). Moreover, women of high socio-economic status are the strongest supporters of abortion rights (Medoff 1989).

Following the process used for the previous issues, I evaluate the subconstituency politics theory's predictions for House and Senate candidates in one- and two-group districts and states. The availability of state-level opinion data on abortion also allows for powerful statistical tests of the competing theories.

To test the implications of subconstituency politics, we need to identify states and districts that fit each of the group constellations. Populations of Super-Educated Women are available from the U.S. Census. To estimate Evangelical Protestant populations by state and congressional district, I employed the 2000 National Annenberg Election Study, which allows the identification of single- and multiple-group districts that contain the various combinations of The Faithful and Super-Educated Women.[37]

Cases were selected by classifying districts and states according to the proportion who identified as The Faithful or as Super-Educated Women. For each scenario, I selected five cases that were closest to the conditions identified by the theoretical predictions of the model. Among two-group districts, cases were selected by dividing the proportion of Super-Educated Women by the proportion of The Faithful and identifying those districts and states that had ratios closest to one, indicating that the groups were about the same size in each district. Conversely, one-group districts composed of The Faithful were identified by selecting those districts with the smallest ratios, indicating relatively few Super-Educated Women and many Faithful. Conversely, single-group districts with only Super-Educated Women were those with the largest ratios.

The analysis in this section focuses on candidates' statements about whether they were pro-choice (i.e., supported *Roe*) or pro-life (i.e., opposed *Roe*). Although *Roe* was the dominant abortion issue discussed during this period, it mapped somewhat inconsistently to the issue of partial-birth abortion in that some candidates who were pro-choice also opposed this procedure, while people who were pro-life always opposed partial-birth abortion.

Subconstituency politics theory holds that in districts with only Super-Educated Women, both candidates will take the pro-choice position. In districts with only The Faithful, all candidates will take a pro-life position. In districts with both The Faithful and Super-Educated Women, Democrats will take the pro-choice position, while Republicans will take the pro-life position.

It is more difficult to assess the competing predictions of the demand model in single-group House districts because we do not have good measures of opinion. In most cases, the predictions of this model are observationally equivalent to the predictions of the subconstituency politics theory. The theories differ in two-group districts, however, in that the demand model implies that candidates should take the same position in each race. To test these predictions, I examined a handful of cases typical of those districts in which both Super-Educated Women and The Faithful exist in meaningful numbers.[38]

The Single-Group Case

Single-group cases were chosen for examination by selecting districts with the largest imbalance between the groups (i.e., the ratio of one group to the other was largest). This left a set of five, mostly Southern, House districts in which The Faithful were the sole group, as well as five districts in the Northeast in which Super-Educated Women were dominant. The Faithful were the dominant political group on abortion in Mississippi's 1st district, Tennessee's 4th district, Texas's 4th district, South Carolina's 3rd district, and Ohio's 18th district. Super-Educated Women were the sole group in New York's 4th, 5th, 12th, and 16th districts, as well as in Massachusetts's 8th district.

Subconstituency politics predicts that in one-group districts, all candidates will take the position preferred by the dominant group. Consequently, in districts in which The Faithful are predominant, all candidates will advocate pro-life positions. In the districts that contain only Super-Educated Women, all legislators should advocate pro-choice positions. As in the earlier case studies, I was unable to confidently identify the predictions of the demand model in one-group cases, because these legislators should follow majority opinion. The positions of candidates in single-group House districts are in Table 4.10.

TABLE 4.10   POSITIONS ON *ROE V. WADE* OF HOUSE CANDIDATES FROM SINGLE-GROUP DISTRICTS

Year	State	District	Candidate	Position
			The Faithful	
2004	Mississippi	1st	Roger Wicker (R)	Opposed
			Barbara Washer (Ref.)	•
2002			Roger Wicker (R)	Opposed
			Rex Weathers (D)	•
2004	Tennessee	4th	Lincoln Davis (D)	Opposed
			Janice Bowling (R)	Opposed
2004	Texas	4th	Ralph Hall (R)	Opposed
			Jim Nickerson (D)	•
2002			Ralph Hall (R)	Opposed
			John Graves (D)	Opposed
2002	South Carolina	3rd	Gresham Barrett (R)	Opposed
			George Brightharp (D)	•
2004	Ohio	18th	Bob Ney (R)	Opposed
			Brian Thomas (D)	•
			Super-Educated Women	
2004	New York	16th	Jose Serrano (D)	Supported
			Ali Muhammad (R)	•
2002			Jose Serrano (D)	Supported
			Frank Dellavalle (R)	•
2004		5th	Gary Ackerman (D)	Supported
			Stephen Graves (R)	Opposed
2002			Gary Ackerman (D)	Supported
			Perry Reich (C)	•
2004		4th	Carolyn McCarthy (D)	Supported
			James Garner (R)	•
2002			Carolyn McCarthy (D)	Supported
			Marilyn O'Grady (R)	Opposed
2004		12th	Nydia Velazquez (D)	Supported
			Paul Rodriguez (R)	•
2002			Nydia Velazquez (D)	Supported
			Cesar Estevez (C)	•
2004	Illinois	1st	Bobby Rush (D)	Supported
			Raymond Wardingly (R)	Opposed

Note: R, Republican Party; Ref., Reform Party; D, Democratic Party; C, Conservative Party. Positions are for candidates who faced challengers. Districts chosen had the greatest ratio of majority-group members to minority-group members (where the minority made up less than 10 percent of the district). Under the selection criteria employed, for example, Massachusetts's 8th district would rank fourth, but it was dropped in favor of Illinois's 1st district, because Democratic Congressman Michael E. Capuano of Massachusetts's 8th district has not faced an opponent since 1998. (Note, however, that Capuano's behavior is consistent with the model—that is, he is pro-choice.) A bullet indicates no position announced.

Examining one-group districts in which The Faithful were the only active group, one sees seven races for which nine issue positions were obtained. In every case (100 percent), candidates adopt pro-life positions in these districts. In contrast, districts dominated by Super-Educated Women show less consistent but still strong support for the theory, as 75 percent (9 of 12) of candidates supported the pro-choice position. Overall, the results for these cases are highly statistically significant ($p < .001$), as the theory predicts correctly in 86 percent of cases (18 of 21).

One interesting aspect of these results is that these single-group cases show relatively high levels of missing data. It is especially difficult to obtain positions on abortion for challengers to what are very safe Democrats in the districts dominated by Super-Educated Women. In fact, each of the three prediction errors comes from Republican challengers to incumbent Democrats in districts in which the Democrats are extremely safe. Given the low level of news coverage, especially of the New York races, it would not be surprising to discover that reporters limit their coverage to issues on which the candidates disagree.

Subconstituency politics predicts that all candidates in states dominated by The Faithful will advocate a pro-life position, while all candidates in states with only Super-Educated Women will advocate a pro-choice position. Positions taken by Senate candidates in single-district states are in Table 4.11.

Once again, these significant results ($p < .001$) are highly consistent with the predictions of the subconstituency politics theory. The results vary by district type, however, as we see that in three of the four districts dominated by The Faithful (75 percent), and in 89 percent (17 of 19) of the positions examined in the states dominated by Super-Educated Women, candidates took positions consistent with the theory.

The Multiple-Group Case

I begin by examining candidates' positions in multiple-group House districts. The districts were selected so they would be of roughly equal size to provide a "typical case" of a multi-group district. The five that were most balanced were California's 38th district, Colorado's 6th district, Texas's 20th district, Florida's 22nd district, and Oregon's 1st district. For each case I attempted to obtain candidates' positions for the two most recent races held in the district following the 2000 election.[39]

Recall that the subconstituency politics theory predicts that Democratic candidates in these districts will take pro-choice positions and support *Roe*, while Republicans will take pro-life positions and oppose *Roe*. The demand model suggests that all candidates will take the same position in their attempt to appeal to district opinion.

TABLE 4.11   POSITION ON *ROE V. WADE* OF SENATE CANDIDATES
FROM SINGLE-GROUP STATES

Year	State	Candidate	Position
		The Faithful	
2004	North Dakota	Byron Dorgan (D)	Supported
		Mike Liffrig (R)	Opposed
2000		Kent Conrad (D)	Opposed
		Duane Sand (R)	Opposed
		Super-Educated Women	
2004	Connecticut	Chris Dodd (D)	Supported
		Jack Orchulli (R)	Supported
2002		Joe Lieberman (D)	Supported
		Phil Giordano (R)	Supported
2000	Massachusetts	Edward Kennedy (D)	Supported
		Jack E. Robinson (R)	Supported
2002		John Kerry (D)	Supported
		Michael Cloud (L)	•
2002	New Jersey	Frank Lautenberg (D)	Supported
		Douglas Forrester (R)	Supported
2000		Jon Corzine (D)	Supported
		Bob Franks (R)	Supported
2004	New York	Charles Schumer (D)	Supported
		Howard Mills (R)	Supported
2000		Hillary Clinton (D)	Supported
		Rick Lazio (R)	Supported
2002	Rhode Island	Jack Reed (D)	Supported
		Robert Tingle (R)	Opposed
2000		Lincoln Chaffee (R)	Supported
		Robert Weygand (D)	Opposed

Note: D, Democratic Party; R, Republican Party; L, Libertarian Party. Positions are for candidates who ran against opponents. A bullet indicates no position announced.

The positions of House candidates presented in Table 4.12 are consistent with the predictions of the subconstituency politics theory. Of the eight races and sixteen possible positions, twelve were ascertained. Subconstituency politics predicts correctly in about 92 percent (11 of 12) of cases ($p < .001$). While the predictions of the demand model are less specific, in only one of the four races for which both candidates' positions were available does the result support it.

The one case that both subconstituency politics and the demand model predicts incorrectly is Goli Ameri's position in the 2004 race in Oregon's 1st district. While Ameri describes herself as pro-choice, she also favors increased restrictions on abortion, such as parental notification, and opposes federal funding for

TABLE 4.12   POSITIONS ON *ROE V. WADE* OF CANDIDATES FROM MULTIPLE-GROUP DISTRICTS

Year	State	District	Candidate	Position
2002	California	38th	Grace Napolitano (D)	Supported
			Alex Burrola (R)	Opposed
2004	Colorado	6th	Tom Tancredo (R)	Opposed
			Joanna Conti (D)	Supported
2002			Tom Tancredo (R)	Opposed
			Lance Wright (D)	•
2004	Texas	20th	Charles Gonzalez (D)	Supported
			Roger Scott (R)	•
2004	Florida	22nd	Clay Shaw (R)	Opposed
			Robin Rorapaugh (D)	•
2002			Clay Shaw (R)	Opposed
			Carol Roberts (D)	Supported
2004	Oregon	1st	David Wu (D)	Supported
			Goli Ameri (R)	Supported
2002			David Wu (D)	Supported
			Jim Greenfield (R)	•

Note: D, Democratic Party; R, Republican Party. Positions are for candidates who ran against opponents. Districts are listed in order of the degree to which The Faithful and Super-Educated Women are of equal size in a district (i.e., the ratio is closest to 1), and both are greater than 10 percent. A bullet indicates no position announced.

abortions (Cole 2004). Ameri also accepted a $1,000 contribution from the Oregon Right to Life political action committee. In combination, these factors suggest that, contrary to the demand model, Ameri attempted to differentiate herself from the incumbent David Wu on abortion, even though she describes herself as pro-choice.

Turning to the Senate, I apply the same selection criteria employed for House candidates. The five states with the most balanced proportions of Super-Educated Women and The Faithful are Illinois, Delaware, California, Wisconsin, and Minnesota. As with the House races, I attempted to obtain positions for candidates in races held between 2000 and 2004, which are in Table 4.13.

These results are very similar to those observed for the House and are highly consistent with the subconstituency politics theory. Overall, 95 percent of candidates (19 of 20) took positions consistent with the theory's predictions ($p < .001$). The sole incorrect prediction is the pro-choice position taken by California's Republican Representative Tom Campbell, a former economics professor at the University of Chicago, who had represented a progressive congressional district prior to his runs for statewide office. For Campbell, taking a pro-life position would have required switching from his previous position.

Importantly, of the fifteen contests in which both candidates' positions were available, in only two were the results consistent with the prediction of

TABLE 4.13   POSITIONS ON *ROE V. WADE* OF SENATE CANDIDATES
FROM MULTIPLE-GROUP STATES

Year	State	Candidate	Position
2004	Illinois	Barack Obama (D)	Supported
		Alan Keyes (R)	Opposed
2002		Richard Durbin (D)	Supported
		Jim Durkin (R)	Opposed
2002	Delaware	Joseph Biden (D)	Supported
		Raymond Clatworthy (R)	Opposed
2000		Thomas Carper (D)	Supported
		William Roth (R)	Opposed
2004	California	Barbara Boxer (D)	Supported
		Bill Jones (R)	Opposed
2000		Dianne Feinstein (D)	Supported
		Tom Campbell (R)	Supported
2004	Wisconsin	Russell Feingold (D)	Supported
		Tim Michels (R)	Opposed
2000		Herb Kohl (D)	Supported
		John Gillespie (R)	Opposed
2002	Minnesota	Norm Coleman (R)	Opposed
		Walter Mondale (D)	Supported
2000		Mark Dayton (D)	Supported
		Rod Grams (R)	Opposed

Note: D, Democratic Party; R, Republican Party. Districts are listed in order of the degree to which the populations of The Faithful and Super-Educated Women were of equal size in a district (i.e., the ratio was closest to 1), and both were greater than 10 percent.

the demand model. This result is highly statistically significant ($p < .01$), since candidates should take the same position in about seven or eight races due to chance alone.

Evaluation

Taken in combination, these results present a consistent picture of candidates' positioning across states and districts. When positions are combined across single- and multi-group cases, the model correctly predicts a highly statistically significant 89 percent ($p < .001$) of candidates' positions (68 of 76). Moreover, the error rates do not differ much across chambers, as Senate candidates' positions are correctly predicted at about a 93 percent ($p < .001$) rate, while about 88 percent of predictions for House candidates are correct ($p < .001$). Similarly, the difference across districts is relatively small. The model correctly predicts single-group districts at an 89 percent rate ($p < .001$) and two-group districts at a 94 percent rate ($p < .001$).

It is also important to note that in the one domain in which the demand model makes a prediction that clearly differs from the subconstituency politics theory, the results do not support it. The demand model poorly explains candidates' positioning on abortion in campaigns.

Statistical Analysis

As with the case of the assault-weapons ban, employing a statistical framework allows evaluation of the competing theories across states while accounting for bias resulting from selection effects.[40] More specifically, the availability of group-level opinion data allows investigation of whether majority or group opinion better explains candidate positions on abortion. Employing the statistical component is especially important for examining candidates' positioning because deciding whether to take a position may be influenced by strategic factors.

The dependent variable is candidates' positions on abortion, which were obtained by searching newspaper and Internet sources for Senate races that occurred between 2000 and 2004. These sources produced positions for 172 of the 209 Senate candidates who ran for the Senate during this period. Positions on abortion were measured on a 7-point scale that ranged from "abortion should always be legal" to "abortion should be illegal under all circumstances." Higher scores correspond to increased support for restrictions on abortion. Scores for each position on the scale are seen in Appendix 4C.

To evaluate the subconstituency politics theory, active groups must be identified so that subconstituency opinion can be estimated. As discussed earlier, Greenberg (2004) identifies two groups that feel especially strongly about abortion: Super-Educated Women and The Faithful.[41] Greenberg's work provides a strong theoretical basis (and empirical confirmation) to identify The Faithful and Super-Educated Women as active on abortion.

Estimates of state-level opinion on abortion for both the Faithful and Super-Educated Women subconstituencies, as well as for the population as a whole, are obtained using the 2000 National Annenberg Election Study, which surveyed 79,458 respondents.[42] The large sample size allows for reliable estimation of subconstituency opinion.

The opinion measures are constructed in the same manner as in the previous section. *Average Opinion* is mean state opinion on abortion, reflecting the demand model, which predicts that candidates should appeal to majority opinion in the district. In contrast, *Subconstituency Opinion* reflects the mean opinion on abortion among members of the groups to whom candidates in the state appeal. This measure applies the expectations for candidates' positioning to identify the subconstituencies that candidates represent. Specifically, it posits that in districts where both The Faithful and Super-Educated Women are prominent, the Democrat will advocate the opinion of Super-Educated Women, while the Republican will take the mean opinion of The Faithful. In districts in which only one group exists, both candidates will take the mean opinion of that group.

Both of the opinion measures are coded so that higher values are associated with increased restrictions on abortion. The questions used to construct this index are seen in Appendix 4D.

Several additional factors likely influence a candidate's position on abortion. *Female* candidates, who are usually Super-Educated Women, are likely to hold less restrictive positions on abortion. The *Partisanship* of the state electorate may also influence candidates' positions, as states that are more Democratic are more likely to oppose restrictions on abortion. States with larger populations may be associated with fewer restrictions on abortion, since less populous states tend to be more socially conservative. The variable *Population* captures this and should be negatively signed. Higher levels of *Education* may also influence positions on abortion. A final binary variable accounts for the distinctive legacy of the *South* in American politics because the South tends to be more conservative than other parts of the country (e.g., Achen 1978).

As noted in the previous section, candidates' positions may be missing due to strategic avoidance or to a lack of news coverage. Positions that are missing may not occur randomly, a fact that must be considered to ensure unbiased estimates. To account for such selection effects, I employ a Heckman model where the selection equation estimates whether or not we observe a position on abortion, while the main equation estimates each candidate's abortion position.

With few exceptions, the factors held to influence whether we observe candidates' positions are the same as in the case of the assault-weapons ban. *Female* candidates may be more likely to take a position on abortion. In addition, the proportion of the electorate that identifies as white Evangelicals or as Super-Educated Women might affect whether or not a candidate adopts a position. Candidates should be more likely to take a position as the size of these groups increase. Finally, *Candidates' Spending* might influence whether or not a candidate takes a position on abortion. Candidates who spend more money may feel that the excess cash gives them a freedom to talk about only the issues they choose. The results of this analysis are in Table 4.14.

These results reinforce those presented in the case studies. Subconstituency opinion is highly significant, and the coefficient appears relatively large, suggesting that candidates are highly sensitive to the preferences of subgroups. Moreover, *Average Opinion,* the primary alternative hypothesis reflecting the demand model, has no apparent statistical effect. In addition, female candidates are more supportive of abortion rights, as are those from larger and better-educated states.

The results of the selection equation (seen in the column of Table 4.14 titled "Did Candidate Take a Position?") suggest that both strategic decisions and media effects influence whether or not candidates take a position on abortion. Strategically, we see that the decision about whether or not to take a position is heavily influenced by the competitiveness of the race. *Incumbent* is significant

TABLE 4.14 HECKMAN REGRESSION OF CONSTITUENCIES' INFLUENCE ON SENATE CANDIDATES' POSITIONS ON ABORTION, 2000–2004

	Position	Did Candidate Take a Position?
Constant	6.04* (4.30)	−.73 (.88)
Average opinion	−.49 (.64)	
Subconstituency opinion	1.64† (.19)	
Population	−4.74† (1.69)	
Education	−1.62* (.89)	
Partisanship	−.01 (.01)	
Female	−.67* (.28)	−.20 (.31)
South	.41 (.36)	
Competitiveness		.45† (.16)
The Faithful		−.93 (.94)
Super-Educated Women		8.92* (4.68)
Lexis-Nexis sources		−.11* (.06)
Newspapers		.09* (.04)
Candidates' spending (in millions)		3.56 (4.83)
Incumbent		−.39 (.28)
Rho	.20 (.31)	
Observations	158	189

Note: Two-tailed tests. Standard errors are in parentheses.

* $p < .05$.

† $p < .01$.

and negative, suggesting that incumbents are less likely to take a position on abortion. Candidates are much more likely to take a position in a competitive race. The probability of taking a position also increases with the proportion of Super-Educated Women in a state.

The magnitude of a subconstituency's influence is depicted graphically in Figure 4.1, which shows how a candidate's propensity to oppose any restrictions on abortion varies with the constituency's opinion.

While a candidate's position varies little with average opinion, subconstituency opinion has a large impact. Specifically, if we think of the line at .5 as demarcating the point at which a candidate is likely to switch her position, then a change in subconstituency opinion from supporting abortion with no restrictions to supporting it with some restrictions leads candidates to take different positions.

Conclusion

Candidates adopt positions to appeal to intense groups of voters and build a coalition of supporters by repeating this process across issues. This chapter shows that the implications of the subconstituency politics theory are clearly supported on a wide range of issues that vary both substantively and in terms of their visibility.

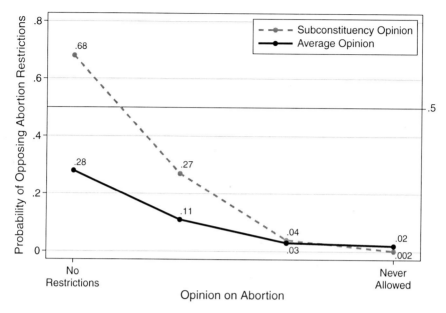

FIGURE 4.1 The probability that a candidate will take the position that abortion should always be legal as opposition within her constituency increases.

Overall, the results, which are summarized in Table 4.15, clearly contradict the predictions of the demand model. On every issue, candidates in constituencies with two active groups did not moderate and take the average position in the district; instead, they supported the more extreme positions advocated by the two active groups. Unfortunately, data do not exist that allow us to ascertain the average opinion of constituents in the one-group districts. The more power-

TABLE 4.15   SUMMARY OF RESULTS OF EMPIRICAL TESTS OF THE DIVERSITY THESIS AND THE SUBCONSTITUENCY POLITICS THEORY IN THE CONTEXT OF CANDIDATE BEHAVIOR

Test	Demand Model	Subconstituency Politics
Non-salient issues: Cuban trade embargo and extension of hate-crimes legislation		
Multiple-group case	–	+
Single-group case		+
Salient issues: Assault-weapons and partial-birth–abortion bans		
Multiple-group case	–	+
Single-group case		+
Combined statistical test	–	+

Note: Blank spaces indicate that the models make no predictions in a context.

ful statistical analyses of the assault-weapons and partial-birth–abortion bans reinforce these results. Candidates do not advocate the preferences of the average voter. Instead, they advocate subconstituencies' preferences.

While the failure of the demand model might be overlooked on the Cuban trade embargo, since the citizenry lacks meaningful preferences on this issue, its failures on the assault-weapons and partial-birth–abortion bans are particularly glaring. Recall that abortion, in particular, is a domestic-policy issue about which the public has well-formed and highly stable preferences. It is on precisely such issues that the demand model should best explain political behavior. Yet contrary to expectations, candidates do not adopt the positions of the average district voter. Instead, they seem to adopt the positions held by intense subconstituencies.

Overall, the results provide strong evidence in favor of the hypothesis that subconstituencies' preferences positively influence candidates' campaign positions. About 90 percent of candidates (35 of 39) took the position that subconstituency politics predicts on the Cuban trade embargo. Similarly strong results were observed on the extension of hate-crimes legislation and abortion: in both cases, about 90 percent of the predictions are correct. The theory best predicts behavior on the assault-weapons ban, where it correctly predicts every case. Even in the case in which it predicts most poorly—that of positions on hate-crimes legislation in one-group districts—it correctly predicts two-thirds of candidates' positions.

These results set the stage for additional testing of the subconstituency politics theory by examining whether candidates continue to service these subconstituencies once elected. The next chapter investigates this question by examining roll-call voting and co-sponsorship on these four issues.

APPENDIX 4A
Database Information

Candidates' positions were researched using Lexis-Nexis, America's Newspapers, and the Google search engine. The newspaper databases contain 406 and 516 newspaper sources, respectively. While Lexis-Nexis's sources are concentrated in heavily populated areas, particularly east of the Mississippi, the sources in the America's Newspapers database are mainly derived from local newspapers and are more evenly distributed around the country. Furthermore, Lexis-Nexis includes the AP Newswire as a source (often the only source for a particular state), while America's Newspapers does not archive the AP Newswire or the *New York Times* as sources.

APPENDIX 4B
Summary of Variables Used in Chapter 4

Variable	Source	Operationalization
Average opinion	2000 National Annenberg Election Study	Average opinion of all citizens in the district. See Appendix 4D for details
Subconstituency opinion	2000 National Annenberg Election Study	Average opinion of group members in the district. See Appendix 4D for details
Population	U.S. Census	Measured in millions
Education	2000 National Annenberg Election Study	7-point scale on which higher scores correspond to increased levels of education
Partisanship	Erikson et al. 1993	Proportion of Democratic identifiers; proportion of Republican identifiers
Female	*Congressional Quarterly Weekly Reports*	1 (candidate is female); 0 (candidate is not female)
South	The eleven states of the Confederacy	1 (southern state); 0 (not southern state)
Competitiveness	*Congressional Quarterly Weekly Reports*	4-point scale in which higher scores are more competitive. This is the folded version of the 7-point scale (1 = safe; 2 = weak; 3 = lean; 4 = toss up)
The Faithful	2000 National Annenberg Election Study	Respondents who self-identified as born-again Christians or as Evangelical and white
Super-Educated Women	2000 National Annenberg Election Study	Self-identified women with at least a four-year college degree
Lexis-Nexis Sources	Lexis-Nexis	The number of news sources included in the Lexis-Nexis electronic database for each state
Newspapers	America's Newspapers	The number of sources included in the America's Newspapers database for each state
Secular Warriors	2004 National Annenberg Election Study	Respondents who do not own guns or attend church
F-You Boys	2004 National Annenberg Election Study	White, married men under fifty without a college degree
Gay	Wilson Institute, University of California, Los Angeles, Law School	Estimated gay, lesbian, and bisexual population from 2005 American Community Study, by district
Born-again	2004 National Annenberg Election Study	Respondents who identified themselves as born-again Christians
Candidate's spending (in millions)	Federal Election Commission	In dollars
Incumbent	*Congressional Quarterly*	1 (incumbent); 0 (not the incumbent)

APPENDIX 4C
Scale for Measuring Candidates' Abortion Position

1: ALWAYS LEGAL

A candidate will receive a score of 1 if he unconditionally supports abortion and the right to choose. Candidates who make this position clear, along with candidates who have a history of never voting to restrict abortion, will receive this score. A candidate who states that he is "100 percent pro-choice" without specifying any exceptions will fall into this category (e.g., Barbara Boxer in 2004).

2: SUPPORTS *ROE V. WADE*

A candidate will receive this score if he supports the Supreme Court's decision in *Roe v. Wade*. Candidates who personally oppose abortion but do not want to see the court's decision overturned will likely fall into this category or into category 3. Unless a candidate has made it clear that he will seek no restrictions on abortion, he will not receive a score of 1 and will fall into this category (e.g., Betty Castor in 2004).

3: OPPOSED TO PARTIAL-BIRTH/LATE-TERM ABORTIONS

A candidate will receive a score of 3 if he generally supports abortion rights, with the exception of late-term or partial-birth abortions. Candidates who are opposed to third-trimester abortions will fall into this category. Candidates in this category typically support most other cases of abortion (e.g., Blanche L. Lincoln in 2004).

4: OPPOSED TO ABORTIONS AFTER THE FIRST TRIMESTER

A candidate will receive a score of 4 if he is opposed to abortions that occur after the first trimester of pregnancy. These candidates will typically advocate rare, safe, and legal abortions done as early as possible. Candidates in this category are opposed to partial-birth and late-term abortions and typically favor some other restrictions, such as waiting periods, parental notification, or barring minors from getting abortions. This category will most likely be filled with candidates who have simply stated where they stand on abortion (e.g., Edward Pipkin in 2004).

5: OPPOSED TO ABORTION UNLESS DUE TO RAPE OR INCEST

A candidate will receive a score of 5 if he believes that abortions should be legal or permissible only for pregnancies that arise as a product of rape or incest. Candidates in this category believe that abortion is wrong under other circumstances, except to protect the life of the mother (e.g., John McCain in 2004).

6: OPPOSED TO ABORTION UNLESS THE MOTHER'S HEALTH IS IN DANGER

A candidate in this category believes that abortion is wrong under nearly all circumstances, except to save the life of the mother (e.g., Harry Reid in 2004).

7: ALWAYS OPPOSED TO ABORTION

A candidate will receive a score of 7 if he opposes abortion in all cases. Candidates who make statements such as "abortion is murder" or liken abortion to infanticide will fall into this category. In addition, candidates who state that they are "100 percent pro-life," without any specific exceptions, will fall into this category (e.g., Pete Coors in 2004).

APPENDIX 4D
The Wording of Questions for Opinion Variables Used in Chapter 4

COMPONENTS OF THE ABORTION INDEX FROM THE 2000 NATIONAL ANNENBERG ELECTION STUDY

Item Number	Wording of Question
CBF01	Do you personally favor or oppose making it harder for a woman to get an abortion? 1 (favor); 0 (oppose)
CBF02	Make it harder for a woman to get an abortion—should the federal government do this or not? 1 (favor); 0 (oppose)
CBF03	Ban all abortions—should the federal government do this or not? 1 (favor); 0 (oppose)

Note: Scores range from 0 to 3, with higher scores corresponding to increased support for restrictions on abortion.

QUESTIONS ABOUT THE ASSAULT-WEAPONS BAN FROM THE 2004 NATIONAL ANNENBERG ELECTION STUDY

Item Number	Wording of Question
cCE32	The current federal law banning assault weapons is about to expire. Do you think the U.S. Congress should pass this law again, or not? 1 (yes); 0 (no)
cCE33	Extending the federal law banning assault weapons—do you favor or oppose this? 1 (favor); 0 (oppose)
cCE34	Extending the federal law banning assault weapons—do you favor or oppose this? 1 (strongly favor); 2 (somewhat favor); 3 (somewhat oppose); 4 (strongly oppose); 5 (neither favor nor oppose)

Note: Questions were combined to obtain an estimate for the proportion who favored extending the assault-weapons ban. The last two items were each asked of opposite halves of the sample. Consequently, there are two items in the scale.

5

Subconstituencies in Congress

In the fall of 1989, following years of controversy surrounding deaths associated with an amino acid supplement called tryptophane, Congressman Henry Waxman (D-Calif.) proposed the Nutrition Labeling and Education Act (NLEA) of 1990. The bill required food labels to list nutritional content and prohibited manufacturers from making health claims until the Food and Drug Administration (FDA) determined that "significant scientific agreement" justified them. The NLEA became law in November 1990.

Building on this success, Waxman turned his attention to increasing the FDA's regulatory authority over vitamins and dietary supplements. In August 1992, Waxman proposed a bill extending the FDA's authority to impose fines and embargo products that flouted FDA regulations by making claims for which there was no scientific consensus (Williams 1992).

The scientific-consensus standard requires that vitamin and supplement manufacturers provide evidence to justify health claims. Since only a few products have been studied for their health benefits, the rule effectively requires manufacturers to sponsor research to validate their claims, an expensive and time-consuming process that could substantially raise prices and lead to products' being pulled from shelves.

Waxman's leadership on the issue of food and vitamin regulation is unsurprising. He is one of the staunchest liberals in the House and a strong advocate of consumer protections, and enhancing food safety seemed a natural target for a man who was "about as powerful as a House member can be" (Barone and Ujifusa 1994, 161).

Waxman's leadership on the vitamin and supplement laws backfired, however. Almost immediately after introducing his bill, Congress was inundated with mail from health-conscious consumers fearing that the FDA was going to ban the sale of vitamins whose manufacturers made unsubstantiated claims—a concern that seems to have had some merit ("FDA Places Vitamins" 1993). Waxman was met by a barrage of criticism. Public meetings were packed with protestors from Waxman's West Los Angeles district, a community with a large population of vitamin consumers. Waxman quickly dropped his support for stiff penalties, and by October 7, 1992, he had struck a deal with Utah Senator Orrin Hatch on the Dietary Supplement Act, which granted vitamin manufacturers a one-year moratorium on complying with the new labeling requirements. In a debate later that month, Waxman recanted his support for regulating vitamins and dietary supplements (Kramer 1992).

While the issue continued to play out over the next two years, the combination of intense constituents and trade organizations for the vitamin industry turned around one of the most powerful members of Congress. In October 1994, reflecting Waxman's more recent view, the House passed his compromise bill that rolled back the FDA's ability to regulate vitamin supplements.

The story of Waxman's positioning on vitamin regulation illustrates the power of latent constituencies. While Waxman's misstep had few electoral consequences—he was handily reelected from an overwhelmingly safe Democratic district—the issue cost him substantial time and effort and the lowest vote percentage (61 percent) in his thirty-four–year House career. It also led to his being challenged both by Democrats in the 1994 primary and by Republicans in the 1992 and 1994 general elections, all of whom cited his stand on vitamin and supplement regulation in their campaigns against him.

Theories of legislative representation have difficulty explaining events like Waxman's experience with vitamin and supplement regulation. Representation theories tend to characterize legislators as delegates, trustees, or politicos (e.g., Eulau et al. 1959) who heed their own preferences, their district's majority-preferred preferences, or some synthesis of the two depending on the circumstances. Sometimes, however, legislators are caught by surprise, as when a latent subconstituency becomes active and opposes a position their legislator has advocated.

Subconstituencies in Congress

The conflicting and disorganized findings about the degree to which citizens control their legislators is an enduring puzzle (e.g., Fiorina 1974; Goff and Grier 1993; Miller and Stokes 1963; Shannon 1968). In many facets of their jobs, legislators emphasize constituents' importance by performing casework, addressing issues important to constituents, and obtaining funding for district projects.[1] As we saw in Chapter 2, studies of policy responsiveness that examine roll-call voting behavior, however, reach less conclusive results depending on the policies examined and the alternative explanations considered (e.g., Hall 1996).[2] Moreover, studies that examine policy responsiveness to subconstituencies find much more consistent evidence for responsiveness than do those that examine responsiveness to majority district opinion (Uslaner 1999).[3]

Subconstituency politics explains how, why, and when politicians appeal to specific groups rather than the majority district position. By recognizing that the subconstituencies to whom candidates appeal vary across issues and districts, subconstituency politics explains the conflicting results observed in past studies as a function of the distribution of group preferences in the district. First, since subconstituencies are not present on most issues in most districts, legislators in those districts use cues other than constituency preferences, such as party or ideology, to make voting decisions. Second, in districts in which only one group cares about an issue, all politicians advocate that group's position. In districts with more than one group, candidates adopt conflicting positions closest to those of their party or ideology. Candidates in these districts are most likely to advocate a position opposed by the majority and, once elected, continue to service that group.

Implications for Congressional Behavior

Subconstituency politics generates three testable implications about legislators' behavior in Congress. First, legislators should cast roll-call votes in a manner consistent with their coalition groups' preferences. The *responsiveness hypothesis* holds that legislators will vote their subconstituency preference rather than moderate their position to appeal to the district majority. Second, the *consistency hypothesis* holds that legislators' positions on roll-call votes should remain the same as their campaign positions as they serve their supporting subconstituencies. Third, the *activity hypothesis* holds that legislators should be more active on issues that are important to groups in their electoral coalition. In essence, subconstituency politics implies that legislators continue to appeal to the groups that got them elected. In the remainder of this section, I explain why the subconstituency politics theory leads to these predictions and then test them using the four cases examined in Chapter 4.

The responsiveness, consistency, and activity hypotheses all stem from the idea that reelection-minded legislators need to maintain their electoral coalitions to ensure their future success. Candidates win by cultivating coalitions of groups. Once elected, legislators work to satisfy these coalition members. To do otherwise is to risk angering the groups and losing their support in the next election. Moreover, appealing to other groups after election is less efficient. Politicians develop reputations on issues, and groups are less likely to trust a legislator who changes a long-held position to get their support.

Legislators satisfy coalitions by casting roll-call votes that are consistent with groups' preferences and by playing a leadership role in developing favorable legislation. While much of this behavior occurs behind the scenes, its manifestation is visible through sponsorship. Helping to initiate legislation signals group members that a legislator is proactive on issues central to her key constituency groups.

In the sections that follow, I test the implications of the competing theories by examining whether congressional behavior is more consistent with the demand model or subconstituency politics on each of the four issues examined in the previous chapter. These tests are performed by examining whether the candidates elected from the states and districts identified in Chapter 4 cast roll-call votes consistent with their subconstituencies' preferences and their campaign positions.

Legislative Representation and the Cuban Trade Embargo

The responsiveness hypothesis holds that legislators vote consistently with their subconstituencies' preferences. According to subconstituency politics, a legislator's position depends on the constellation of groups in a district. In one-group districts, legislators are expected to take the position of that group. Recall that in the case of Cuban trade, most single-group districts are agricultural, while a handful have only old Cubans. Farm-state legislators should vote to reduce trade restrictions. In old Cuban districts (e.g., New Jersey's 13th), however, legislators should support the sanctions. In two-group districts, legislators should advocate the position of the group that supported them. In this case, we expect the Florida legislators to advocate the old Cubans' positions. The model makes no prediction about the behavior of legislators whose districts lack active groups.[4]

The consistency hypothesis holds that legislators continue to advocate the positions taken in the campaign when casting their roll-call votes. If true, we should see a high level of correspondence between legislators' campaign positions and their roll-call votes. To evaluate this hypothesis, we can compare legislators' statements from the campaign with their roll-call behavior. Here, the most interesting test examines those legislators elected from two-group districts because they face the greatest pressure to moderate their positions.

Between 2000 and 2004, House members were given the opportunity to vote on numerous bills pertaining to Cuba, while the Senate had no recorded votes during this period.[5] To test subconstituency politics theory, legislators' votes on the embargo were used to assess their position, wherever possible. It is important to note, however, that the constellation of interests is such that, except in the old

TABLE 5.1   POSITIONS ON REDUCING SANCTIONS FOR LEGISLATORS FROM FLORIDA'S MULTIPLE-GROUP DISTRICTS

District	Legislator	Constituency's Preference	Campaign Position	Roll-Call Position
Senate	Mel Martinez (R)	Opposed	Opposed	•
	Bill Nelson (D)	Supported	Opposed	•
18th	Ileana Ros-Lehtinen (R)	Opposed	Opposed	Opposed
21st	Lincoln R. Diaz-Balart (R)	Opposed	Opposed	Opposed
25th	Mario Diaz-Balart (R)	Opposed	Opposed	Opposed

Note: R, Republican Party; D, Democratic Party. A bullet indicates no position announced.

Cuban districts in New Jersey and Florida, constituent preferences are aligned so that legislators who supported liberalizing travel also support liberalizing trade.[6] Consequently, one can infer that any legislator from an agricultural district willing to co-sponsor bills liberalizing the travel restrictions also supported trade liberalization. This allows us to infer positions for a handful of legislators for whom embargo positions are unavailable. Senators who oppose liberalization need not act at all, as the status quo was illiberal policy toward Cuba. A list of roll-call votes between 1998 and 2004 from which legislators' positions on Cuban trade were ascertained are described in Appendix 5A.

Tests of the responsiveness and consistency hypotheses in the multiple-group districts are seen in Tables 5.1 and 5.2. Recall from Chapter 1 that majority opinion in these states and districts opposes the embargo and travel ban. Consequently, the demand model and subconstituency politics offer competing predictions for these legislators.

The behavior of legislators from multiple-group districts is seen in Table 5.1. Consistent with their constituents' preferences and their campaign promises, every legislator from the multiple-group districts voted to oppose liberalization of Cuba policy. Moreover, since every legislator opposed these policies, none of them co-sponsored any of the bills that came before their chambers.[7] These statistically significant results are consistent with both the responsiveness ($p < .13$) and consistency ($p < .05$) hypotheses.[8] Moreover, the three representatives from two-group districts voted opposite their districts' majority, contrary to the demand model.[9]

The votes cast by legislators from one-group districts are depicted in Table 5.2. All of the legislators from one-group agricultural states and districts are expected to cast votes liberalizing relations with Cuba, while those from the old Cuban districts should oppose these bills.

The results for single group districts also support the subconstituency politics theory. Consistent with the responsiveness hypothesis, every legislator except one (17 of 18) voted with her constituents' preferences ($p < .001$).[10] The consistency hypothesis is also supported as every legislator (15 of 15) voted consistently with her campaign positions ($p < .001$). These results strongly support two key implications of the subconstituency politics theory.

TABLE 5.2 POSITIONS ON REDUCING SANCTIONS FOR LEGISLATORS FROM
SINGLE-GROUP DISTRICTS

State	District	Legislator	Constituency's Preference	Campaign Position	Roll-Call Position
		Agricultural Districts			
Idaho	Senate	Michael Crapo (R)	Supported	Supported	Supported
		Larry Craig (R)	Supported	Supported	Supported
	1st	Butch Otter (R)	Supported	Supported	Supported
	2nd	Mike Simpson (R)	Supported	Supported	•*
Iowa	Senate	Charles Grassley (R)	Supported	Supported	•
		Tom Harkin (D)	Supported	Supported	Supported
	4th	Tom Latham (R)	Supported	Supported	Supported†
	5th	Steve King (R)	Supported	Opposed	Opposed
Montana	Senate	Max Baucus (D)	Supported	Supported	Supported
		Conrad Burns (R)	Supported	•	•
	1st	Dennis Rehberg (R)	Supported	Supported	Supported†
Nebraska	Senate	Chuck Hagel (R)	Supported	Supported	Supported
		Ben Nelson (D)	Supported	•	Supported
	3rd	Tom Osborne (R)	Supported	Supported	Supported
North Dakota	Senate	Kent Conrad (D)	Supported	Supported	•
		Byron Dorgan (D)	Supported	Supported	Supported
	House	Earl Pomeroy (D)	Supported	Supported	Supported
		Old Cuban Districts			
New Jersey	13th	Robert Menendez (D)	Opposed	Opposed	Opposed
Florida	11th	Jim Davis (D)	Supported	Opposed	Opposed‡
	17th	Kendrick Meek (D)	Supported	•	Opposed
	20th	Debbie Wasserman Schultz (D)	Supported	Opposed	•
		Peter Deutsch (D)	Supported	Opposed	Opposed
	22nd	Clay Shaw (R)	Supported	Opposed	Opposed

Note: R, Republican Party; D, Democratic Party. Debbie Wasserman Schultz was elected to an open seat in 2004. There has not been a vote on the embargo since she entered Congress.
* Simpson only had the opportunity to vote on reducing the travel restrictions, which he opposed.
† Opposed trade restrictions but not travel restrictions.
‡ Opposed travel restrictions but strongly supported the embargo.

When the results of one- and two-group districts are taken together, the results provide very strong evidence for subconstituency politics theory, as 97 percent of legislators voted their subconstituency's preference on this low-visibility issue. Moreover, all of the positions legislators voted in Congress were identical to those they took in their campaign.

While the number of cases is limited, it appears that legislators from multiple-group districts were just as likely, if not more likely, to take the clearly identifiable positions held by intense subgroups in the campaign. This is contrary to the implications of spatial voting theory which suggests that legislators attempt to moderate their positions. Moreover, candidates' attempts to obfuscate (e.g., Senator Burns's attempts to liberalize trade) were not limited to campaigns. After all, the Senate chose to hold unrecorded voice votes rather than roll-call votes on

Cuba policy, a fact that may have been motivated by the conflict between the GOP's position and the pressure constituents placed on farm-state Republicans.

Evaluation

Evidence from legislators' behavior on U.S. foreign policy toward Cuba strongly supports the responsiveness and consistency hypotheses. By voting as they had promised, legislators represented the groups to which they had appealed during their campaigns. Even under conditions in which they might have been expected to moderate their positions, as when competing groups existed in a district, the pattern is unmistakable. Equally important, the evidence is also inconsistent with the predictions of the demand model. As we saw in Chapter 1, majority opinion opposes the embargo. Despite this, legislators from two-group states and districts supported it in every case.

Legislative Representation and Hate Crimes

In the 110th Congress, legislation expanding the definition of hate crimes to include people based on sexual orientation, gender, and disability passed both the House and the Senate. After years of failed attempts to garner a floor vote, the House passed H.R. 1592 on May 3, 2007. In the Senate, the bill passed by voice vote following the 60–39 defeat of a filibuster on September 27, 2007. The Democratic leadership attached the bill to a defense-appropriations package to obviate the president's threatened veto. The defense package stalled, however, when liberals who supported hate-crimes legislation opposed the defense-appropriation bill ("Caving in on Hate Crimes" 2007).

These votes allow for the testing of subconstituency-politics and demand-model predictions in the context of hate-crimes legislation. Recall that subconstituency politics holds that in one-group districts, legislators should vote the dominant group's preferences. In two-group districts, legislators should vote the position of the group they appealed to in the campaign, which is usually the group closest to their party's traditional position. In the case of hate crimes, Democrats in two-group districts should support the hate-crimes protections, while Republicans should oppose them.

Two key constituencies that news accounts suggest were active on the issue were gays and born-again Christians. The gay community was sensitive to the issue because Matthew Shepard had been targeted and tortured because of his sexual orientation, an identity that members of this community share. Born-again Christians were activated on the issue because their religious identity holds that a gay lifestyle directly contradicts God's will and that hate-crimes protections based on sexual identity are designed to silence their criticism.

I began testing the implications of the responsiveness and consistency hypotheses on hate crimes by examining whether legislators voted with their

TABLE 5.3   POSITIONS ON HATE-CRIMES LEGISLATION (H.R. 1592) OF CANDIDATES
FROM SINGLE-GROUP DISTRICTS, 2007

State	District	Candidate	Constituency's Preference	Campaign Position	Roll-Call Position
		Born-Again Districts			
Kentucky	1st	Ed Whitfield (R)	Opposed	•	Opposed
Tennessee	1st	David Davis (R)	Opposed	Opposed	Opposed
Alabama	6th	Spencer Bachus (R)	Opposed	•	Opposed
		Gay District			
California	9th	Barbara Lee (D)	Supported	Supported	Supported

Note: R, Republican Party; D, Democratic Party. A bullet indicates no position announced.

subconstituencies and campaign positions. The results from one-group districts are in Table 5.3.

While the number of cases is limited owing to the lack of single-group gay districts, these results are consistent with both the activity and the consistency hypotheses. Each of the four legislators voted with her district's preference ($p < .07$), and both David Davis and Barbara Lee, the only two legislators for whom campaign positions could be obtained, voted consistent with those positions.[11]

The results in Table 5.4 are stronger, as all five of the legislators from multiple-group districts voted both with their constituents and their campaign positions ($p < .04$). Unlike the case of the Cuban trade embargo, however, we are unable to discern whether the results are consistent with the demand model because opinion data are unavailable by state and district on the issue. In Washington State, for instance, both senators were Democrats and thus took the same position, which may well be the position preferred by the state's citizenry.

Taken together, the results from the one- and two-group districts on legislation extending hate-crimes protections based on sexual orientation provide a second low-visibility issue on which legislators' positions are consistent with subconstituency politics. While the results from the one- and two-group districts

TABLE 5.4   POSITIONS ON HATE-CRIMES LEGISLATION (H.R. 1592, S.AMDT. 3035) OF
CANDIDATES FROM MULTIPLE-GROUP DISTRICTS, 2007

State	District	Candidate	Constituency's Preference	Campaign Position	Roll-Call Position
Texas	26th	Michael Burgess (R)	Opposed	Opposed	Opposed
	31st	John Carter (R)	Opposed	Opposed	Opposed
Michigan	2nd	Pete Hoekstra (R)	Opposed	Opposed	Opposed
Washington	Senate	Maria Cantwell (D)	Supported	Supported	Supported
		Patty Murray (D)	Supported	Supported	Supported

Note: R, Republican Party; D, Democratic Party. Positions for House candidates (except incumbents) are unavailable before 2006.

are far beyond what we would expect to see from chance alone ($p < .002$), they poorly discriminate between theories, because it is hard to ascertain majority opinion in the two-group districts. Similarly, in the one-group districts, the theories also predict the same outcome.

Legislative Representation and the Assault-Weapons Ban

The assault-weapons ban sought to extend the 1994 restrictions on semiautomatic weapons, which expired in 2004. The issue provides a difficult test for the subconstituency politics theory because the issue's overwhelming popularity forces legislators from districts with F-You Boys to take the position opposite that preferred by the majority. (A majority of voters in every state favored the extension.) Moreover, as we saw in Chapter 1, it is also a fairly visible issue, indicative of those on which the demand model suggests politicians should be most responsive to majority will. Recall from Chapter 4 that the two active groups on gun issues are F-You Boys and Secular Warriors. The large size differential between these groups creates a case in which F-You Boys are outnumbered in every state and district by Secular Warriors, so that no one-group districts exist that contain only F-You Boys.

Because state-level public-opinion data on the assault-weapons ban are available to test the theories, we can employ both statistical analyses and case studies to test them. In 2004, the Senate held a vote to reauthorize the assault-weapons ban. The House, however, has not held a roll call on the issue since the ban passed in 1994, as the GOP majority leadership opposed the ban. Despite this, some representatives' positions can be identified though co-sponsorship or support of a discharge petition to force the bill out of committee and to the floor for a vote, because these are actions that one would expect only from supporters.[12] To test the responsiveness and consistency hypotheses, I examined whether legislators in these one- and two-group districts advocated the position preferred by their constituents and the position they advocated in their campaigns, respectively.

Table 5.5 presents legislators' positions on extending the assault-weapons ban as obtained through examination of roll-call votes, co-sponsorship, or their signing of a discharge petition. The legislators' behavior corresponds perfectly to both their constituents' preferences (7 of 7) and the positions they advocated in the campaign (5 of 5). These statistically significant results ($p < .01$) support the responsiveness and the consistency hypotheses. Importantly, the results are consistent with both the subconstituency politics and demand models, given that the public overwhelmingly favors the assault-weapons ban. The two-group districts, however, provide a crucial test.

While the two-group case directly pits the theories against each other, the value of the case study is somewhat diminished, because positions for four House

TABLE 5.5 POSITIONS ON THE EXTENSION OF THE ASSAULT-WEAPONS BAN (H.R. 1022)
OF CANDIDATES FROM SINGLE-GROUP DISTRICTS

State	District	Candidate	Constituency's Preference	Campaign Position	Roll-Call Position
New York	14th	Carolyn Maloney (D)	Supported	Supported	Supported
	11th	Yvette Clark (D)	Supported	•	Supported
California	12th	Tom Lantos (D)	Supported	•	Supported
Georgia	4th	Hank Johnson (D)	Supported	•	Supported
Florida	20th	Debbie Wasserman Schultz (D)	Supported	Supported	Supported
Connecticut	Senate	Joe Lieberman (Ind.)	Supported	Supported	Supported
		Chris Dodd (D)	Supported	Supported	Supported

Note: D, Democratic Party; Ind., Independent Party. One-group districts contain Secular Warriors only; no one-group districts with only F-You Boys exist. A bullet indicates no position announced.

members are unavailable. Table 5.6 shows that three of these are Democrats who did not co-sponsor or sign the 2004 discharge petition, and two are Republicans whom one would not expect to see co-sponsor or support the discharge petition because subconstituency politics suggests they should oppose the bill. Two senators, Bernie Sanders and Ken Salazar, joined the Senate after the 2004 vote and have not co-sponsored the bill in the years that have followed.

The results of the two-group test provide additional support for the responsiveness hypothesis ($p < .16$), as 80 percent of legislators (4 of 5) took the expected positions. Unfortunately, owing to a combination of missing information about candidates' positions and roll-call votes, we have fewer cases with which to evaluate the consistency hypothesis, but in both cases for which we can compare them, they match (2 of 2; $p < .25$). While these results are not as strong

TABLE 5.6 POSITIONS ON THE EXTENSION OF THE ASSAULT-WEAPONS BAN
(S.AMDT. 2637) OF CANDIDATES FROM MULTIPLE-GROUP DISTRICTS

State	District	Candidate	Constituency's Preference	Campaign Position	Roll-Call Position
Massachusetts	3rd	Jim McGovern (D)	Supported	Supported	Supported
New York	22nd	Maurice Hinchey (D)	Supported	•	•
Maine	1st	Tom Allen (D)	Supported	Supported	•
New Hampshire	2nd	Paul Hodes (D)	Supported	Supported	•
Nevada	3rd	Jon Porter (R)	Opposed	•	•
Vermont	Senate	Bernie Sanders (S)	Supported	•	•
		Patrick Leahy (D)	Supported	Supported	Supported
Oregon	Senate	Ron Wyden (D)	Supported	•	Supported
		Gordon Smith (R)	Opposed	•	Supported
Colorado	Senate	Ken Salazar (D)	Supported	Supported	•
		Wayne Allard (R)	Opposed	•	Opposed

Note: D, Democratic Party; R, Republican Party; S, Socialist Party. S.Amdt. 2637 was taken in 2004. Positions are for 2002 and 2004. A bullet indicates no position announced. The House did not vote on this bill.

as those in the previous sections, they are highly consistent with the model and, taken together, are statistically significant ($p < .06$).

Fortunately, the problems of missing data are largely overcome by examining senators' behavior. The availability of opinion data allows us to statistically analyze senators' behavior across one- and two-group states while accounting for alternative explanations for roll-call voting. The key variables in the analyses are estimates of *Average Opinion,* which reflects a district's majority opinion, and *Subconstituency Opinion,* which operationalizes the opinions of the groups that senators represent depending on the constellation of group preferences in their states. Higher scores correspond to support for increased restrictions on guns. In states in which Secular Warriors are dominant, senators of both parties rely on their opinion as a cue, while in two-group states, Republicans rely on the opinion of F-You Boys. Opinion on gun control is obtained from the 2004 National Annenberg Election Study.

As in the previous statistical analyses, controls are included to account for influences on legislators' behavior, such as *South, Education, Population,* and state net Democratic *Partisanship.* The measurement of all variables is described in Appendix 5B. As the dependent variable—senators' roll-call votes on the 2004 extension of the assault-weapons ban—is binary, I employ probit to estimate the results.[13]

The substantive results of the statistical analyses are shown in the first two graphs in Figure 5.1, which depict the influence of a shift in the *Subconstituency Opinion* and in *Average Opinion* variables from advocating "fewer" gun-control restrictions to advocating "the same" restrictions that exist under current law (i.e., shifting from 2 to 3 on the 4-point gun-opinion scale) while holding all other variables at their median values.[14] The statistical results on which all three of these figures are based are in Appendix 5C.

While the statistical results show that both *Average Opinion* and *Subconstituency Opinion* are statistically significant predictors of legislators' votes on the assault-weapons ban, their effects vary dramatically. In the subconstituency opinion plot, a small shift in subconstituency opinion leads to a massive 50 percent change in the probability that a senator will support the ban. If we think of legislators with probabilities higher than .5 as likely to vote for the assault-weapons ban and those with probabilities lower than .5 of as likely to vote against it, then this shift is quite powerful in that it implies that the typical legislator will change her vote in response to a change in subconstituency opinion. In contrast, the change that results from shifting average opinion by the same amount leads to a smaller change that is unlikely to change the legislator's vote. These results suggest that subconstituency opinion has a much larger impact on legislator behavior than does district majority opinion, as measured through average opinion.

The third plot in Figure 5.1 simulates the impact of shifting a legislator's campaign position from opposing all forms of gun control (i.e., a 1- to 7-point

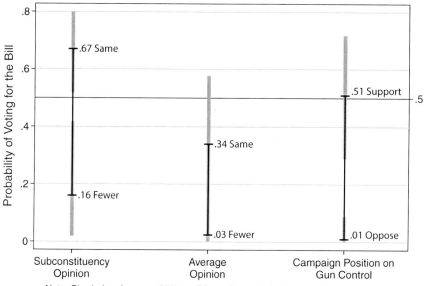

Note: Shaded regions are 95% confidence intervals for the predicted probabilities.

FIGURE 5.1   Change in the probability of voting for the assault-weapons ban.

gun scale) to supporting the assault-weapons ban (scored 3), holding all other variables at their median. Here we see a huge shift of about 50 points in the probability of voting for the bill, although the large range of uncertainty overlaps .5, and thus we cannot be confident that a change in campaign position is associated with a change in a senator's vote. Unsurprisingly, legislators who took a campaign position in which they claimed they opposed gun control had about a 1 percent likelihood of supporting the assault-weapons ban, while those who claimed to support the ban were more likely than not to vote for it.[15]

Legislators' behavior on the highly visible issue of the assault-weapons ban supports the subconstituency politics theory. While legislators are responsive to both average and subconstituency opinion, these results show that they are much more sensitive to their dominant group's preferences. In addition, their roll-call votes are highly consistent with the positions they advocated in their campaigns, which, in turn, is consistent with the consistency hypothesis.

Legislative Representation and Abortion

The fourth case, abortion, is the most highly visible of the issues examined, and like gun control, it should pose a difficult test for subconstituency politics and an easier test for the demand model. To test the responsiveness, consistency, and activity hypotheses, I examined legislators' behavior on abortion-related roll-call votes held in the 106th–108th Congresses (1999–2004). Recall that the active subconstituencies on abortion are Super-Educated Women, who support *Roe v. Wade*, and The Faithful, who oppose it.

In the House, two key issues pertaining to abortion were addressed during this period. The most visible issue was the ban on partial-birth abortion (H.R. 4965). A second key bill, H.R. 4691, brought by pro-life advocates, sought to prevent federal and state governments from discriminating against health-care providers that do not provide coverage for abortions. In the Senate, five bills received votes during this period. Three pertained to the attempt to pass a ban on partial-birth abortion (S. 1692, S. 3, S. 3 Conference Report), and two were Senate amendments to the ban on partial-birth–abortion bills that averred the Senate's support of *Roe v. Wade* (S.Amdt. 2320, S.Amdt. 260). Importantly, the Abortion Non-Discrimination Act of 2002 (H.R. 4691), which passed the House but was not considered by the Senate, and the sense of the Senate amendment on *Roe v. Wade*, which was not considered in the House, provide a comparable baseline for evaluating the hypotheses across chambers on abortion because they both serve as a referendum on *Roe*.[16] All of these votes are described in Appendix 5A.

Employing a combination of case studies and statistical analyses, this section tests the competing theories by looking at the House and Senate roll-call voting behavior of legislators elected from the districts examined in Chapter 4. I employ case studies so the theory can be evaluated for House members for whom district-level estimates of opinion on abortion are unavailable.[17] Finally, since opinion data exist for states, and all states have active groups on abortion, I employ quantitative statistical techniques to simultaneously evaluate the competing representation theories and account for alternative influences on senators' behavior.

One-Group States

As mentioned earlier, two issues reflected legislators' stands on abortion during this period. In the House, the Abortion Non-Discrimination Act was proposed to protect pro-life health-care providers from losing government contracts simply because they choose not to perform abortions. In the Senate, the amendment to the partial-birth–abortion ban expressed senators' support for the *Roe v. Wade* court decision. Subconstituency politics holds that legislators from one-group districts should vote with that group. In districts with The Faithful, legislators should take the pro-life position. In districts dominated by Super-Educated Women, legislators should vote pro-choice.

We begin by examining House members' voting behavior on the Abortion Non-Discrimination Act (H.R. 4691) in single-group districts. Recall from the preceding chapter that The Faithful are the dominant group in Mississippi's 1st district, Tennessee's 4th district, Texas's 4th district, South Carolina's 3rd district, and Ohio's 18th district. Super-Educated Women are the dominant group

TABLE 5.7   POSITIONS ON ABORTION LEGISLATION (H.R. 4691) OF HOUSE
CANDIDATES FROM MULTIPLE-GROUP DISTRICTS, 2002

State	District	Candidate	Constituency's Preference	Campaign Position	Roll-Call Position
California	38th	Grace Napolitano (D)	Pro-choice	Pro-choice	Pro-choice
Colorado	6th	Tom Tancredo (R)	Pro-life	Pro-life	Pro-life
Texas	20th	Charles Gonzalez (D)	Pro-choice	Pro-choice	Pro-choice
Florida	22nd	Clay Shaw (R)	Pro-life	Pro-life	Pro-life
Oregon	1st	David Wu (D)	Pro-choice	Pro-choice	Pro-choice

Note: D, Democratic Party; R, Republican Party.

in New York's 4th, 5th, 12th, and 16th districts, as well as in Illinois's 1st district. House members' roll-call votes on H.R. 4691 are shown in Table 5.7.

These statistically significant results ($p < .001$) strongly support the responsiveness and consistency hypotheses. In the districts dominated by The Faithful, all of the members voted pro-life, as expected. Similarly, in districts dominated by Super-Educated Women, all of the members voted the pro-choice position. In total, representatives from every district voted with their district's dominant group. Finally, the consistency hypothesis is also supported ($p < .001$), as every member voted consistently with her campaign position.

The Senate case study differs from the House in that there are only a handful of single-constituency states, of which only North Dakota is dominated by The Faithful. Connecticut, Massachusetts, New Jersey, and Rhode Island are states with only Super-Educated Women. Senators' votes on the *Roe* amendment are in Table 5.8.

These results also strongly support the responsiveness and consistency hypotheses. While all ten senators from districts in which Super-Educated Women were active voted consistently with their stated campaign positions, Byron Dorgan and Kent Conrad voted contrary to the position espoused by The Faithful. Even so, a statistically significant 83 percent of cases ($p < .05$) are consistent with the predictions of the responsiveness hypothesis, while all of the cases (100 percent) support the consistency hypothesis ($p < .001$).

Multiple-Group Districts

The responsiveness hypothesis predicts that legislators from multiple-group districts will vote their subconstituencies' position on the issue. Specifically, Republican legislators from two-group districts should advocate the pro-life position, while Democrats should advocate the pro-choice position. Subconstituency politics also holds that all legislators should vote in a manner consistent with the position they advocated in the campaign.

TABLE 5.8 POSITIONS ON ABORTION LEGISLATION (S.AMDT. 260) OF SENATE CANDIDATES FROM MULTIPLE-GROUP DISTRICTS

Year	State	Candidate	Constituency's Preference	Campaign Position	Senate Vote
2004	Illinois	Barack Obama (D)	Pro-choice	Pro-choice	•
2002		Richard Durbin (D)	Pro-choice	Pro-choice	Pro-choice
2002	Delaware	Joseph Biden (D)	Pro-choice	Pro-choice	•
2000		Thomas Carper (D)	Pro-choice	Pro-choice	Pro-choice
2004	California	Barbara Boxer (D)	Pro-choice	Pro-choice	Pro-choice
2000		Dianne Feinstein (D)	Pro-choice	Pro-choice	Pro-choice
2004	Wisconsin	Russell Feingold (D)	Pro-choice	Pro-choice	Pro-choice
2000		Herb Kohl (D)	Pro-choice	Pro-choice	Pro-choice
2002	Minnesota	Norm Coleman (R)	Pro-life	Pro-life	Pro-life
2000		Mark Dayton (D)	Pro-choice	Pro-choice	Pro-choice

Note: D, Democratic Party; R, Republican Party. A bullet indicates no position announced.

Recall that districts are chosen so that competing groups are equally matched in terms of size. For the House, the two-group districts are California's 38th, Colorado's 6th, Texas's 20th, Florida's 22nd, and Oregon's 1st. The House members' positions on the Abortion Non-Discrimination Act, as well as the abortion position they took in the campaign, are in Table 5.9.

These statistically significant results are consistent with both the responsiveness ($p < .05$) and consistency ($p < .05$) hypotheses. Every legislator (100 percent)

TABLE 5.9 POSITIONS ON ABORTION LEGISLATION (H.R. 4691) OF HOUSE CANDIDATES FROM SINGLE-GROUP DISTRICTS, 2002

State	District	Candidate	Constituency's Preference	Campaign Position	House Vote
The Faithful					
Mississippi	1st	Roger Wicker (R)	Pro-life	Pro-life	Pro-life
Tennessee	4th	Lincoln Davis (D)	Pro-life	Pro-life	•
		Van Hilleary (R)	Pro-life	•	Pro-life
Texas	4th	Ralph Hall (R)	Pro-life	Pro-life	Pro-life
South Carolina	3rd	Gresham Barrett (R)	Pro-life	Pro-life	•
		Lindsey Graham (R)	Pro-life	•	Pro-life
Ohio	18th	Bob Ney (R)	Pro-life	Pro-life	Pro-life
Super-Educated Women					
New York	16th	Jose Serrano (D)	Pro-choice	Pro-choice	Pro-choice
	5th	Gary Ackerman (D)	Pro-choice	Pro-choice	Pro-choice
	4th	Carolyn McCarthy (D)	Pro-choice	Pro-choice	Pro-choice
	12th	Nydia Velazquez (D)	Pro-choice	Pro-choice	Pro-choice
Illinois	1st	Bobby Rush (D)	Pro-choice	Pro-choice	Pro-choice

Note: R, Republican Party; D, Democratic Party. Positions are for candidates who ran against opponents. A roll-call vote was taken in 2002. Van Hilleary and Lindsey Graham left office the term after the vote. A bullet indicates no position announced.

TABLE 5.10   POSITIONS ON ABORTION LEGISLATION (S.AMDT. 260) OF SENATORS FROM
SINGLE-GROUP DISTRICTS

Year	State	Candidate	Constituency's Preference	Campaign Position	Senate Vote
		The Faithful			
2004	North Dakota	Byron Dorgan (D)	Pro-life	Pro-choice	Pro-choice
2000		Kent Conrad (D)	Pro-life	•	Pro-choice
		Super-Educated Women			
2004	Connecticut	Chris Dodd (D)	Pro-choice	Pro-choice	Pro-choice
2002		Joe Lieberman (D)	Pro-choice	Pro-choice	Pro-choice
2000	Massachusetts	John Kerry (D)	Pro-choice	Pro-choice	Pro-choice
2002		Edward Kennedy (D)	Pro-choice	Pro-choice	Pro-choice
2000	New Jersey	Frank Lautenberg (D)	Pro-choice	Pro-choice	Pro-choice
2004		Jon Corzine (D)	Pro-choice	Pro-choice	Pro-choice
2000	New York	Charles Schumer (D)	Pro-choice	Pro-choice	Pro-choice
2002		Hillary Clinton (D)	Pro-choice	Pro-choice	Pro-choice
2000	Rhode Island	Jack Reed (D)	Pro-choice	Pro-choice	Pro-choice
		Lincoln Chaffee (R)	Pro-choice	Pro-choice	Pro-choice

Note: D, Democratic Party; R, Republican Party. Positions in 2000, 2002, and 2004 are for candidates who faced opposition. A bullet indicates no position announced.

voted as subconstituency politics predicts, as all votes were consistent with the legislators' campaign position and their subconstituency's preferences.

For analysis of the Senate, the multiple-group states are Illinois, Delaware, California, Wisconsin, and Minnesota. The relevant Senate vote was on S.Amdt. 260, a statement of support for *Roe v. Wade* that was added to the ban on partial-birth abortion, which passed 52–46 on March 12, 2003. The amendment was identical to one attached to the partial-birth–abortion ban that had passed four years earlier. Senators' positions and roll-call votes are in Table 5.10.

These significant results are also consistent with subconstituency politics theory, as both the responsiveness ($p < .01$) and consistency ($p < .001$) hypotheses are supported. All of the eight senators who cast roll calls voted consistently with their subconstituencies' preference, as well as with their stated campaign positions. There are two legislators for whom positions were unavailable.[18]

Evaluation

Taken in combination, these cases provide exceptionally strong evidence for the subconstituency politics theory, as the results for legislators' behavior are even stronger than for candidates' position taking. Across chambers and district types, legislators behaved as the responsiveness hypothesis predicts in about 94 percent of cases (49 of 52; $p < .001$). The consistency hypothesis is even more strongly supported as every abortion vote was consistent with the legislators' campaign positions ($p < .001$).

While these case studies provide strong results, their focus on a single type of district and their inability to simultaneously account for rival hypotheses and for probabilistic relationships limits their generalizability. Employing a statistical framework allows us to test competing hypotheses across district types by studying the impact of subconstituency and majority district opinion on senators' roll-call votes.

Statistical Analyses

In contrast to the case studies, statistical analysis allows simultaneous testing of the responsiveness and consistency hypotheses across the one- and two-group districts. Recall that in single-constituency states, subconstituency politics holds that both candidates will advocate the position of that group. There are six single-constituency states. In two-constituency states, subconstituency politics holds that legislators will advocate the position most closely tied to their traditional party position. Forty-four states have both groups.

The key dependent variables for testing the competing theories are the amendments that assess support for *Roe v. Wade*. These two amendments are consistent with the stands on position taking used throughout the book. Moreover, it is the issue of *Roe* about which Super-Educated Women and The Faithful are active and intense.

A second series of abortion bills pertaining to the ban on partial-birth abortion are also of interest. These bills relate less well to Super-Educated Women's activated group identity because these women do not oppose it to the degree that they oppose repealing *Roe*.[19] Consequently, we might expect weaker findings for subconstituency influence.

The dependent variables are roll-call votes on each of the five abortion bills. Votes for the bill are scored "1," while votes against are scored "0." In the 106th Senate, two votes qualified for examination. The first, on S. 1692, banned partial-birth abortions. It passed 63–34 but was later vetoed by President Bill Clinton. The second bill was the Harkin Amendment, S.Amdt. 2320, which expressed the "sense of Congress" in support of *Roe v. Wade*. This bill passed 51–47. No abortion bills were considered in the 107th Senate. In the 108th Senate, three abortion bills received roll-call votes. The ban on partial-birth abortion (S. 3) was considered again and passed 64–33. As in the 106th Congress, the Harkin Amendment supporting *Roe v. Wade* was attached as an amendment (S.Amdt. 260). Finally, the conference report reconciling the House and Senate versions of the partial-birth–abortion bill (which omitted the amendment asserting Congress's support for *Roe*) also passed (64–34).[20]

The demand model is operationalized using the variable *Average Opinion*, which reflects majority opinion as measured using states' mean opinion on abortion. The subconstituency politics theory is operationalized using *Sub-*

constituency Opinion. Higher scores on the opinion measures correspond to increased opposition to abortion. In two-group states, *Subconstituency Opinion* is the mean opinion of The Faithful for GOP senators and the average opinion of Super-Educated Women for Democrats. In one-group states, the average opinion of the active group is used regardless of the senator's party. Consequently, the opinion estimate used depends on the nature of the district and, in two-group states, on the senators' party. *Population* is measured in millions. *Education* is measured according to the average level of school completed. *Partisanship* is measured using net Democratic partisanship (Erikson et al. 1993). The two binary variables, *Female* and *South,* are scored "1" if a senator is female or comes from one of the eleven southern states. The construction and measurement of each of these variables is described in Appendix 5B. As the dependent variable is binary, the model is estimated using probit.

The responsiveness hypothesis asserts that opinion measures should be negatively associated with support for *Roe* but positively associated with support for the partial-birth–abortion ban. Since the partial-birth–abortion bills make it more difficult for women to obtain an abortion, *Female* should be negatively signed on these bills but positively signed on *Roe.* Similarly, the Democratic *Partisanship* variable should be negatively signed on the partial-birth–abortion bills and positive on the *Roe* legislation. Conversely, the *South* variable should be positively signed on these bills and negatively signed on the *Roe* bill. There is no clear expectation about either the *Population* or the *Education* variable. Statistical results for these estimations are in Appendix 5D.

The results show that subconstituency opinion is highly significant, but we are unable to detect any role for average opinion on the *Roe* votes. The results in Figure 5.2 depict the magnitude of the influence of subconstituency opinion on senators' votes on abortion legislation. To estimate the size of the influence, I simulate the effect of shifting subconstituency opinion for an average, "hypothetical" legislator imbued with characteristics of the median legislator from each state for each of the variables included in the model. The influence of subconstituency on the probability of voting for the bill is shown in Figure 5.2.

Figure 5.2 graphically depicts the predicted change in a senator's behavior that results from a very modest shift in subconstituency opinion—from favoring slightly fewer restrictions to favoring slightly more restrictions. The results are stunning. Looking at the *Roe* votes in the first two columns, the probability of a legislator supporting this amendment goes from about 71 percent to about 14 percent, a staggering 57-point decline. If one imagines that a legislator will vote for a bill when the probability is greater than .5, then this shift in subconstituency opinion causes legislators to shift their votes.

The simulated results for the partial-birth–abortion ban, while not as strong, also depict substantial influence for constituency opinion, as the change in a

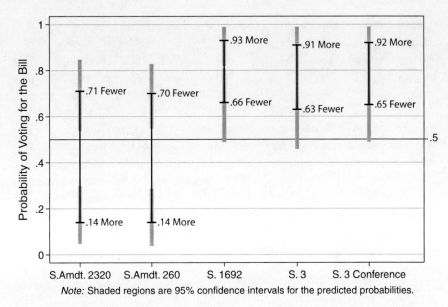

FIGURE 5.2 Change in the probability of voting "yea" when opinion shifts from slightly fewer to slightly more restrictions on abortion.

legislator's probability of voting for the ban averages about 28 percent. While this change never seems to shift the median legislator's vote, it is nonetheless large in absolute terms. Legislators' roll-call votes are better explained by sub-constituency politics than by appeals to the district as a whole.

The consistency hypothesis is evaluated by adding legislators' campaign positions to the model estimated earlier. The full results are in Appendix 5E and clearly support the consistency hypothesis, as legislators' behavior is highly consistent with their campaign positions, even after controlling for alternative explanations. On each vote, the position legislators took in the campaign is both correctly signed and highly significant.

Figure 5.3 depicts the magnitude of the impact that a change in a candidate's abortion position has on the vote. These estimates are calculated by holding all other variables at their medians and shifting a legislator's campaign position from opposing partial-birth abortion to opposing abortion after the first trimester.

Once again, we see massive changes in the probability of voting for the *Roe* bills and smaller, but still quite large, effects on the partial-birth–abortion bills. While the uncertainty is higher because of the reduced number of campaign positions on S.Amdt. 260, a shift in campaign position corresponds to a change in one's vote. While the same result is likely on S.Amdt. 2320, we cannot be confident of this, because the uncertainty bars intersect the .5 line. Even on the partial-birth–abortion votes, the magnitude of the shifts is large, averaging

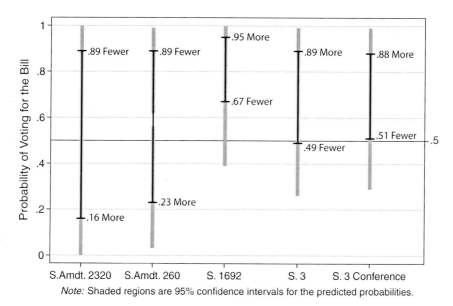

FIGURE 5.3 Probability of voting "yea" when campaign position shifts from supporting *Roe v. Wade* to opposing it, with exceptions.

24 points. Moreover, it is important to note that the shifts in campaign positioning that lead to these results are so subtle that in both cases the campaign position taken is one in favor of legalized abortions under at least some narrow circumstances.

Overall, the results on the abortion issue strongly support the responsiveness and consistency hypotheses. Legislators appeal to their subconstituencies and cast roll-call votes that are consistent with their campaign positions. Perhaps equally important, we see little evidence that legislators appeal to the district's majority opinion.

Co-sponsorship and Subconstituency Politics: A Test of the Activity Hypothesis

The activity hypothesis holds that legislators should be more active on issues that are important to subconstituencies in their states and districts. Activity levels are difficult to gauge, as most work is done behind the scenes and off the *Congressional Record*. One indicator for such activity, however, is the decision to sponsor or co-sponsor legislation.

Co-sponsoring legislation signals that the issue is important and serves as a proxy for the intensity of a legislator's preference. There are myriad reasons to agree to co-sponsor, however, above and beyond being influenced by a strong subconstituency (e.g., Koger 2003). As Barry Burden (2007) points out, legislators' decisions about which issues to work on often stem from their personal evaluations of what is important.

Recall that subconstituency politics holds that politicians both reflect the views of the intense groups in their districts and work to deliver policy to them on the issues they feel strongly about. The activity hypothesis suggests that co-sponsorship rates among legislators with active district groups should be higher than rates for legislators who lack such groups. To test the activity hypothesis, co-sponsorship data and data that allow us to identify a legislator's dominant district group are needed. Data are available to examine co-sponsorship on the hate-crimes, assault-weapons, and abortion issues.

The movement to extend hate-crimes protections to cover sexual orientation is advocated by gay groups and opposed by born-again Christians. The activity hypothesis implies that legislators who represent districts in which gays are the dominant group should work to pass this legislation and to signal their disproportionately strong support to this subconstituency. Consequently, the proportion of legislators from gay districts who co-sponsor legislation should be larger than the proportion of those from districts dominated by born-again Christians.

To test this hypothesis I examined co-sponsorship on three bills introduced in the 110th Congress (2007). Sponsored by John Conyers, H.R. 1592 collected 171 co-sponsors (37 percent) in the House.[21] In the Senate, Ted Kennedy sponsored both S. 3035, which was offered as an amendment to a large defense-appropriations bill, and was co-sponsored by thirty-four senators (34 percent), and S. 1105, a stand-alone bill that was co-sponsored by forty-four senators (44 percent).

The proportion of senators representing each constituency who co-sponsored hate-crimes legislation is shown in Table 5.11. On each of the three bills, the proportion of co-sponsors from gay-dominated districts dwarfs the proportion from born-again–dominated districts, as subconstituency politics predicts. On every bill, the difference in co-sponsorship rates across groups is highly statistically significant. Moreover, on both Senate votes, the rate of co-sponsorship is about double that of the Senate as a whole. In the House, however, the rate of co-sponsorship among the gay districts is about the same as for

TABLE 5.11 PERCENTAGE OF LEGISLATORS CO-SPONSORING HATE-CRIMES LEGISLATION, BY DOMINANT GROUP, 2007

Bill	Gay (%)	Born-Again (%)	Difference (%)
H.R. 1592 (171)	40	8	32*
S. 3035 (34)	87	26	61*
S. 1105 (44)	93	35	58*

Note: One-tailed tests. The number of co-sponsors is in parentheses.

$*p < .01$.

TABLE 5.12   PERCENTAGE OF LEGISLATORS CO-SPONSORING
ASSAULT-WEAPONS LEGISLATION, BY DOMINANT GROUP

Year	Bill	Secular Warriors (%)	F-You Boys (%)	Difference (%)
2004	S. 2637 (13)	22	6	16*
2007	H.R. 1022 (60)	21	0	21†

Note: One-tailed tests. The number of co-sponsors is in parentheses.
* $p < .05$.
† $p < .01$.

the House as a whole (39 percent). These results support the activity hypothesis in the context of hate-crimes legislation.

In the case of the assault-weapons ban, the activated subconstituencies are Secular Warriors, who support the legislation, and F-You Boys, who oppose it. The two bills on which co-sponsorship data are available are the 2004 Senate vote on the assault-weapons ban, S. 2637, which had 13 co-sponsors (13 percent), and the 2007 House bill H.R. 1002, which had 60 co-sponsors (14 percent). The activity hypothesis holds that legislators serving Secular Warriors should sponsor at higher rates than those serving F-You Boys.

Co-sponsorship on the assault-weapons ban also supports the activity hypothesis. Table 5.12 shows that in both chambers, the difference in co-sponsorship rates is significantly higher for legislators serving Secular Warriors than for those catering to F-You Boys. Moreover, in both cases these rates are also about 50 percent higher than the rate of co-sponsorship for the House and Senate as whole.

Co-sponsorship information is available for two of the five Senate votes on partial-birth abortion (S. 1962, S. 3), as well as on the 2002 Abortion Non-Discrimination Act (H.R. 4691) in the House. While the Senate bills were both co-sponsored by about 45 percent of the chamber, only 22 percent of the House co-sponsored H.R. 4691. The activity hypothesis holds that legislators from states in which The Faithful are the dominant group are more likely to co-sponsor legislation that restricts abortion. Faithful districts are those in which The Faithful are the only group, as in a one-group district, or in two-group districts that are represented by a Republican. The activity hypothesis holds that the proportion of legislators who co-sponsor from districts dominated by The Faithful should be much larger than the proportion who co-sponsor from districts dominated by Super-Educated Women.

The results in Table 5.13 are the largest we have seen in the three issue areas and are highly consistent with the activity hypothesis. Legislators from Faithful districts are significantly more likely to co-sponsor pro-life legislation. In each case, the levels of support for senators serving The Faithful are about double the rate of the Senate as a whole, while House members co-sponsor at a rate about 50 percent higher than that for the average representative.

TABLE 5.13   PERCENTAGE OF LEGISLATORS CO-SPONSORING
ABORTION LEGISLATION, BY DOMINANT GROUP

Year	Bill	The Faithful (%)	Super-Educated Women (%)	Difference (%)
1999	S.1962 (46)	78	7	71*
2002	H.R. 4691 (95)	38	5	33*
2003	S.3 (44)	84	4	80*

Note: One-tailed tests. The number of co-sponsors is in parentheses.
* $p < .01$.

Summary and Conclusion

Despite his power and electoral security, Henry Waxman switched his position on vitamin and supplement regulation because he unknowingly activated a sub-constituency on an issue for which there was only one intense group in his district. This example demonstrates the power the people wield when they feel intensely enough to overcome their lack of interest in politics.

One of the central questions of representation examines the degree to which the citizens can control their elected officials. This chapter shows that legislators' behavior in Congress is strongly influenced by intense groups rather than by the average voter and that, once elected, legislators continue to support the positions they advocated in their campaigns. The results also show that legislators are disproportionately active on issues important to groups in their districts, as the activity hypothesis suggests. Table 5.14 summarizes the results of the tests about legislators' behavior performed in this chapter.

The evidence supports the subconstituency politics theory in every test and is inconsistent with the demand model in almost every test in which the competing theories generate differing predictions. The results appear to be very robust, as similar findings are observed across four very different issues that run the gamut from civil rights and domestic policy to ethnic politics and foreign policy. While the average citizen often appears to go unrepresented, legislators' responsiveness to subconstituencies suggests that the people have the means to rein in their elected officials. Congressman Henry Waxman's position change on vitamin labeling illustrates the people's power by showing that subconstituencies can affect even very safe legislators.

When combined with evidence from the preceding two chapters, these results undermine the demand model. The individual-level assumptions relating to the issue visibility thesis—that individuals who are more highly exposed to news are more knowledgeable—find no support. In contrast, members of groups with activated identities know more about issues related to those identities, even when those active groups are drawn from among the least knowledge-

TABLE 5.14 SUMMARY OF RESULTS FOR TESTS OF THE DEMAND
MODEL AND THE SUBCONSTITUENCY POLITICS THEORY IN THE
CONTEXT OF LEGISLATOR BEHAVIOR

Test	Demand Model	Subconstituency Politics
Cuban Trade		
Responsiveness	–	+
Consistency		+
Hate Crimes		
Responsiveness		+
Consistency		+
Activity		+
Assault Weapons		
Responsiveness	Mixed	+
Consistency		+
Activity		+
Abortion		
Responsiveness	–	+
Consistency		+
Activity		+

Note: Blank spaces indicate that the models make no predictions in a context.

able in the populace. Moreover, as we have seen, the campaign- and institutional-level results strongly support the subconstituency politics theory and are inconsistent with the demand model. Neither candidates nor legislators advocate the views of the average voter in their districts. Instead, where subconstituencies exist, candidates in campaigns and legislators in Congress advocate the views of those intense groups to whom they appealed in their campaigns.

These findings are extremely robust across the aspect of democracy, the issue, and the methodology examined. The analysis presented in this chapter examines four issues that conventional explanations suggest might lead to different levels of constituency influence. The examination of responsiveness, both in campaigns and in Congress, shows that rather than adopting a mealy mouthed moderate position, legislators in multi-group districts adopt these groups' policy positions.

The notion that politicians appeal to smaller, intense groups on less visible issues such as the Cuban trade embargo and hate-crimes legislation may seem unsurprising. Assault weapons and abortion policy, however, represent issues about which citizens are knowledgeable and on which politicians are thought to be least able to shirk. Here too, however, legislators ignore their districts' majority preferences and appeal to active subconstituencies both in campaigns and in Congress. It is not likely that these differences are attributable to methodology, because different methods are used to examine these policies, and in all cases the same results are achieved. Subconstituency politics explains candidates' positioning in campaigns and in Congress better than does the demand model.

The next section of the book employs subconstituency politics to examine whether legislative responsiveness varies according to the diversity of the citizenry in the district and whether legislators are more responsive on more visible issues.

APPENDIX 5A
Summary and Description of Relevant Roll-Call Votes

VOTES ON THE CUBAN TRADE EMBARGO

106th Congress

H.R. 4871, Treasury and General Government Appropriations Act, 2001. This appropriations bill featured many amendments dealing with Cuba.

H.Amdt. 1023, offered by Representative Charles Rangel (D-N.Y.), to prohibit funds from being used to enforce the economic embargo. It failed 174–241 in roll call no. 424.

107th Congress

H.R. 2590, Treasury and General Government Appropriations Act, 2002.

H.Amdt. 242, offered by Representative Charles Rangel (D-N.Y.), called for the lifting of the Cuban embargo. It failed 201–227 in roll call no. 271.

H.R. 5120, Treasury and General Government Appropriations Act, 2003.

H.Amdt. 552, offered by Representative Jeff Flake (R-Ariz.), restricted funding to enforce the travel ban to Cuba. It passed 262–167 in roll call no. 331.

H.Amdt. 555, offered by Representative Charles Rangel (D-N.Y.), called for a lifting of the embargo. It failed 204–226 in roll call no. 333.

108th Congress

S.Amdt. 1900, offered by Senator Byron Dorgan (D-N.D.), called for lifting the travel ban. It was agreed to by a voice vote.

H.Amdt. 772, sponsored by Representative Charles Rangel (D-N.Y.), prohibited funding from going to enforce the embargo. It failed 188–225 in record vote no. 461.

VOTES ON EXTENDING HATE-CRIMES PROTECTIONS

110th Congress

H.R. 1592, sponsored by Representative John Conyers Jr. (D-Mich.), garnered 171 cosponsors. It passed 237–180 in record vote no. 299.

S. 3035, sponsored by Senator Edward Kennedy (D-Mass.), garnered thirty-four cosponsors. It passed on a voice vote after cloture was invoked by vote of 60–39 in roll call no. 350. It was later stripped from the larger bill.

S. 1105, sponsored by Senator Edward Kennedy (D-Mass.), garnered forty-four cosponsors. No action had been taken at the time of this writing.

VOTES ON THE ASSAULT-WEAPONS BAN

108th Congress

H.R. 2038, reauthorization of the assault-weapons ban, sponsored by Representative Carolyn McCarthy (D-N.Y.), garnered 111 co-sponsors. It never received a vote, as a discharge petition failed with seventy-two signatures.

S. 2637, sponsored by Senator Dianne Feinstein (D-Calif.), garnered thirteen co-sponsors. It passed 52–47 on record vote no. 24.

109th Congress

H.R. 1312, reauthorization of the assault-weapons ban, sponsored by Representative Carolyn McCarthy (D-N.Y.), garnered ninety-four co-sponsors, but never received a vote.

110th Congress

H.R. 1022, sponsored by Representative Carolyn McCarthy (D-N.Y.), garnered sixty co-sponsors but has not yet received a vote.

VOTES ON ABORTION

106th Congress

S. 1692, Partial-Birth Abortion Ban Act of 2000, sponsored by Senator Rick Santorum (R-Penn.), passed 63–34 in record vote no. 340. The bill was was later vetoed by President Bill Clinton.

S.Amdt. 2320, an amendment to S. 1692 sponsored by Tom Harkin (D-Iowa), expressed the sense of Congress in support the Supreme Court's decision in *Roe v. Wade*. It passed 51–47 in record vote no. 337.

107th Congress

No Senate bills concerning abortion made it to a roll-call vote in the Senate during the 107th Congress.

H.R. 4691, Abortion Non-Discrimination Act of 2002, prevented federal and state governments that receive federal assistance from discriminating against health-care providers solely because they do not pay for or provide coverage for abortion procedures. It passed 229–189 in roll-call vote no. 412.

H.R. 4965, Partial-Birth Abortion Ban Act of 2002, sponsored by Representative Steve Chabot (R-Ohio). It passed 274–151 in vote no. 343.

108th Congress

S. 3, Partial-Birth Abortion Ban of 2003, sponsored by Senator Rick Santorum (R-Penn.). It passed 64–33 in record vote no. 51. The House version of the bill was H.R. 760, which passed 282–139 in record vote no. 242. Because these bills differed, they went to conference, which struck S.Amdt. 260.

S.Amdt. 260, expressing the sense of Congress in support of *Roe v. Wade,* was similar to the Harkin Amendment attached to the previous bill banning partial-birth abortion. It passed 52–46 in record vote no. 48.

S. 3 Conference Report, the conference report to S. 3, passed 64–34 in record vote no. 402. The bill also passed in the House 281–142 in record vote number 530.

APPENDIX 5B
Construction and Measurement of Variables in Regression Models

Variable Name	Description
Average opinion	
Gun control	Average state opinion on the 4-point question on gun control is from the 2004 National Annenberg Election Study (NAES), item cce31, rescaled so that higher scores correspond to support for increased restrictions. Opinion on the assault-weapons ban (employed in Appendix 5C) is from the 2004 NAES, items cce32 and cce33.
Abortion	Mean state opinion on abortion is from the 2000 NAES; the variable was constructed using items cbf01 and cbf02 to create a 4-point scale in which higher scores correspond to increased restrictions on abortion.
Campaign position	
Gun control	Legislator's placement (based on campaign position) on the 7-point scale in which 1 is anti–gun control and 7 favors banning handguns. Precise coding details are in Appendix 4B.
Abortion	Legislator's placement (based on campaign position) on the 7-point scale in which 1 corresponds to no restrictions on abortion and 7 corresponds to a complete ban on abortion. Precise coding details are in Appendix 4B.
Education	7-point scale of educational attainment; higher scores correspond to increased education levels.
Female	Scored 1 (legislator is female) or 0 (legislator is not female).
Partisanship	State's net Democratic partisanship using the scores in Erikson et al. 1991; for House districts, estimates were created using the 2000 NAES.
Population (in millions)	From the U.S. Census.
South	Scored 1 (legislator represents any of the eleven Confederate states) or 0 (legislator does not represent one of these states).
Subconstituency opinion	
Gun control	Subconstituency opinion on the 4-point gun-control question from the 2004 NAES, item cce31, rescaled so that higher scores correspond to support for increased restrictions. In states with F-You Boys as the dominant group, this measure records the opinion of respondents who are F-You Boys. Where Secular Warriors are the dominant group, the measure records the average opinion of those respondents. Opinion on the assault-weapons ban (employed in Appendix 5C) is from the 2004 NAES, items cce32 and cce33.
Abortion	Subconstituency opinion on the abortion measure is described as above, except that instead of calculating states' average opinion on abortion, average opinion for each subconstituency was calculated. For states with only Super-Educated Women, the score is their mean score. For states in which The Faithful are the dominant group, the score is the mean abortion score.

Variable Name	Description
Subconstituency opinion (*continued*)	
Super-Educated Women	Proportion of a district's population that consists of women with college degrees or higher estimated using the U.S. Census.
Gay	Estimated percentage of each state and district that is gay, lesbian, or bisexual. Figures are from the Wilson Institute at University of California, Los Angeles, School of Law and based on the 2005 American Community Survey from the U.S. Census.
F-You Boys	White, married men under fifty with less than a college degree, from the 2004 NAES.
Born-again	Respondents who self-identified in the 2004 NAES as "born-again."
Secular Warriors	Respondents who never go to church and do not own a gun, from the 2004 NAES.
The Faithful	Proportion of the district's population that consists of white Protestants, estimated using the 2000 NAES.

APPENDIX 5C
Probit of Subconstituency and Average Opinion on Senators' Votes on the Assault-Weapons Ban

	Opinion on Assault Weapons	Opinion on Gun Control	Campaign Positions on Gun Control
Average opinion	10.86‡ (5.63)	3.26* (1.35)	1.23 (1.80)
Subconstituency opinion	6.01† (1.51)	1.53† (.39)	1.96† (.63)
Campaign position		.20‡ (.11)	
Education	−.86 (1.20)	−.71 (1.25)	.43 (1.67)
Partisanship	.01 (.02)	.01 (.02)	.02 (.03)
Population (in millions)	−.02 (.03)	−.02 (.03)	.02 (.04)
South	−1.14* (.53)	−1.14* (.53)	−1.15 (.73)
Constant	−8.16 (5.17)	−11.99* (5.04)	−12.38‡ (6.57)
Observations	93	93	64
Log-likelihood	−40.44	−41.64	−24.06

Note: Standard errors are in parentheses.
* $p < .05$.
† $p < .01$.
‡ $p < .10$.

APPENDIX 5D

Probit of Senate Abortion Votes from the 106th and 108th Congresses

	Roe Bills		Partial-Birth–Abortion Bills		
	S.Amdt. 2320	S.Amdt. 260	S. 1692	S. 3	S. 3 Conference Report
Average opinion	.30 (1.09)	.55 (.98)	1.16 (1.04)	1.90‡ (1.04)	1.91‡ (1.06)
Subconstituency opinion	−1.64† (.34)	−1.65† (.34)	1.20† (.34)	1.14† (.35)	1.13† (.35)
Female	1.22 (.79)		−.65 (.59)	−1.08‡ (.62)	−1.39‡ (.72)
Education	.98 (1.42)	1.14 (1.34)	−.97 (1.45)	−.52 (1.54)	−.49 (1.56)
Partisanship	.03 (.02)	.03 (.02)	−.04‡ (.02)	−.07‡ (.03)	−.07* (.03)
Population (in millions)	.00 (.04)	.06 (.04)	−.02 (.03)	−.10* (.05)	−.12* (.05)
South	−1.22* (.59)	−1.21* (.58)	.92 (.64)	2.25* (.85)	2.24* (.87)
Constant	−.78 (6.96)	−2.10 (6.40)	−.10 (6.97)	−2.68 (7.29)	−2.70 (7.37)
Observations	93	94	92	93	94
Log-likelihood	−36.36	−39.54	−33.34	−28.75	−28.04

Note: Standard errors are in parentheses.

* p < .05.

† p < .01.

‡ p < .10.

APPENDIX 5E
Probit of the Influence of Campaign Positions on Roll-Call Votes

	Roe Bills			Partial-Birth–Abortion Bills	
	S.Amdt. 2320	S.Amdt. 260	S. 1692	S. 3	S. 3 Conference Report
Average opinion	.69 (2.75)	-.94 (2.29)	2.79‡ (1.68)	3.13‡ (1.61)	3.08‡ (1.61)
Subconstituency opinion	-2.52* (1.27)	-2.26† (.83)	1.52* (.74)	1.27* (.56)	1.27* (.55)
Campaign position	-1.76* (.79)	-1.10† (.32)	.76* (.32)	.72† (.26)	.69† (.26)
Female	1.83 (4.00)		-.13 (.84)	-.53 (.82)	-.73 (.92)
Education	-2.80 (3.32)	-.20 (2.60)	1.17 (2.89)	1.29 (3.00)	1.16 (3.03)
Partisanship	-.10 (.11)	-.05 (.06)	-.09‡ (.05)	-.08‡ (.05)	-.08‡ (.05)
Population (in millions)	-.08 (.14)	.05 (.06)	-.18‡ (.09)	-.16* (.07)	-.17* (.07)
South	-.27 (1.43)	1.07 (1.54)	2.13 (1.46)	2.66‡ (1.38)	2.63‡ (1.38)
Constant	22.91 (20.07)	11.94 (14.34)	-13.83 (14.00)	-14.49 (14.40)	-13.67 (14.57)
Observations	70	80	69	79	80
Log-likelihood	-7.83	-13.77	-15.11	-16.01	-15.95

Note: Standard errors are in parentheses.

* $p < .05$.

† $p < .01$.

‡ $p < .10$.

6

Heterogeneity and Representation Reconsidered

CONSTITUENT: *"You don't represent me, and that's supposed to be your job."*
SENATOR SANTORUM: *"Obviously, I can't represent everybody's viewpoint. . . .*
My job is to respect everybody's viewpoint, and I do."
—EXCHANGE BETWEEN AN ANGRY CONSTITUENT AND SENATOR RICK SANTORUM,
AS REPORTED IN THE *PITTSBURGH POST-GAZETTE*, MARCH 27, 2003

Since the time of Aristotle, elites have claimed that diversity in a polity is an inherent good, with more always being preferred to less. James Madison saw diversity of peoples and interests as the solution to the problem of majority tyranny. In today's society, American governmental and educational institutions promote policies designed to embrace, and enhance, diversity to take advantage of its benefits. Others suggest that increased diversity allows for the consideration of a greater range of potential solutions to the problems that face a polity (Sunstein 1993).

Social scientists routinely find, however, that the role of diversity is quite complex. In some instances, diversity has negative effects. Diverse societies show higher levels of civil conflict and political instability (Geertz 1973; Rabushka and Shepsle 1972). Some find that the effects vary with different types of institutions (e.g., Collier 2000) and have varying effects in different venues (e.g., Hero and Tolbert 1995a). Others suggest that for reducing inequality, some types of diversity are more effective than others (e.g., Wilson 1987).

Interest in diversity has also led to the investigation of its relationship to representation. Unsurprisingly, these results are also complex. Scholars have long recognized that diversity affects particular aspects of representation (e.g., Fenno 1978; Rohde 1991). Some programs designed to enhance descriptive diversity lead to outcomes that appear to reduce substantive representation (e.g., Lublin 1997). Moreover, politicians elected from diverse constituencies, for instance, are less responsive than those from more homogeneous constituencies (e.g., Bailey and Brady 1998; Bishin et al. 2006, but see Gulati 2004). Taken broadly, these studies suggest that enhanced diversity is associated with decreased levels of legislative representation, a finding that seems inconsistent with the central value of liberalism which underlies democracy.

Liberalism, the idea that all people in society should have equal voice, has become central to modern conceptions of democracy, and virtually all studies of representation assume that politicians equally consider the views of all of their constituents.[1] This chapter examines whether the relationship between political diversity (see Appendix 6A) and representation is affected by overlooking the importance and role of subconstituencies. The problem introduced by electoral diversity is that as an electorate becomes diverse in its preferences, politicians are forced to choose among the positions held by their constituents.[2] As illustrated by Senator Santorum's remark, perfect substantive representation is impossible when constituents disagree.[3] In such cases, politicians must choose whom to represent. As a result, diversity bears critically on studies of responsiveness—the degree to which legislators' behavior reflects the preferences of the citizenry.

The examination of representation in campaigns and in Congress in the preceding chapters makes it clear that, contrary to conventional wisdom, states and districts are not easily stereotyped as diverse or homogeneous. On the issues of Cuban trade and assault weapons, for example, Florida's 20th district is homogeneous, with only one group that feels strongly about those issues. On issues of abortion and extending hate-crimes protections, however, the district has multiple groups holding competing viewpoints. Clearly, scholars need to be cautious when making generalizations about diversity.

The conflicting results about the role of diversity are problematic, as they suggest that the quality of representation provided to citizens varies depending on factors outside of their own, and their elected officials', immediate control. The preferences of institutions such as state legislatures, which both manipulate the political characteristics of the district and are far removed from citizens' control, interfere with the relationship between the citizenry and its' elected officials. To the extent that these institutions diminish the quality of representation that they receive, democratic responsiveness is compromised. If so, then rules designed to ensure electoral fairness, such as "one man, one vote" or rules proscribing "racial redistricting" or requiring "compactness" are not enough to ensure that citizens in different districts will be equally well represented. Consequently, these findings have important implications for political scientists and policymakers alike.

This chapter examines whether the deleterious effects of diversity still hold once subconstituency effects are considered. Since scholars who observe adverse effects from diversity fail to account for subconstituencies, it seems quite possible that their conclusions may prove erroneous once subconstituencies are considered. The failure to account for subconstituencies may lead to the mistaken conclusion that diversity inhibits democracy.

The findings and conclusions of past research are based on the assumption that politicians represent the will of the majority, which is operationalized by considering all citizens' views. As we have seen, this assumption is ill-founded, as politicians appeal to groups rather than to the public as a whole. Moreover, whenever there is disagreement in a district, politicians must choose among competing perspectives.

I begin by examining the concept of representation and investigate the finding that diversity diminishes it, which is called the diversity thesis. The subconstituency responsiveness hypothesis provides an alternative explanation for the findings about the diversity thesis. Owing to data limitations, however, I create a new measure of representation and test its implications. The results show that candidates and legislators from homogeneous versus heterogeneous districts show no systematic difference in the degree to which their behavior corresponds to their subconstituencies' preference.

Measuring Representation

The term "represent" reflects the idea that public officials should make present one or more aspects of the citizenry that elects them (e.g., Pitkin 1967). While there is considerable discussion of the different ways in which politicians represent the citizenry (e.g., symbolic or descriptive), most research focuses on substantive representation, which is the attempt to make citizens' preferences present through a politician's actions (Pitkin 1967). Thus, political scientists who examine substantive representation are concerned with the degree to which the behavior of elected officials reflects the preferences of their constituents.

One measure of substantive representation is *responsiveness,* which assesses the degree to which politicians change their behavior as their constituents change their preferences (Achen 1978). This measure assesses how well politicians in a legislature take positions that co-vary with those of their constituents, but it does not evaluate politicians' absolute policy positions. Usually, responsiveness is evaluated either over time, where we look to see whether, for instance, the behavior of members of Congress changes with their constituents' preferences, or cross-sectionally, as when members from more conservative districts behave in a more conservative manner than do those from other, less conservative districts. The notion of responsiveness is thought to reflect the democratic principle that "what people decide must influence the outcome" (Achen 1978, 490).[4] It is important to note, however, that this operationalization may not be consistent with a lay person's intuition of responsiveness, which seems to require that politicians do what their constituents' want.

Responsiveness is not the only aspect of representation, however. Christopher Achen (1978) identifies two other aspects of representation that describe the degree to which individual legislators can represent the citizenry. *Proximity* reflects the idea that legislators should be ideologically close to, or ideologically resemble, their citizens. Because proximity depends on the distribution of citizens' preferences, legislators from homogeneous districts will always necessarily be closer to their constituents than will those from diverse districts, simply because a heterogeneous citizenry is more widely dispersed (Achen 1978). A weakness in this measure is that proximity is dependent on factors outside the politician's control. An alternative conception of representation, called *centrism*, assesses the degree to which a legislator's position is located in the center of the distribution of constituents' preferences and reflects the liberal-democratic norm of fairness or equal consideration of all views (Achen 1978).

One limitation of these measures is that they require data that are seldom available. Proximity and centrism require estimates of opinion and candidates' positions on identical scales. Even responsiveness requires estimates of constituents' opinion on the same issue as legislators' behavior, which is only occasionally available and even then only at the state rather than district level of analysis. To overcome these limitations, I employ a new measure that allows for the testing of hypotheses about representation that existing measures do not.

Correspondence: Voting Correctly

Representation can be assessed by evaluating whether legislators take the position preferred by a majority of the people in the district. This standard, called *correspondence*, is based on Richard Lau and David Redlawsk's (2006) work on "voting correctly" (Bishin and Park 2008). A legislator's behavior corresponds to his constituents' preference when he casts a roll-call vote on an issue that is identical to the position preferred by the majority of his constituents. Correspondence has an important advantage over responsiveness in that it requires politicians not just to move with constituents, but also to act precisely as constituents want them to act.[5] By evaluating whether legislators are carrying out their constituents' wishes, correspondence bridges a gap between people's perception of what responsiveness means and the concept scholars are evaluating. In fact, correspondence can be thought of as a special case in which there is "perfect" responsiveness that occurs when the position of a legislator and the district are identical.

Rather than requiring knowledge of citizens' and legislators' precise preferences to calculate policy distances, correspondence requires only that we know whether politicians advocate the same position preferred by their constituents.

While any individual's specific policy preference is often unknown, the preferences of active groups or even the district as a whole are often known, so in some cases we can use this information to test the subconstituency representation hypothesis.

Take, for instance, the example of Cuban American politics examined in Chapter 1. While district-level public-opinion data for the south Florida congressional districts do not exist, news reports of county-level data (which essentially comprise three districts) and data released by the campaigns provide some leverage. When these reports are consistent with the public statements of group members, we can draw inferences about the preferences of groups in the county.

Heterogeneity and Representation

Despite its importance, the degree to which diversity conditions politicians' responses to citizens' preferences has received relatively scant attention. Legislators seem very responsive in terms of Heinz Eulau and Paul Karps's (1977) symbolic, allocative, and service criteria, irrespective of district diversity. In the domain of policy responsiveness, however, differences emerge.

Studies of policy responsiveness show that representation varies with diversity within a state. Michael Bailey and David Brady (1998), for instance, find that the influences on legislators' roll-call votes on the General Agreement on Tariffs and Trade and the North American Free-Trade Agreement differ significantly between homogeneous and diverse states.[6] More specifically, they find that legislators in states ranked among the twenty-five least diverse are driven by constituents' interests, while the behavior of those from the twenty-five most heterogeneous states is largely driven by political-party and personal ideology. The authors conclude that "the representative process is different in homogenous and heterogeneous states" (Bailey and Brady 1998, 536). Similar results are observed in the context of campaign position taking, where both ideological and descriptive diversity affect candidates' responsiveness (Bishin et al. 2006).[7] Taken in combination, I refer to the finding that diversity diminishes responsiveness as the *diversity thesis*.

Others examine diversity and responsiveness in racial, ethnic, and economic groups. In particular, studies of African Americans and Latinos highlight the benefits (and tradeoffs) that result from creating majority-minority districts that are more racially or ethnically homogeneous to ensure that these traditionally disadvantaged groups are represented descriptively (e.g., Lublin 1999). While some scholars disagree (e.g., Shotts 2003), these studies generally show that increasing the number of group members in a district beyond a certain point adversely affects that group's ability to obtain favorable policy. Instead, once a certain threshold of diversity (i.e., percentage of the population) is reached, a legislator will be substantively responsive to the group (Lublin 1999).

Other studies of African Americans examine how the size of a group in a district affects responsiveness (e.g., Hutchings 1998; Whitby 1997).[8]

The results of these studies suggest that both responsiveness and the cues legislators use to make decisions vary depending on the diversity of the district. In some districts, the party platform may dominate, while in others, constituents' views drive behavior. To date, however, not a single study of how legislators behave *in their districts* suggests that legislators in diverse districts behave any differently, or are motivated by different goals, from those in homogeneous districts. To the contrary, those who have observed legislators emphasize the similarity of their behavior across district types (e.g., Fenno 1978, 1996; Kingdon 1971). Moreover, even those scholars who find that diversity matters fail to offer a theoretical mechanism that explains why citizens' preferences should matter less in diverse states or districts.

A Subconstituency-Based Explanation

The lack of evidence explaining reduced responsiveness combined with the finding that politicians appeal to groups rather than to districts as a whole suggests that an alternative explanation for these results may exist. A group-politics explanation also seems consistent with the finding that diversity conditions responsiveness.

At its core, preference heterogeneity deals with group interests, as individuals can be categorized into groups of citizens who support, oppose, or ignore issues on the agenda. Subconstituency politics holds that politicians appeal to, represent, and build coalitions of individuals to gain support. Groups form when several individuals share an intense preference on one or more issues. Their intensity gives them political power disproportionate to their size (Dahl 1956; Olson 1971). Heterogeneity describes the diversity of preferences on an issue in a district.

Subconstituency politics accounts for groups and provides an alternative to the diversity thesis. Instead of resulting from different representational processes, the findings from existing research may be a product of the distribution of group preferences. If legislators appeal to groups in both homogeneous and heterogeneous states, then assuming that politicians appeal to the average district voter may introduce bias in our estimates of citizens' preferences—the difference between the opinion of the average citizen and the opinion of the group—into the estimates of citizens' preferences.

Implications, Methods, and Data

The subconstituency politics theory generates two testable implications to evaluate whether diversity affects responsiveness. First, it provides a mechanism that explains the results obtained by scholars relying on average district data. Second, it implies that once subconstituencies are considered, we should not observe any systematic differences in responsiveness across levels of district diversity.

Case Selection

To draw inferences about diversity and representation that are not contaminated by the effect of issue visibility, I selected two cases that vary dramatically in their visibility. Doing so helps to ensure that the results can be generalized and that, to the extent that the results we observe are the same across issues (whether politicians are responsive or not), they cannot be attributed to issue visibility. The low-salience issue I examine is the Cuban trade embargo, of which the public seems largely unaware, while the high-salience issue is abortion, on which virtually every citizen has a well-considered opinion (Jelen and Wilcox 2003). Controlling for issue visibility in this way allows us to draw firmer conclusions about the effects of diversity on representation.[9]

For similar reasons, wherever possible, representation is tested by examining politicians' behavior through their campaign position taking and roll-call voting. While most studies of representation examine only a single chamber of Congress, democratic theory suggests that representatives might be more representative than are senators. Therefore, to ensure that the variation was not dependent on the chamber of Congress or the setting in which the behavior was examined, wherever possible I examined the relationship between representation and diversity across these settings.

Does Diversity Reduce Responsiveness?

Why might we observe diminished responsiveness in diverse polities? One explanation is measurement error. Imagine that legislators are equally responsive to the dominant district group in both homogeneous and heterogeneous districts. Measures of average district opinion better reflect constituents' influence in homogeneous districts, where the group's preference is more similar to the preferences of the rest of the district.[10] Similarly, the difference between the dominant district group and the average voter is greater in heterogeneous districts. In this circumstance, statistical models that incorporate average district measures are less likely to find legislators from these heterogeneous districts to be as responsive. Simply put, studies that overlook subconstituency appeals are more likely to mismeasure citizens' preferences in diverse districts, and therefore lead to a mistaken conclusion about the effect of diversity. The manner through which this occurs is illustrated in Figure 6.1.

Figure 6.1 illustrates that the distance between the average citizen's opinion and the opinion of the average member of the subconstituency is smaller in the

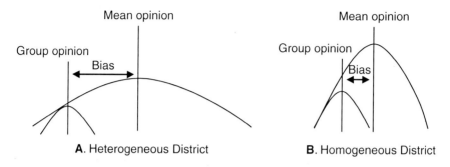

A. Heterogeneous District   **B**. Homogeneous District

FIGURE 6.1   (A) Bias in a heterogeneous district; (B) bias in a homogeneous district.

homogeneous district than in the heterogeneous one. This occurs because, in homogeneous constituencies, there is less variation around the average opinion of the state or district. While measures of the average citizen's preferences are biased in both scenarios, the bias is much larger for estimates taken from heterogeneous districts than for homogeneous ones, because the preference of the group in the homogeneous district is likely to differ less from the preference of the district as a whole. One consequence is that average district opinion should be much more closely related to legislators' behavior in homogeneous districts, not because legislators are any more responsive, but because measures of constituencies' preferences are less biased under these conditions.

It is noteworthy that even in homogeneous districts, politicians appeal to segments of their constituency rather than to the public as a whole.[11] Since there are very few issues on which all constituents agree, politicians frequently confront the dilemma that Senator Santorum faced. In both homogeneous and diverse districts, legislators may respond by reflecting the preference of the largest group of citizens with a position on the issue.[12] If scholars mistakenly estimate constituents' preferences by accounting for the preferences of all citizens, rather than only the group to whom legislators actually appeal, the representative in the heterogeneous state mistakenly appears less faithful to the electorate than does the legislator representing the homogeneous state.

We can test this implication in a simple way. If the mechanism identified by the subconstituency politics theory is correct, then the distance between the opinion of a subconstituency and the average voter in a district should be greater in heterogeneous districts than in homogeneous ones. Fortunately, data are available to test this prediction at the state level using the measures of subconstituency opinion and average district opinion on abortion employed in Chapters 4 and 5. Specifically, we can estimate the distance between average district opinion and the opinion of the subconstituency represented by each legislator and compare these distances across state types.[13] Our expectation is that the difference between average district opinion and subconstituency opinion should

TABLE 6.1   ABSOLUTE VALUE OF THE DIFFERENCE BETWEEN AVERAGE AND
SUBCONSTITUENCY OPINION ON ABORTION, BY STATE

	Single-Group Districts	Multiple-Group Districts	Difference
The Faithful	.18 (1)	.63 (24)	−.44*
Super-Educated Women	.12 (6)	.39 (16)	−.27 [p < .01]
Combined	.13 (7)	.53 (40)	−.40 [p < .001]

Note: The number of states is in parentheses. Probability (p) values are based on one-tailed difference of means tests, with samples assumed to have unequal variances.

* Unable to estimate significance due to lack of single-group cases.

be small to nonexistent in homogeneous (one-group) states, and much larger in heterogeneous (two-group) states. Consequently, the difference between these (within state) differences should be negative and significant if the sub-constituency politics theory is correct. The results of these analyses are shown in Table 6.1.

Table 6.1 depicts the differences in opinion on abortion first, by active group across levels of diversity (e.g., Super-Educated Women in one-group versus two-group states); and second, by comparing average opinion distances across one- and two-group states. The results are highly consistent with the subconstituency politics mechanism. Regardless of the group, the difference between average and subconstituency opinion is negative, a finding consistent with expectations in every case. Moreover, in those cases for which enough data exist to estimate statistical significance, the results are always highly significant. In homogeneous states, we see smaller differences that are about one third the size of the differences observed in the heterogeneous states. When we combine these results across groups, the average difference is highly significant as well. These results are consistent with the subconstituency politics-based explanation for the finding that diversity conditions responsiveness.

It is important to note, however, that the results are not inconsistent with the diversity thesis, since it is possible that legislators from diverse districts are less proximate to the citizens but more responsive relative to legislators from other districts. Legislators from homogeneous districts might be closer to the citizenry but might not move with them quite as well.

Testing Subconstituency Responsiveness

If politicians from homogeneous and heterogeneous states are equally representative, then the differences in responsiveness that we observe when using average district opinion should disappear when we examine responsiveness to subconstituencies. Moreover, contrary to past research, we should find that legislators are responsive regardless of the level of diversity within the district. These implications lead to the *subconstituency responsiveness* hypothesis, which holds that there is a strong positive relationship between politicians' behavior and the preferences of subconstituency groups, regardless of district diversity.

Following the strategy pursued throughout the book, I try to test the theory in as many contexts as possible to ensure robustness while using methods similar to those employed in past research to ensure that the findings are comparable. Past research has relied on Herfandahl indices of descriptive diversity such as the Sullivan Diversity Index (e.g., Bailey and Brady 1998; Sullivan 1973) or measures of ideological dispersion such as the variance around mean state ideology (e.g., Bishin et al. 2006; Gronke 2001; Jones 2003). These studies classify states as diverse if they are above the median on these indices and homogeneous if they are below the median. Since states do not necessarily coalesce into diverse and homogeneous groups at equal rates (of twenty-five) on all issues, considering the constellation of district groups provides a more intuitive approach.[14] We can classify states according to whether only one group is active, more than one group is active, or no groups are active on the issue.[15] Homogeneous states are those with only one active group on the issue. Heterogeneous states are those with two opposing groups that are active on the issue.

Unfortunately, two major limitations inhibit the application of standard statistical models for assessing responsiveness in roll-call voting. First, the lack of variation in state diversity on abortion and Cuban trade inhibit estimation of statistical models of senators' roll-call–voting behavior. Second, public-opinion data are available only on the abortion issue and only at the state level. While the lack of variation in state diversity might be overcome by examining House members' behavior to obtain more cases, the absence of reliable opinion data impedes the use of statistical models of House roll-call voting behavior.[16]

Given these limitations, I tested the subconstituency responsiveness hypotheses in two ways. On the Cuban trade embargo, I examined whether the correspondence between politicians' behavior varied with district diversity in campaign positioning and legislators' roll-call voting. On abortion, I examined correspondence on legislators' roll-call votes. Moreover, the more nuanced positions recorded in candidates' public statements allow an assessment of responsiveness on abortion in campaigns.

Diversity and Representation in Campaigns

The first test of the subconstituency responsiveness hypothesis examines whether diversity conditions candidates' representativeness in the positions they adopt in their campaigns. If diversity is inconsequential, then candidates' positions should not vary across levels of district diversity when holding constituents' preferences constant. Specifically, candidates who represent a specific group should hold that group's position, regardless of whether they are running for office in homogeneous or heterogeneous districts.

We begin by examining whether candidates' positions on abortion vary with district diversity. Candidates' positions on abortion are obtained from news coverage of campaigns and are rated on a 7-point scale ranging from "abortion should always be legal" to "abortion should be illegal under all circumstances." Higher scores correspond to increased support for restrictions on abortion. (Scores for each position on the scale are described in Table 2.1.)

States are classified as diverse or homogeneous according to whether they have more than one active group in the district. Diverse states are those two-group states in which both The Faithful and Super-Educated Women are prominent.[17] Subconstituency politics predicts that in such states, the Democrat will take the position advocated by Super-Educated Women, while the Republican will take the position of The Faithful. In contrast, homogeneous states are those in which only one group exists. There, candidates from both parties will take the position of that group.

We can examine whether responsiveness varies with constituency diversity by comparing candidates' positions on abortion across districts within the two different constellations of groups. Specifically, we can look to see whether the average position taken by a legislator from a two-group state differs from that taken by a legislator in a one-group state. By comparing candidates representing the same groups across levels of state diversity we can see whether diversity leads to differences in positioning on issues.

The subconstituency responsiveness hypothesis clearly implies that we should observe no difference in candidates' positions across districts. The diversity thesis implies that we should observe differences in responsiveness across states while the influence of constituents' opinion remains the same. In two-group (i.e., diverse) states, the diversity thesis suggests candidates will take more moderate positions than in one-group states.[18] Consequently, since legislators are appealing to the entire district, two-group states should produce candidates with more moderate positions on abortion.[19]

The expectations from the diversity thesis suggest that a constituency's views moderate as diversity within a district increases. Candidates from two-group districts representing The Faithful should have lower scores, indicating support for relatively fewer restrictions on abortion, than those from single-group districts. Conversely, candidates from two-group districts representing Super-Educated Women should have higher scores, indicating increased support for increased abortion restrictions than those from single-group districts.[20] To summarize, if diversity affects responsiveness, then we should see differences across columns and within rows in Table 6.2.

TABLE 6.2   SENATE CANDIDATES' AVERAGE POSITIONS ON ABORTION, BY STATE
DIVERSITY AND GROUP

	Single-Group Districts	Multiple-Group Districts	Difference
The Faithful	5.3 (3)	5.2 (77)	.1 [$p < .98$]
Super-Educated Women	2.3 (18)	2.6 (71)	−.3 [$p < .37$]

Note: The number of candidates is in parentheses. For positions on the abortion scale, see Chapter 4. P values are based on one-tailed difference of means tests, with samples assumed to have unequal variances.

The results in Table 6.2 are interesting on several levels. While there are only a handful of candidates from one-group states, the positions held by candidates in single group cases do not seem to be any different from the positions held by those in diverse districts. The differences in positions held by candidates representing the different groups, however, as indicated by comparing scores within columns and across rows, are quite substantial. Candidates from states dominated by Super-Educated Women support *Roe v. Wade,* while candidates from districts dominated by The Faithful hold that abortion should never be legal except when due to rape or incest. Substantively, these results are consistent with our expectation that candidates who respond to a particular constituency in a diverse state should respond to the same constituency in the same way as they would in a homogeneous state.

We can perform a similar test using candidates' positions on the Cuban trade embargo. Because we have less nuanced positions in the case of the embargo, we can only examine the frequency with which candidates' positions are the same as constituents in different types of districts. More precisely, we can test for correspondence by examining whether the difference between the proportions of candidates taking the corresponding position varies across one- and two-group districts. Since there are relatively few states and districts with active groups on the issues, we examine House candidates' positions across districts. Recall from Chapter 4 that diverse districts are those with both old and new Cubans in the 18th, 21st, and 25th districts of south Florida. Homogeneous districts are those with just old Cubans (New Jersey's 13th and Florida's 11th, 17th, 20th, and 22nd) and the farming districts located primarily in the Midwest.[21] If the subconstituency responsiveness thesis is correct, then we should see no difference in correspondence in one- versus two-group districts.[22]

The results from Table 6.3, while instructive, are far from definitive. First, the distribution of groups is such that farmers are found only in homogeneous districts that lack old and new Cubans. Conversely, new Cubans are found only in districts that also have old Cubans. Old Cubans are found in both homogeneous and diverse districts. Because of the small number of districts and their concentration, it is hard to compare across categories. When we compare totals,

TABLE 6.3 PROPORTION OF HOUSE CANDIDATES' CORRESPONDING EMBARGO
POSITIONS, BY STATE DIVERSITY AND GROUP

	One-Group Districts	Two-Group Districts	Difference
Farmers	90% (10)	No cases	
Old Cubans	100% (5)	100% (3)	0
New Cubans	No cases	100% (3)	
Combined	93% (15)	100% (6)	7% [$p < .73$]

Note: The number of candidates is in parentheses. For positions on the embargo, see Chapter 4. Lacking directional
hypotheses, p values are based on one-tailed difference of means tests, with samples assumed to have unequal variances.

however, we see that 93 percent of candidates from one-group states took a
position that corresponded with the subconstituency position, while all candidates (100 percent) from diverse districts did so, a relatively small and statistically insignificant difference ($p < .71$).[23] Taken in combination with the abor-
tion-positioning results, these findings are consistent with the subconstituency
responsiveness hypothesis.

Diversity and Correspondence in Congress

Do legislators from homogeneous states cast corresponding roll-call votes at
greater rates than do those from heterogeneous states? For abortion, I examine
legislators' roll-call votes pertaining to *Roe v. Wade*, issues addressed in the 106th
and 108th Senates and the 107th House.[24] For the Cuban trade embargo, relevant roll calls were taken only in the 106th and 107th Houses, and no roll calls
were taken in the Senate, between 1999 and 2004.

To investigate the impact of diversity on responsiveness, I examine the
abortion bills introduced in Chapter 5. Recall that during this period, there
were five Senate roll-call votes on abortion. Three pertained to attempts to ban
partial-birth abortion (i.e., S. 1692, S. 3, S. 3 Conference Report), sponsored by
Senator Rick Santorum. The other two bills (S.Amdt. 2320, S.Amdt. 260)
expressed the sense of the Senate on the *Roe v. Wade* court case.[25] A 107th
House bill that closely matches the *Roe* amendments is H.R. 4691, the Abortion
Non-Discrimination Act of 2002, which was designed to prevent discrimination in the allocation of federal or state funding against health-care providers
who refuse to perform abortions. The bill passed the House handily but died
in committee after introduction in the Senate. I focus on the *Roe* bill and
amendments because, as shown in Chapter 3, Super-Educated Women and
The Faithful are active and interested in *Roe*, while Super-Educated Women
are less unified on partial-birth abortion.

In the remainder of this section, I test whether legislators from single-group
districts had greater rates of correspondence than those from two-group states.

TABLE 6.4   PERCENTAGE OF "CORRECT" VOTES ON ABORTION CAST IN THE
HOUSE AND SENATE, BY DIVERSITY

	Single-Group Districts	Multiple-Group Districts	Difference
106th Congress			
S.Amdt. 2320	83% (12)	89% (84)	−6% [$p = .69$]
107th Congress			
H.R. 4691	76% (93)	85% (318)	−9% [$p < .95$]
108th Congress			
S.Amdt. 260	83% (12)	85% (84)	−2% [$p < .54$]
Combined	78% (117)	86% (486)	−8% [$p < .97$]

Note: The number of legislators who voted is in parentheses. Lacking directional hypotheses, p values are based on two-tailed difference of means tests, with samples assumed to have unequal variances. H.R. 4691 was cast in the House. All other votes were taken in the Senate.

For legislators from states in which The Faithful are dominant, a corresponding vote is the pro-life position on these bills. For those from states and districts in which Super-Educated Women are dominant, a pro-choice vote is correct. Applying this rubric, we can simply compare whether the proportion of corresponding votes varied across district types on the various abortion bills. Recall that the subconstituency responsiveness hypothesis predicts that there should be no difference across district type.[26] The results are in Table 6.4.

The results in Table 6.4 show very high levels of correspondence across states. On average, more than 80 percent of legislators voted correctly on abortion. Comparing across district types, however, the results show no definitive pattern, though the differences are slightly negative in each case, implying that, if anything, legislators from heterogeneous states might be more representative. Of course, these results are inconsistent with what we would expect to observe if the findings of the diversity thesis were broadly generalizable.

We can examine correspondence on legislators' votes on the Cuban trade embargo as well. While there were no Senate roll-call votes on the issue during the time period under study, there were three relevant votes in the House in the 106th (H.Amdt. 1031) and 107th (H.Amdt. 242, H.Amdt. 555) Congresses.[27] For strategic reasons, each of these votes came in the form of an amendment to an appropriations bill. Rather than repealing the embargo itself, each of these amendments was designed to de-fund the enforcement of the embargo on issues pertaining to food, agriculture, and pharmaceutical supplies. The first of these amendments, H.Amdt. 1031, passed in the 106th House. The two amendments offered in the 107th failed.

Our expectation on the House votes is that representatives from the one-group agricultural districts should vote for these amendments, while those from the old Cuban districts (New Jersey's 13th and Florida's 11th, 17th, 20th, and 22nd) should oppose it. Florida's 25th district was not created until the 108th

TABLE 6.5 PERCENTAGE OF "CORRECT" VOTES ON THE CUBAN TRADE EMBARGO
CAST BY REPRESENTATIVES, BY DIVERSITY

	Single-Group Districts	Multiple-Group Districts	Difference
106th House			
H.Amdt. 1031	92% (12)	100% (2)	$-8\%\ [p < .65]$
107th House			
H.R. 242	100% (12)	100% (2)	0
H.R. 555	92% (12)	100% (2)	$-8\%\ [p < .65]$
Combined	94% (36)	100% (6)	$-6\%\ [p < .71]$

Note: The number of legislators who cast votes is in parentheses. For positions on the embargo, see Chapter 4. Lacking directional hypotheses, p values are based on two-tailed difference of means tests, with samples assumed to have unequal variances.

Congress, so in the 106th and 107th Congresses, there were only two diverse districts (Florida's 18th and 21st). Since both of these districts were represented by Republicans—Ileana Ros-Lehtinen and Lincoln Diaz-Balart—they should have opposed these amendments. The subconstituency responsiveness hypothesis holds that we should see no difference in the frequency of correspondence across levels of diversity. These results are in Table 6.5.

Overall, the results seem quite consistent with the subconstituency responsiveness hypothesis, as the differences across districts are small, and when they do exist, they are in the direction opposite that implied by the diversity thesis: Representatives from homogeneous states had lower levels of correspondence than did those from heterogeneous districts. In no case are these differences significant, and when combined across all votes, an overwhelming proportion of representatives (94 percent) voted correctly on each of the three bills.

While these results must be taken with caution, given the small number of cases, nonetheless there is no discernible pattern to indicate that legislators from one-group states and districts cast votes that corresponded with their constituents' preferences at higher rates than did their counterparts from diverse states. Given the breadth and consistency of the findings, the results seem likely to be generalizable. Moreover, the analyses evaluate the relationship between diversity and representation across a broad range of contexts, including campaigns and Congress, both in the House and Senate, as well as visible (abortion) and less visible (Cuban trade) issues.

Despite these findings, it is important to reemphasize that the results in Tables 6.3–6.5 do not allow for the evaluation of the effect of diversity on *responsiveness* and thus are not directly comparable to past research. Instead of rejecting or overturning these past findings, the test of correspondence only allows one to conclude that, under one reasonable standard of representation—correspondence (which equates to perfect responsiveness)—legislators from diverse states behave consistently with their subconstituencies' preferences at about the same rate as do those from homogeneous states. In addition, the conclusions of the diversity thesis do not extend to correspondence. In every case in which we observed a difference, diverse states had higher levels of correspondence.

Discussion and Conclusion

Whether in campaigns or in Congress, politicians are equally representative in homogeneous and diverse districts. Subconstituency politics seems to explain why previous studies may have found otherwise. Politicians everywhere are forced to make choices when constituents disagree, which they virtually always do. On both the Cuban trade embargo and the issue of abortion, not only does representation frequently occur but we also observe little variation in the degree to which it varies across districts.

By evaluating the degree to which the elected do what the people want, the measure of representation called "correspondence" better reflects citizens' conception of representation and thereby avoids the paradox of responsiveness. Moreover, using correspondence, we are better able to describe the degree to which a system is representative and to identify those legislators whose behavior is inconsistent with citizens' preferences.

When examining correspondence, or the degree to which legislators do what their constituents want them to, no difference between diverse and homogeneous districts emerges. Legislators vote as their subconstituencies demand at approximately the same rate in diverse and homogeneous districts. Both in the positions they take in campaigns and the votes legislators cast in Congress, politicians appeal to subconstituencies regardless of district diversity. Each of the results, when taken case by case, provides modest support for the subconstituency responsiveness hypothesis. Given the unanimity of the findings, however, the results of the four tests provide much stronger support. By implication, these results also support the subconstituency politics theory. The findings from these tests are summarized in Table 6.6.

These results are sensitive to the aspect of representation being examined. For example, Achen (1978) shows that through no fault of their own, legislators from diverse states are necessarily less proximate to their constituents, because they have little control over the dispersion of citizens' preferences in their district. It appears, however, that legislators have a great deal more control over the degree to which they are centrist or responsive or to which their behavior corresponds to the preferences of the citizenry. Taken in this context, the results raise new questions about the degree to which the elected are responsive to the citizenry as a whole rather than just to those with intense preferences. This finding, while independent of the degree of diversity, is most easily seen in diverse districts, because it is in such venues that politicians face hard choices on issues precisely because constituents disagree.

TABLE 6.6 SUMMARY OF RESULTS OF EMPIRICAL TESTS OF THE DIVERSITY THESIS AND THE SUBCONSTITUENCY POLITICS THEORY

Test	Diversity Thesis	Subconstituency Politics Theory
Mechanism		+
Candidates' behavior		
Abortion	−	+
Cuban trade embargo		+
Legislators' behavior		
Abortion		+
Cuban trade embargo		+

Note: Blank spaces indicate that the models make no predictions in a context.

These differences across indicators of representation suggest that scholars need to be much clearer in their analysis and consideration of the implications of different aspects of representation. Because the different measures have different implications and, as Achen shows, can lead to very different results, scholars must be especially attentive to the characteristics of representation being considered and their relevance to the question of interest.

The concept of diversity also requires reconsideration. Pundits and scholars frequently describe districts and people as diverse without fully considering the context in which the judgment is being made. As we saw with the example of Florida's 20th district at the beginning of this chapter, a district that is diverse on one issue may not be on some other issue. Moreover, measures of diversity based on descriptive characteristics have the potential to be especially misleading, since physical or economic diversity may not correspond to diversity in preferences on any particular issue. Students of representation would do well to consider that diversity is contextual and depends on the issue under consideration, as well as on the aspect of representation being evaluated.

Finally, it is worthwhile to consider the normative implications of the relationship between the concepts of responsiveness and correspondence. As noted, correspondence is identical to responsiveness in the case where legislators' behavior is identical to constituents' preferences. In a sense, then, correspondence reflects an ideal type or level of representation in which citizens always get what they want. In the legislative setting, this standard might be an appropriate one for assessing the degree to which a system is responsive. On many issues, however, it is impossible to evaluate the degree to which correspondence occurs, because information about constituents' preferences is seldom assessed in a manner that is directly comparable with legislators' behavior. Of course, since correspondence requires less precise information than alternative measures, this problem also inhibits the assessment of centrism, responsiveness, and proximity.

In contrast to the diversity research described in Chapter 1, these results suggest a surprisingly simple and consistent finding about the relationship between diversity and representation. In contrast to the complexities demonstrated in past work, in which diversity matters for some aspects of democracy and development but not for others, these results show remarkable uniformity. Diversity seems to matter not at all for representation. Regardless of the issue being examined or the venue of democracy in which representation is being assessed, and whether in candidates' campaign positions or the chamber of Congress, legislators seem equally responsive regardless of the level of diversity.

APPENDIX 6A
Measuring Diversity

Classifying states as diverse or as not diverse using broad indicators such as ideology or indices based on demographic characteristics may be problematic when these measures translate poorly to specific issues. Consider, for example, the distribution of opinion on abortion across states. As we saw in Chapter 5, the overwhelming majority of states (88 percent) have two competing intense groups on this issue, while only six states are homogeneous in that they have only one group that cares strongly about the issue. Similar problems arise when looking at opinion on the Cuban trade embargo. There, only Florida, and only three of its districts are diverse on the issue. Every other state or district has either no active group or has only one group and is thus homogeneous. Application of the diversity criterion used in past studies would incorrectly impose the assumption of homogeneity on nineteen states that have competing and active groups on abortion, and on Cuban trade, it would lead to twenty-four states' being misclassified as diverse.

Following the process used in previous chapters, I employ Stanley Greenberg's classification of group preferences to identify active groups on abortion. Recall that Greenberg (2004) identifies two active intense groups on abortion: The Faithful, who consist of white religious Protestants who attend church weekly and are strongly pro-life, and an opposing group called Super-Educated Women, or women who hold bachelor's degrees and are staunchly pro-choice.[28] On Cuban trade, the active groups are old Cubans, who immigrated to the United States before 1980; new Cubans, who immigrated after 1980; and farmers.

As noted, identification of active groups on abortion indicates that states are more diverse than House districts. While 88 percent of states have two active groups, 78 percent of House districts do, which, when applied to the large number of districts, provides more opportunities to compare responsiveness across district type. The distribution of groups on the Cuban trade embargo is also interesting. Cubans tend to be geographically concentrated, exceeding 5 percent of the population in only four districts nationally, but only in Florida do their numbers exceed 5 percent of a state (5.6 percent). Farmers, while almost 50 percent larger than Cubans in absolute numbers (.62 percent versus .44 percent of the U.S. population), are even more geographically dispersed. Only one congressional district, Nebraska's 3rd, exceeds 5 percent farmers, and no state comes close.

7

The Myth of Issue Visibility

Friends don't let friends commit crimes against humanity.
—Representative Chris Smith (R-N.J.), quoted in
Dana Milbank, "Belatedly, the House's History Lesson"

After years of opposition from the Clinton and Bush administrations and the Republican-controlled House, supporters of a resolution recognizing the Armenian genocide mobilized in 2007.[1] The mobilization was sparked when Democrats took control of the House and elected Representative Nancy Pelosi of California's 8th district, who supported the resolution, as speaker of the House (Huse 2007). House Resolution 106 was introduced on January 30, 2007, by Representative Adam Schiff of California's 29th district. By late summer, 229 representatives had signed on as co-sponsors. With only 218 votes necessary for passage, broad support expected even among those who were not co-sponsors, and Speaker Pelosi's support, its passage seemed certain.

By October, however, the Turkish government and President Bush had initiated an intense lobbying campaign designed to kill the bill. Opposition reached a high point on October 10, following narrow approval by the Foreign Affairs Committee (27–21). In response, Turkey recalled its ambassador to the United States and threatened to expel U.S. forces, a move that would deal a crippling blow to the nation's ability to support the wars in Iraq and Afghanistan because about 75 percent of war materiel flows through Turkey (Sebnem and Knowlton 2007). An issue that was scarcely covered in the media was suddenly thrust into the national spotlight, as virtually every major newspaper and most major television news outlets ran stories about the Armenian Genocide Resolution.

Almost immediately, members of Congress began to withdraw their support. In a little over a month, support changed so dramatically that Speaker Pelosi told Representative Schiff that she would delay a vote until a time of his choosing. Lacking the votes needed to ensure passage of a bill that seemed to be a sure thing just six months before, it was unclear whether a vote would be held at all.

The Armenian Genocide Resolution is yet one more example in which increased issue visibility appears to have forced legislators to behave as constituents wanted. Before the issue was visible, an overwhelming majority of legislators supported the resolution, but once it became visible and public opinion seemed to turn, passage was no longer assured. After all, who would want to face a challenger alleging that the incumbent had jeopardized the safety of American soldiers and inhibited their ability to get the supplies needed to defend their country from Islamic terrorists?

At a glance, the role of public opinion on the Armenian Genocide Resolution is consistent with the conventional wisdom about issue visibility and legislative responsiveness. Constituents' preferences seem to have served as a powerful constraint on legislators who might otherwise have voted to recognize events that most consider to be a clear case of genocide. Legislators are thought to be most responsive on visible issues because the public is most likely to notice their misdeeds. Consequently, explanations of the failure of this non-binding resolution, after passage seemed assured, have to consider the role of public opinion.

The contention that legislators are more responsive on visible issues results from scholars' discovery that, on many issues, legislators do not seem to represent their constituents. These mixed findings are inconsistent with the expectations of the demand model, which holds that legislators respond to district majorities. Scholars explaining their inconsistent or negative findings about responsiveness offer issue visibility to explain why legislators are responsive on some issues but not on others. This perspective is called the issue visibility thesis.

While scholars frequently offer issue visibility as an explanation for their inconsistent findings, studies of the influence of visibility on representation are scarce, and most evidence offered in its favor is ad hoc. This chapter investigates whether issue visibility conditions legislative responsiveness. While the questions are similar, in contrast to Chapter 3, which suggests that that citizens are no better able to hold legislators accountable on visible issues, this chapter examines whether *legislators* behave more responsively on visible issues.

The question of whether legislators are more responsive on more visible issues allows for an interesting application of the subconstituency politics theory, as it provides an alternative explanation for why scholars might perceive increased responsiveness on visible issues. In some cases, visible issues may serve to socially prime a group identity and thus lead to increased opinion homogeneity. In the months following September 11, 2001, for instance, the country was swept up in a wave of patriotism that research shows was indicative of a national identity (Huddy et al. 2005). If visible issues are frequently characterized by large groups of people acting on the basis of a shared identity, then we would expect legislators to respond to this large active group. In other cases, visible issues may be more contentious and characterized by group conflict. Subconstituency politics holds that when opinions conflict, legislators represent these groups rather than the opinion of a district's majority.

This chapter describes the logic underlying the issue visibility thesis and investigates the degree to which visibility is associated with responsiveness. Then I develop expectations about the relationship between visibility and responsiveness using the demand model and the subconstituency politics theory. These predictions are investigated by examining the relationship between visibility and responsiveness across different kinds of legislation and by conducting a natural experiment to isolate the impact of visibility on responsiveness. The results provide little evidence to suggest that legislators are any more responsive on visible issues than on less visible ones. Instead, legislators appear to respond to the preferences of groups regardless of the level of issue visibility.

The Issue Visibility Thesis

Citizens are thought to be best able to hold their elected officials responsible when the issues under consideration are most visible (e.g., Arnold 1990). Since not all bills are especially visible to the public, responsiveness is thought to vary with the degree to which they are visible (Bianco 1994; Bianco et al. 1996; Burstein 2003; Hutchings 1998, 2001; Hutchings et al. 2004; Kuklinski and Elling 1977; McCrone and Kuklinski 1979; Page and Shapiro 1993; Theriault 2005). Hence, visibility has come to be seen as central to explanations like the demand model, which describes how legislative representation works.[2] The visibility thesis refers to the hypothesis that policy responsiveness increases with issue visibility.

The fact that representation studies reach conflicting results suggests that extant theories poorly explain legislators' behavior. For decades, scholars have tried to explain why studies of legislators' behavior based on the demand model reach conflicting results about whether legislators respond to constituents' preferences (e.g., Bishin 2000; Krehbiel 1999; Miller and Stokes 1963; Shannon 1968; Uslaner 1999). Issue visibility is an extension of the demand model and explains these conflicting results by suggesting that responsiveness varies according to the ease with which the people can hold their representatives accountable on specific issues. As an issue becomes increasingly visible, citizens are better able to compare their legislators' behavior to their own personal preferences.

The logic underlying the visibility thesis is straightforward. Congress faces thousands of issues each year, far more than the average citizen (or member of Congress) can follow. Citizens are more likely to become informed about legislators' behavior as visibility increases. Legislators, fearing the possibility of citizen action should they misstep, respond to constituents' preferences on visible issues because the probability of retribution is high relative to that of nonvisible issues. As Kim Quaile Hill and Patricia Hurley (1999, 305) note, the thesis holds that "increased salience leads to increased demands, which lead to good representation."

Recall that the evidence presented in Chapter 3 raises serious questions about whether citizens are more knowledgeable about more visible issues. It is entirely possible, however, for visibility to condition legislators' behavior even if the process through which citizens hold elected officials responsible does not work as scholars expect, or as the demand model implies. Legislators might be more responsive on visible issues despite citizens' lack of knowledge about them, for instance, because they perceive that citizens will notice their misdeeds regardless of whether citizens actually do. Legislators may behave more responsibly on more visible issues because they mistakenly think that citizens are more likely to notice and exact retribution.[3]

Issue visibility also provides an alternative mechanism for explaining representation that is inconsistent with subconstituency politics. Subconstituency politics offers no special role for issue visibility except in the instance where visibility serves to activate a previously latent group identity. In most cases, group members are already sensitive to information about issues relating to their identity, as well as more likely to seek out information on issues relevant to it because of their increased intensity. Consequently, there is no reason to expect legislators to be increasingly responsive, since they already respond to the group members who are most likely to notice their behavior.

The distinction between the competing explanations of who is represented has important implications for representation and democracy. If legislators respond to constituents only on visible issues, then the inconsistent findings about legislators' responsiveness imply that representation does not occur on most issues because they are not visible. As we will see in the next section, however, it is not clear that studies of less visible bills are less likely to find that representation occurs.

Does Visibility Enhance Responsiveness?

Since Warren Miller and Donald Stokes (1963) observed that responsiveness varies across issues, visibility has become central to explanations of how the representation process works (e.g., Bianco 1994; Bianco et al. 1996; Burstein 2003; Froman 1963; Hutchings 1998, 2001; Hutchings et al. 2004; Kingdon 1971; Page and Shapiro 1993; Theriault 2005). Scholars frequently note that the degree to which legislators' and constituents' views of issues are congruent seem to vary by issue depending on their visibility (e.g., Froman 1963; Miller and Stokes 1963). In one of the few attempts to examine the impact of intensity on specific bills, John Kingdon uses visibility as a proxy for constituents' intensity and argues that constituency should matter most "on the most visible issues."[4]

While claims supporting the role of visibility are extensive, they are also largely anecdotal. Kingdon's (1971) conclusions, for instance, are based primarily on his own observations about visibility. Larry Bartels's (1991) study of representation examined defense spending precisely because it was a visible issue. Vincent Hutchings (1998) argues that legislators' responsiveness to black constituents in the South was greater on the visible Civil Rights Act of 1990 than on the important but less visible Michel-LaFalce Amendment to the same bill. William Adams and Paul Ferber (1980) offer visibility as a post hoc explanation after finding substantial difference in responsiveness among Texas state legislators in reducing restrictions on liquor versus creating a year-round legislature. James Kuklinski and Richard Elling (1977) use salience to explain conflicting results about responsiveness and conclude that legislators appear more responsive on more salient issues.[5]

While the view that visibility conditions responsiveness is widely held, a growing literature produces evidence inconsistent with the implications of the issue visibility thesis. Studies frequently show that constituents influence legislators on issues that are not visible. Foreign-policy issues are frequently of low visibility (e.g., Almond 1950; Dahl 1956), but research on foreign-policy issues increasingly finds legislators to be responsive to constituents on them (e.g., Bailey 2001; Bailey and Brady 1998; Bishin 2003; Overby 1991). Adding to the confusion, others find that many legislators are not responsive on visible foreign-policy votes (e.g., Gleek 1947). Eric Uslaner (1999, 46) finds consistent responsiveness on foreign-policy issues but observes that the role of ideology appears to be greater on such votes because "such issues are of lesser concern to voters than are domestic concerns." Consequently, James Lindsay and Randall Ripley's (1992, 422) assertion that "the relationship between public opinion and Congressional behavior is not simple, at least not on foreign policy issues" seems apt.

Studies of issues other than foreign policy also raise questions about the role of visibility. While Kingdon (1971) finds a large role for constituencies on highly visible votes, for instance, he also finds that constituents have a major influence on 25 percent of low-visibility issues. Bryan Jones (1973) finds that Texas legislators are least responsive on the highly visible sales-tax issue. Other studies that examine a variety of bills that vary substantially in their visibility also find strong support for constituents' influence (e.g., Bishin 2000; Uslaner 1999). In sum, the body of scholarly knowledge suggests that legislators' responsiveness to constituencies occurs intermittently on both visible and non-visible bills.

Since the relationship between visibility and responsiveness has not been directly examined, it is impossible to ascertain whether the finding for visibility results from other factors. It seems likely that visible bills are more likely to be studied partly because interest in them is high. Such bills are also easier to study because the data necessary to examine them, such as those pertaining to public opinion, are more likely to be available. As Paul Burstein (2003) points out, there has not yet been a study that samples the universe of bills to determine the degree to which visibility conditions representation. The remainder of the chapter assesses the empirical evidence for the visibility thesis.

Expectation and Implications

Studying the visibility of issues requires measures of both visibility and responsiveness, neither of which is widely available. Measures of issue visibility used to study variation in visibility across states or congressional districts do not yet exist. Measures of representation or representativeness are also scarce because they require measures, both of citizens' preferences and of legislators' behavior on comparable issues. Existing measures allow the examination of visibility and responsiveness at the national level, however. Doing so allows examination of the relationship between responsiveness and visibility across issues rather than across legislators.

A second approach is to employ a natural experiment using an issue that becomes visible after legislators take a position.[6] This type of case study allows inferences similar to those seen in the idealized experiment described above. Most important, many of the competing influences on responsiveness are effectively held constant (e.g., party identification, legislators' ideology) before and after visibility increases.

While the data that allow the testing of the competing representation theories are far from ideal, implications of the issue visibility thesis and subconstituency politics can be examined to determine whether, and to what degree, issue visibility conditions responsiveness. In the sections that follow, I employ the methods described to investigate the implications of the two perspectives.

Visibility and Representation: A Natural Experiment

The Armenian Genocide Resolution is an issue that saw a huge increase in visibility for reasons outside legislators' control, and on which legislators took recorded positions both before and after the issue became visible. The resolution was initially of very low visibility partly because there was little opposition from any segment of the American public: The staunchest opponent was the Turkish government. The recall of the Turkish ambassador, along with the threat of barring the United States from using Turkey to stage the wars in Iraq and Afghanistan, brought tremendous visibility to the issue. Expecting the resolution to pass easily, many legislators gladly signed on as co-sponsors but publicly withdrew

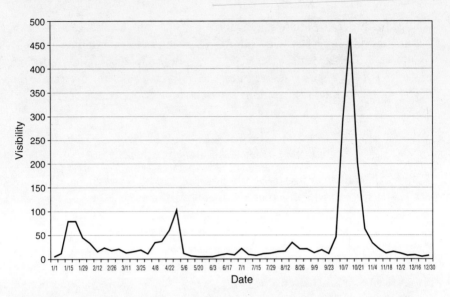

FIGURE 7.1 Number of articles mentioning the Armenian genocide by week in 2007.

their support once the issue became visible. Legislators' decisions to co-sponsor and to withdraw their co-sponsorship provide an indication of support for the resolution both before and after it became visible.

The resolution was introduced in early 2007. By late summer, the bill had 229 co-sponsors, and support in the House of Representatives was thought to be even higher. By October, the Turks and the administration had intensified their lobbying against the bill. The bill was voted out of the Foreign Relations Committee by a vote of 27–21 on October 10, at which point the Turkish government withdrew its ambassador and publicly threatened to block the United States from using its bases to stage the wars in Iraq and Afghanistan. Between October 1 and November 1, eighteen co-sponsors had withdrawn. By January 2008, the resolution had only 211 co-sponsors, some of whom appeared to be wavering. It was no longer clear whether the bill had the votes to pass. The dramatic increase in visibility that occurred is depicted in Figure 7.1.

The issue visibility thesis and subconstituency politics theory offer competing perspectives on how legislators should respond to these circumstances. Issue visibility suggests that because legislators are less responsive on less visible issues, factors such as party pressure and personal ideology should matter more when bills are less visible, and constituency preferences should matter once the bill becomes visible.

Subconstituency politics, in contrast, holds that visibility matters only to the extent that it serves to activate identities and that, regardless of the level of issue

TABLE 7.1   DIFFERENCES IN DISTRICT CHARACTERISTICS BETWEEN
THOSE WHO WITHDREW AS CO-SPONSORS AND THOSE WHO DID NOT

	Co-sponsors	Co-sponsors Who Withdrew	Difference
Republican	28.8%	23.5%	5.3%
Legislator liberalism	71.57	70.59	.98
District ideology	2.92	2.79	.14*
Number of veterans	31,743	39,506	−7,763*

Note: Two-tailed test.
* $p < .01$.

visibility, legislators should appeal to subconstituencies' preferences. In the case of the genocide resolution, the active groups legislators should appeal to are Armenians, who intensely supported the resolution, and Turkish Americans, who opposed it. Once the issue became visible, threats about restricting military access to Turkish airbases may well have activated veterans, a group especially likely to be sensitive to developments that may endanger the troops.

To examine whether issue visibility led to a change in responsiveness, we can compare the characteristics of legislators who withdrew their co-sponsorship after the issue became visible with those who did not. Four hypotheses might explain the change in the decision to co-sponsor. First, increased pressure by the president should cause Republicans to withdraw at a higher rate. Second, conservative legislators, who are more likely to support the war in Iraq, should be more likely to withdraw. Third, legislators from conservative districts should be more likely to withdraw co-sponsorship. Finally, legislators with more veterans in their districts should be more likely to withdraw co-sponsorship. Differences in the characteristics of districts and legislators who co-sponsored with those seventeen representatives who withdrew their co-sponsorship after October 1, when the issue became visible, are summarized in Table 7.1.[7]

The table reports differences across districts between those legislators who withdrew co-sponsorship and those who did not for factors thought to affect legislators' behavior after the resolution became visible. The first row shows that the proportion of legislators who were Republican was roughly similar among those who withdrew and those who did not, suggesting that the Bush administration's renewed calls to oppose the resolution had little impact. Similarly, legislators who withdrew co-sponsorship were about as liberal as those who did not, according to the 2007 index compiled by the interest group Americans for Democratic Action.[8] The two constituency variables show larger differences. Legislators who withdrew support represented constituencies that were very slightly, but statistically significantly, more conservative on a 5-point ideology scale.[9] Similarly, consistent with the idea that veterans became active in response to threats by the Turkish government, legislators who withdrew co-sponsorship came from districts with substantially larger populations of veterans than did those who co-sponsored but did not withdraw.

While these data are illustrative, they fail to describe whether the differences in these characteristics of constituencies are large enough to explain the decision to withdraw. Nor do they account for alternative influences on legisla-- tors' co-sponsorship decisions or for the differing influences on the decision to co-sponsor in the first place. To account for these explanations, I examine legislators' decisions co-sponsor and to withdraw as co-sponsors statistically while accounting for the fact that only those who originally agreed to co-sponsor could withdraw.[10]

Subconstituency politics suggests that legislators with more Armenians in their districts will be more likely to co-sponsor, while those with more Turks will be less likely to do so. The demand model holds that, as the average constituent becomes more liberal, legislators will be more likely to co-sponsor. Recall that the issue visibility thesis, as a correction of the demand model, predicts that the impact of the average voter should be larger on visible issues—in this case, the decision to withdraw co-sponsorship—than on less visible issues. We also expect that, given both Republican leaders' and the president's vocal opposition, Republican legislators will be less likely to co-sponsor. In contrast, more liberal legislators should be more likely to co-sponsor.[11]

The issue visibility thesis suggests that average district ideology should influence the decision to withdraw support once the issue becomes visible. Specifically, increased liberalism within the district should be negatively associated with the decision to withdraw. Once the Turkish government publicly threatened American military interests, subconstituency politics suggests that legislators from districts with larger veteran populations should be more likely to withdraw as a co-sponsor. Legislators' liberalism should be negatively associated with the decision to withdraw, while being a Republican should make one more likely to withdraw because of the president's renewed calls to oppose the bill.

The effects of these factors are shown in Table 7.2. Our test examining whether the two models are independent, using a statistic called Rho, is insignificant, meaning that we cannot rule out the possibility that selection effects are not present. Results from the selection model indicating co-sponsorship are depicted in the first column. The subconstituency variables are statistically significant, as the ratio of Armenians to Turks in a district is positively associated with the propensity to co-sponsor.[12] The number of veterans per capita is also a significant predictor of co-sponsorship. As the demand model predicts, district liberalism is positively associated with co-sponsorship. Neither party nor legislator ideology is a significant influence on the decision to co-sponsor.

TABLE 7.2   INFLUENCES ON DECISIONS TO CO-SPONSOR AND WITHDRAW
CO-SPONSORSHIP OF THE ARMENIAN GENOCIDE RESOLUTION

	Full Model		Constituency Model	
	Withdraw	Co-sponsor	Withdraw	Co-sponsor
Constant	.31 (2.76)	−4.86† (1.42)	.79 (2.04)	−4.92† (1.40)
Armenians/Turks	−.02 (.05)	.14† (.03)		.15† (.03)
Republican	−1.30 (1.03)	−.02 (.42)		.12 (.41)
Veterans	.04† (.02)	−.03† (.01)		−.03† (.01)
District liberalism	−.80 (.85)	1.71† (.47)	−.88 (.71)	1.73† (.47)
Legislators' liberalism	−.01 (.01)	.01 (.01)		.01 (.01)
Bills co-sponsored		1.70* (.69)		1.71* (.69)
Observations	221	426	221	426
Log-likelihood	−248.71		−254.06	

Note: One-tailed tests. Standard errors are in parentheses.

$*p < .05.$

$†p < .01.$

The influences on withdrawal of co-sponsorship after the genocide resolution became visible are depicted in the second column. Consistent with the
expectations of subconstituency politics, legislators from districts with more
veterans were more likely to withdraw co-sponsorship. The role of the average
voter's preference is less clear, however. Contrary to the expectations of the issue
visibility thesis, there is no evidence of a role for the average constituent's opinion on the decision to withdraw co-sponsorship.

One explanation for these results is that even omitting the relationship
between the rival explanations and the likely interrelationships between a legislator's party, a legislator's ideology, and a constituency's ideology, the data lack
sufficient power to detect the influence of constituency on co-sponsorship. If
the problem stems from the similarity of the rival explanations and the absence
of data, then we should observe a significant relationship when the variables
reflecting the rival explanations are dropped from the outcome model. The
results presented in the third column show that such an explanation is not supported. Even when these explanations are assumed to have no effect, we fail to
detect any influence of constituency liberalism.

These results consistently support the subconstituency politics theory: All
of the variables tapping subconstituencies' concerns are significant. The implications for the issue visibility thesis and the demand model are less clear.
Defenders of the demand model offer the issue visibility thesis to explain the
perplexing finding that legislators frequently seem to rely on cues other than
constituency when making decisions in Congress. In the case of the Armenian
Genocide Resolution, we find that legislators who represented more liberal
constituencies were more likely to co-sponsor the resolution. Contrary to the

issue visibility thesis, however, we observe no greater role for the average voter's preferences once the issue became highly visible. Constituents had no apparent influence on legislators' decision to withdraw support.[13] Moreover, we find that contrary to the visibility thesis, district liberalism seemed to play a role in affecting legislators' initial decision, as those from more liberal districts were more likely to co-sponsor.

In a sense, it is hard to know what to make of these results, since it is always more difficult to demonstrate that something does not matter than to demonstrate that something does. In this light, two points seem worth considering. One concern is that, owing to the small number of legislators, the model lacks sufficient power to detect the effect of constituency on withdrawal. It bears noting, however, that the same constraints were faced by the *Veterans* variable that was found to be a significant predictor of withdrawal. Moreover, even when we bias the estimation in favor of constituency liberalism by assuming that all other explanations of withdrawal do not matter, its influence is still statistically insignificant. Finally, recall also from Table 7.1 that the difference in district liberalism between those who withdrew and those who co-sponsored but did not withdraw was tiny, constituting less than 20 percent of a one category move on the district-liberalism scale. Nonetheless, we can only say that we are unable to detect any effect of district liberalism on the decision to withdraw.

Visibility and Responsiveness across Issues

The evidence presented above fails to support the contention that legislators become more responsive to the average citizen once an issue becomes visible. Results from the natural experiment presented above constitute only one case, however, and may not be generalizable, as there is no obvious way to assess whether the case of the Armenian Genocide Resolution is typical. Fortunately, data are available to test the visibility thesis across issues, which allows for improved understanding of the degree to which the findings are generalizable.

Responsiveness consists of two components—constituents' preferences and legislators' behavior—and is measured by summarizing the link between them.[14] The constituency data needed to examine responsiveness are available from 1987 through 1992 using the American National Election Study: Pooled Senate Election Study (PSES). The PSES is unique in that it provides estimates of constituent preferences for respondents from each of the fifty states. This sampling strategy allows for the estimation of subconstituency preferences, thereby facilitating comparison of the two theories.

The second component of responsiveness, legislators' behavior, is available for issues that Congress considered during the period covered by the PSES. Senate "key" votes as identified by *Congressional Quarterly* provides an annual sample of about fifteen votes that vary in their visibility. Many of these votes are on obscure amendments that have implications for the outcome of related substantive legislation. The list of bills included in the study is in Appendix 7A.

Responsiveness reflects the degree to which legislators move with constituents' preferences and is assessed by applying roll-call voting data to data on constituency ideology from the PSES. As we are interested in examining the link between constituents and legislators, we need a measure of responsiveness that reflects the influence constituents have on legislators' behavior. We can create such a measure using simulations. The process through which responsiveness is calculated is described in Appendix 7B.

Issue visibility can also be estimated during this period using news coverage, a proxy commonly used across fields to study issue visibility (Epstein and Segal 2000; Kingdon 1971; Mayhew 1991). Employing electronic news databases, Hutchings (1998) examined the incidence of news stories written in major Southern newspapers to demonstrate the relative visibility of two civil-rights bills. Building on this work, I employ the Lexis-Nexis electronic database to estimate issue visibility.

Increased coverage makes constituents more likely to notice misbehavior at the time it occurs and makes it more likely that a potential instigator will mobilize on the issue during the election cycle. To the extent that an issue is visible, a legislator should be more responsive to constituents' preferences. To gauge issue visibility, I examined several combinations of keywords substantively relevant to the bill for their salience. The independent variable *Visibility* is a simple count of the number of articles in which the keywords relevant to the bill appeared in the year preceding the vote.[15] The precise terms used for each of the key votes from 1987 to1992 are listed in Appendix 7A.

Table 7.3 depicts the impact of responsiveness, operationalized using the subconstituency and average district measures of constituency, on visibility.[16] In both cases, the influence of visibility was tiny, and thus we observe no systematic influence of visibility and responsiveness.[17] Moreover, the explained variation is exceptionally low, never exceeding 1 percent. Also noteworthy is that the constant is statistically significant in both models, suggesting that responsiveness

TABLE 7.3 REGRESSION OF THE EFFECT OF RESPONSIVENESS ON ISSUE VISIBILITY

	Subconstituency Responsiveness	District Responsiveness
Visibility	−.00 (.00)	−.00 (.00)
Constant	.23* (.01)	.08* (.01)
R-squared	.00	.00
Observations	93	93

Note: One-tailed tests. Standard errors are in parentheses.
* $p < .01$.

occurs even when issues are not at all visible. Taken together, there is no evidence of a relationship between visibility and responsiveness.

The relative size of the constants across the two models suggests an additional test of the demand and subconstituency models. If legislators respond to the preferences of the party subconstituency rather than to the average district voter, then estimates of subconstituency responsiveness should be larger than for average district responsiveness. A significance test of responsiveness levels shows that, statistically, responsiveness to the partisan subconstituency is significantly larger than responsiveness to the district average ($p < .001$).[18]

Discussion and Conclusion

The issue visibility thesis stems from disagreement about whether legislators represent their constituents. It suggests that legislators are more likely to follow citizens' preferences on visible issues because their misbehavior is more likely to be noticed by constituents.

Two tests were employed to detect an influence of visibility on responsiveness. First, the "natural" experiment employing the Armenian Genocide Resolution exploits the abrupt increase in visibility that accompanied the Turkish government's withdrawal of its ambassador and threat to bar the U.S. military from using the country's bases to supply the wars in Afghanistan and Iraq. This case study allows for the control of alternative explanations, since unobserved factors relating to legislators and districts that might influence the outcome likely remained constant since visibility was exogenous to the legislative process.

While average opinion influenced legislators' decisions to co-sponsor the resolution, we are unable to detect influence on the decision to withdraw co-sponsorship. In contrast, subconstituencies played a significant role in influencing legislators' decisions. The number of Armenians and Turks in a district helps to explain the decision to co-sponsor, while the size of the veteran population helps to explain the decisions both to sponsor and to withdraw. While evidence for the issue visibility thesis's correction to the demand model is scarce, evidence supporting the subconstituency politics theory continues to pile up.

Perhaps most important, subconstituency politics helps explain why the resolution has not yet been scheduled for a vote. While the American public likely knows little about the issue, it seems that many legislators are fearful of the negative consequences of putting American soldiers in harm's way, particularly those who have disproportionately large concentrations of veterans in their districts. While Armenians and Turks make up a tiny portion of the population (far less than 1 percent combined), veterans constitute more than 10 percent of the U.S. population and exist in numbers far greater than Turks and Armenians in 434 congressional districts.

TABLE 7.4   SUMMARY OF RESULTS OF EMPIRICAL TESTS OF
RESPONSIVENESS ON ISSUE VISIBILITY

Test	Subconstituency Politics Theory	Issue Visibility Thesis
Natural experiment	+	−
Cross-issue analysis	+	
Size of responsiveness	+	−

Note: Blank space indicates that the models make no predictions in a context.

While the politics surrounding the Armenian Genocide Resolution may be unique, examination of the relationship between visibility and responsiveness across ninety-three Senate votes over a six-year period depicts no apparent relationship. Moreover, once again, responsiveness to the partisan subconstituency appears to be greater than responsiveness to the average citizen.

The results of this chapter are especially powerful when considered in combination with those presented in Chapter 3. Recall that the rationale for the issue visibility thesis is that legislators are more responsive to citizens on more visible issues because citizens are more likely to discover their misdeeds on such visible issues. In Chapter 3, however, we were unable to detect increased issue knowledge among those who were most exposed to news and media, an observation that calls into question the average citizen's ability to hold legislators accountable for their actions. The negative implications of such a finding, while disappointing for those who aspire to create an informed citizenry capable of holding the elected accountable for their actions, may be overcome if legislators fail to recognize citizens' inability or unwillingness to become informed.

If legislators act as if citizens may become informed, then an uninformed citizenry may be of little consequence. The results summarized in Table 7.4, however, suggest that legislators are no more responsive to the average district voter on visible issues than on invisible ones. There is no evidence that issue visibility provides a corrective that explains the conflicting findings observed in representation studies that employ the demand model. Instead, it appears that politicians appeal to subconstituencies on both visible and invisible issues. The influences on legislators' behavior change with issue visibility only to the extent that visibility serves to activate new group identities with which legislators are forced to reckon. In sum, this chapter provides the first systematic investigation of the issue visibility thesis and finds the influences of visibility on responsiveness are too small to detect.

APPENDIX 7A
Search Terms and Results, 1987–1992

Vote	1987 Bill Number and Title	Keywords	Hits	Hits (t − 1)	District Ideology	Party Ideology
1	H.R. 1 Clean Water Act Reauthorization	Water pollution	883	730	.021	.2
2	H.R. 2 Omnibus Highway Reauthorization	Highway AND federal	1,965	789	.065	.23
3	H.R. 1157 Farm Disaster Assistance	Farm AND aid	945	178	.079	.04
4	H.Con.Res. 93 Fiscal Budget 1988 Resolution	Federal AND budget	6,380	3,379	.051	.37
5	H.R. 3 Omnibus Trade Bill	Tariffs	600	927	.054	.26
6	H.J.Res. 324 Temporary Debt-Limit Increase/ Deficit Targets	Federal AND debt	2,263	2,067	.003	.37
7	S. 2 Senate Campaign Finance	Campaign finance	1,640	1,645	.015	.37
8	S. 1174 Fiscal 1988–1989 Defense Authorization/ Missile System Testing Limits	ABM	334	278	.001	.31
9	S. 1174 Fiscal 1988–1989 Defense Authorization/ Nuclear Testing	Nuclear testing	169	109	.242	.26
10	S. 1174 Fiscal 1988–1989 Defense Authorization/ SALT II Limits	SALT II	120	85	.059	.28
11	S.J.Res. 194 War Powers Compliance	War powers	86	70	.086	.24
12	Bork Nomination	Bork	1,209	1,250	.031	.32
13	H.R. 2700 Energy and Water Appropriations/ Nuclear Waste Repository	Nuclear AND waste	381	400	.039	.3
14	S. 825 Housing and Community Development/ Budget Waiver	Housing AND federal	761	1,598	.107	.29

APPENDIX 7B
Calculating Responsiveness

The statistical model used to estimate responsiveness is the product of the impact citizens' ideology has on each roll-call vote.[19] Two measures of constituency ideology are employed to estimate responsiveness. Using ideological self-placement from the PSES, the average citizen's ideology is calculated for each state, a measure consistent with the demand model, the theory that underlies the visibility thesis. A second measure tapping subconstituencies' preferences is also calculated. Recall from Chapter 2 that one of the most pervasive activated group identities in the context of campaigns is the partisan identity (e.g., Green et al. 2002). Subconstituency ideology is calculated by averaging the ideological self-placement scores of respondents in the incumbent senator's party. This measure is consistent with the widely reported finding that legislators appeal first and foremost to their partisan constituency (e.g., Clinton 2005; Wright 1989).

Once the impact of these ideology measures on senators' roll-call votes is estimated, responsiveness is calculated using vote probabilities obtained using two hypothetical constituencies: one moderately liberal, and one moderately conservative.[20] Responsiveness is the change in the probability that a legislator will vote for each bill when constituents' ideology shifts from moderately liberal to moderately conservative. Specifically, I subtract the probability that a legislator will vote for a bill when his constituency is set to the value of the first quartile on the district ideology variable (moderately liberal) from the probability of a vote for the bill when constituency is set at the third quartile (moderately conservative). For each vote, responsiveness is the absolute value of the shift in the probability of voting for a bill that results from a change in constituency ideology and serves as the dependent variable in the study.

APPENDIX 7C
Variable Coding and Sources

Variable Name	Source	Coding
Veterans	U.S. Census Bureau. 110th Congressional District Summary File (Sample)	Number of veterans by congressional district divided by 1,000
District liberalism	2004 National Annenberg Election Study, question Cma06	"Generally speaking, would you describe your political views as very conservative (1), conservative (2), moderate (3), liberal (4), or very liberal (5)?"
Armenian	U.S. Bureau of the Census, 110th Congressional District Summary File (100 percent file)	Number of Armenians by congressional district divided by 1,000
Armenian/Turkish	U.S. Bureau of the Census, 110th Congressional District Summary File (100 percent file)	Number of Armenians by congressional district per 1,000 residents divided by the number of Turks by congressional district per 1,000 residents

(continued on next page)

APPENDIX 7C (*continued*)

Variable Name	Source	Coding
Turkish	U.S. Bureau of the Census, 110th Congressional District Summary File (100 percent file)	Number of Turks by congressional district per 1,000 residents.
Republican	Office of the Clerk, U.S. House of Representatives	Democrat = 0 Republican = 1
Legislator liberalism	Americans for Democratic Action	Index ranges between 0 (most conservative) and 100 (most liberal)
Bills co-sponsored	Thomas Legislative Search	Total number of bills (sponsored or co-sponsored during 2007)
Co-sponsorship	Thomas Legislative Search (H.R. 106)	Co-sponsor = 1 No co-sponsorship = 0
Withdraw co-sponsorship	Thomas Legislative Search (H.R. 106)	Withdrew co-sponsorship = 1 No withdrawal = 0
Visibility	Lexis-Nexis Electronic News Search (*U.S. News*) conducted 8/1/07 to 8/10/07	Number of articles resulting from a search of keywords relevant to the bill that appeared in the year preceding the vote
Subconstituency responsiveness	American National Election Study: Pooled Senate Election Study (PSES), Senate "key" votes as identified by *Congressional Quarterly* 1987–1992, VPS 547	Votes regressed on subconstituency ideology to compute the change in the probability that a legislator will vote for each bill when constituents' ideology shifts from moderately liberal to moderately conservative
District responsiveness	American National Election Study: Pooled Senate Election Study (PSES), Senate "key" votes as identified by *Congressional Quarterly* 1987–1992, VPS 547	Votes regressed on ideology/average citizen's (district) ideology to compute the change in the probability that a legislator will vote for each bill when constituents' ideology shifts from moderately liberal to moderately conservative

8
Conclusion

A nnie Betancourt fared poorly in her race for Congress, despite taking the majority-preferred position on Cuba—the most visible issue in the election—because the constituents to whom she appealed were less intense than those who supported her opponent. To be sure, factors such as money and a Republican bias inherent in the district almost certainly mattered as well. But the fact that a Cuban American woman with name recognition and previous experience as a state legislator from the same area ran 12 points behind the 2000 Democratic presidential candidate in that district suggests that Betancourt fared especially poorly.[1] Mario Diaz-Balart's supporters were more intense and more willing to work to ensure his election.

To answer the question posed at the beginning of the book: politicians take minority-preferred positions to exploit the benefits of citizens' intensity. This book has developed a new theory of representation that explains why, how, and when these groups' identities are activated and translated into politics. Individuals have multiple, overlapping social identities, most of which are latent at any given time. Politicians take policy and valence positions to activate individuals' social identities and to exploit those identities that are active. These identities prime citizens' responses to the world. Moreover, politicians activate different group identities in different people by taking positions on a series of issues and in this way build a coalition of intense groups of individuals through the development of a platform.

This new conceptualization of why and how politicians appeal to groups takes us far beyond traditional characterizations based solely on partisanship (e.g., Bishin 2000; Clinton 2006; Uslaner 1999; Wright 1989) or the reelection constituency (Clausen 1973; Fenno 1978). Contrary to past conceptualizations of subconstituencies, which largely see groups as static across districts, the theory explains both the supply side of legislators' positions and the demand side of how group identities cause individuals to become interested in and knowledgeable about politics. Unlike these previous theories, it also explains when and why politicians take positions contrary to their partisans' preferences. Thus, the issues and groups to whom legislators appeal are dynamic as they vary across issues and districts.

The evidence shows that citizens are more knowledgeable about issues that relate to their active social identities; that candidates in campaigns often stake out relatively extreme positions to appeal to intense citizens; and that, once elected, legislators continue to service these groups through co-sponsorship and roll-call voting behavior. By describing this process, subconstituency politics provides answers to several unresolved questions of representation.

A major goal of this book is to provide a unified theory of representation that explains how the various components of the American representation process fit together. Too often, scholars focus on individual aspects of the democratic process by focusing on the behavior of individuals, of candidates in campaigns and elections, or of legislators in Congress. While these studies have led to reasonably satisfactory explanations for the behavior of actors within each of these domains, the theories that result are seldom useful for understanding who, when, how, and whether people are represented. Moreover, such theories seldom deal with evidence from aspects of the representation process outside their narrow domain that might call the theory into doubt. Developing a general theory allows the use of the broadest range of evidence to develop and test the mechanisms that underlie the representation process and, in so doing, help us to better understand the limits of republican democracy.

This work also extends the implications of research on issue ownership and campaign effects by suggesting that campaigns affect outcomes not by changing people's minds, but by changing the context in which the campaigns are conducted. In particular, subconstituency politics implies that effective campaigns activate or exploit beneficial social identities. Doing so leads citizens to make decisions on the basis of factors or considerations that give one candidate an advantage over the other.

The results also highlight the importance of treating the concept of diversity in a nuanced manner. Frequently, districts are designated diverse (or not) by fiat based solely on their citizens' ideology, race, or ethnicity. This research shows that the degree to which a district is diverse depends critically on the specific dimension being examined. Districts that are diverse in some ways may be homogeneous in others.

The cases examined were selected to maximize the generalizability of the results. Conflicting results routinely observed in representation studies are frequently justified by the assertion that politicians are more responsive on visible issues. By examining Cuban trade, hate crimes, assault weapons, the Armenian genocide resolution, and abortion, we are able to easily compare the quality of the competing theories, because these issues vary across levels of visibility. In most districts, issues pertaining to Cuba are of low visibility, while gun control and abortion are among the most visible and widely debated issues in contemporary politics. Since the subconstituency politics theory outperforms the demand model on both high-visibility and low-visibility issues, the results seem likely to be widely generalizable. Moreover, they suggest that visibility does not condition responsiveness.

Owing to their generalizability, these results help to explain the policy puzzles posed at the outset. Politicians such as Jeb Bush, Rick Santorum, and Mario Diaz-Balart not only take minority-preferred positions; they also firmly and loudly propound them, even on visible issues—precisely those on which democratic theory predicts otherwise—because these intense minorities can be more valuable than their more numerous but less intense fellow constituents. For good or ill, unorganized citizens who have never met but who share an experience and outlook can be exceptionally powerful. Americans' lack of interest in politics foments the tyranny of the minority.

Tyranny of the Minority?

The Framers of the U.S. Constitution were faced with devising a government that moved away from the king's monarchy and empowered the people while simultaneously ensuring that the people would not use their new power as a majority to run roughshod over the rights of minorities. While the Framers offered institutional prescriptions as well, the most potent solution was that "the society itself will be broken into so many parts, interests, and classes of citizens, that the rights of individuals, or of the minority, will be in little danger from interested combinations of the majority" (Hamilton et al. 2003, 51). James Madison thought that the development of a large and diverse polity would make it difficult for majorities to coalesce "on any other principles than those of justice and the general good" (Hamilton et al. 2003, 51).

As we have seen throughout this book, and as is described more formally in the context of democratic theory (e.g., Dahl 1956), it is the diverse nature of peoples' identities and preferences and the variation of intensities to which they correspond that make it possible for minorities to defeat majorities. Thus, it seems somewhat ironic that, by trying to limit the majority's reach, a government explicitly designed to overcome tyranny by a monarch became susceptible to tyranny by the minority. The development of a large and diverse public sphere enables groups to run roughshod over the will of the majority.

Tyranny of the minority violates several of the most basic tenets of liberal democracy, such as the notion that the will of the majority should prevail and that all people are equal under the law. Using this standard, it is difficult to classify a government as democratic. It is important to emphasize, however, that tyranny by the minority as described here is not the same as tyranny by a monarch or by an oligarchy. The political mechanism illustrated here is more consistent with what Robert Dahl describes as a tyranny of the *minorities,* the distinction being that, rather than a single ruler or group denying the majority across all issues, different minorities rule on different issues because of their disproportionate intensity on those issues. The people have power when they care intensely.

The subconstituency politics theory also explains how the power of a minority's disproportionate intensity is amplified by the majority's ignorance and apathy. This distinction is important, because a tyranny of minorities is democratic in the sense that anytime the majority also feels intensely about an issue, it ultimately prevails. Moreover, membership in these majority and minority groups is not static. People tend to be most knowledgeable and best represented on the issues they care most about (e.g., Lavine et al. 1996).

A tyranny of the minority seems to have unintended benefits to accompany its consequences. As Dahl points out, one benefit of the Madisonian system may be in the stability it provides, in that minority groups have the ability to be heard and to win if they are "active and legitimate" and not opposed by intense majorities. Rather than opting out of a system that always subjugates minority preferences, minorities can not only be heard but can also win when they are intense. Consequently, the costs imposed by the tyranny of the minority might be offset, at least to some degree, by this enhanced stability and in any case can be overcome by an active and interested majority. Such conditions seem little like tyranny at all.

Such a balance seems to require, however, that majorities recognize when their ambition is at odds with that of the minority. Substantial evidence suggests that this is only occasionally the case because of the way in which a particular minority pursues or frames an issue. An intense minority, whether a special-interest or citizens' group, can exploit the apathy and ignorance of the average citizen to pursue policy that is contrary to the majority's interest. Indeed, political scientists have documented how politicians have become expert at obscuring the nature of policy and its traceability to—and, hence, their responsibility for—policy that might have adverse consequences or be wildly unpopular (e.g., Arnold 1990). Thus, a minority might frame a debate or policy in a way that diminishes the ability of the majority to recognize and mobilize opposition.

Pitting interest against interest and faction against faction only works when all parties recognize the issues under consideration. I will return briefly to the importance of transparency in the final section.

Stochastic Representation?

This book also seeks to resolve several empirical questions pertaining to American representation. One of the observations that motivated the development of the subconstituency politics theory of representation was that research examining legislative responsiveness reaches conflicting results as to the degree to which legislators' roll-call voting reflects constituents' preferences. While scholars frequently describe the findings of the representation literature as consistent with the idea that legislators respond to constituents' preferences (e.g., Hutchings 2003), the evidence on this question is quite mixed. Indeed, a close examination of the results of the responsiveness literature shows that even in the most prominent studies, there is evidence that politicians appeal to constituents' preferences on some issues but not on others (e.g., Hall 1996; Miller and Stokes 1963). Considering the strong bias against the publication of null results, these mixed results seem likely to overstate the case that legislators are responsive to public preferences.

The subconstituency politics theory of representation explains these conflicting results as a product of scholars' overlooking the subconstituencies to whom legislators appeal when they take positions. Because issues (and identities) vary in their importance across districts, employing average district data obscures the fact that politicians who have more nuanced views of their constituencies adjust the cues they rely on as issues vary. Failing to account for subconstituencies leads to the finding that only sometimes do legislators reflect their constituents' will.

Studies using average district data seem most likely to find a large role for constituencies on issues where citizens within a district overwhelmingly agree. In contrast, those issues characterized by intra-district disagreement—in short, the hard (and often interesting) issues—are poorly explained. Consequently, the results presented here suggest that studies may reach mixed or negative results because they fail to adequately operationalize the mechanism that underlies politicians' behavior.

The theory also implies a potentially serious problem with using ideology measures or measures of preferences aggregated across issues to summarize either district opinion or politicians' behavior. The use of ideology measures constructed by aggregating positions across these issues necessarily obscures the nuanced manner through which representation occurs, since legislators may appeal to different constituents across multiple dimensions because citizens' intensities, interests, and positions vary issue by issue.

The Myth of the Median Voter

For decades, scholars have noted that empirical tests fail to confirm theoretical predictions of spatial voting models (e.g., Adams et al. 2004; Burden 2004; Groseclose 2001; Lewis and King 2000; Merrill and Grofman 1999; Rabinowitz and MacDonald 1989). Along the way, a wide variety of explanations have been offered that, generally, explain relatively small divergences from the median voter.

The subconstituency politics theory offers a generalizable theory-driven explanation for why candidates offer more extreme positions. Because voters have different propensities to participate and different levels of knowledge about and interest in issues, politicians offer positions to appeal to different intense groups of citizens on different issues. Essentially, differences in intensity and interests lead candidates to act in a multidimensional issue space in which different positions are advocated across different issues (dimensions) to build a coalition that is intensely supportive and thus most likely to participate.

By introducing and documenting this multidimensional issue space that varies across districts, the subconstituency politics theory questions the reliance on the one-dimensional spatial model, which assumes that politicians compete for voters on a single issue or an ideological continuum. Unfortunately, as documented by the literature on the uncovered set, introduction of a multidimensional space fails to produce a single dominant strategy for candidates (e.g., McKelvey and Ordeshook 1976). Moreover, these observations are consistent with current research in social psychology. There may not be a single best strategy for candidates to pursue, because voters' various latent social identities allow candidates to win using a wide range of strategies.

The theory and evidence presented here explain both why and when candidates will offer positions that are relatively extreme from the median. It is important to note, however, that these observations are not inconsistent with Anthony Downs's (1957) original work pertaining to the median voter theorem.[2] Thus, the disjunction between theory and empirical validation stems from scholars' attempts to test simplified implications of his predictions. Specifically, we employ one-dimensional tests of a multidimensional world.

The Puzzle of Citizen Control

Among the most vexing challenges facing students of representation is reconciling our understanding of citizens' knowledge about and lack of interest in politics with their apparent need for knowledge and interest in order to hold their elected officials accountable. Subconstituency politics provides an explanation that accounts for citizens' lack of interest and knowledge.

While the average voter is generally unknowledgeable about politics, subconstituency politics explains that voters are knowledgeable about and interested in particular issues that pertain directly to their activated group identities. In addition, having an activated identity makes one more sensitive to news and information about relevant issues. Consequently, even citizens with relatively low levels of education or news exposure show high levels of political knowledge on issues that are relevant to their activated identities. In stark contrast to the ignorance and apathy of the public at large, these citizens appear to have both the interest and the capacity necessary to hold their elected officials accountable. Neither an instigator ready to alert an inattentive public (e.g., Arnold 1990) nor a fully informed populace (e.g., Bernstein 1989) are required to keep hyper-attentive subconstituencies informed about the behavior of elected officials on the issues these groups care most about.

Diversity Deconstructed

Subconstituency politics also sheds light on the finding that legislators are more responsive to constituents in homogeneous districts than in heterogeneous ones (e.g., Bailey and Brady 1998; Bishin et al. 2006). This finding has important implications about the degree to which American democracy functions effectively and suggests that there is a cost to democratic responsiveness as diversity increases.

Subconstituency politics suggests that the finding of reduced representation may be an artifact of the misconceptualization of representation. Studies that find legislators to be more responsive in homogeneous states assume that politicians appeal to the average voter's preferences. The subconstituency politics theory explicitly rejects this claim and holds instead that in all districts, politicians appeal to subgroups of intense citizens. Consequently, in diverse states, the differences in opinion between the average voter and the average group member are likely to be much greater than in homogeneous districts. As a consequence, estimates of the impact of constituents' influence on political behavior are likely to be attenuated in diverse districts, because the estimates of constituents' preferences are more biased than in homogeneous districts. There is no evidence to suggest that the behavior of politicians from homogeneous states corresponds any more closely to citizens' preferences than does the behavior of those from diverse states.

The Myth of Issue Visibility

A prominent explanation of the conflicting results of representation studies is the issue visibility thesis, which holds that legislators are more responsive on more visible issues. The research presented here provides substantial evidence to refute this claim. Across the four issue areas examined, we find no evidence to suggest that politicians are any more responsive on visible issues such as gun control and abortion than on the Cuban trade embargo and hate crimes. Evidence on the assault-weapons ban is especially instructive, as a majority opinion in every state supports this bill, but it garnered just a little more than a majority in the U.S. Senate and was not brought to a House vote. Moreover, evidence from a natural experiment of the Armenian Genocide Resolution and a large-scale study of ninety-three key issues over six years also fail to detect evidence that supports the visibility thesis. Given these findings, the onus is now on supporters of the theory to present systematic evidence to support it.

Pluralism and the Unorganized

In addition to reconciling the representation puzzles posed at the outset, the subconstituency politics theory provides two especially relevant insights for contemporary students of democracy and representation. Perhaps most important, the theory develops and documents a new definition of a group by describing a largely overlooked but crucially important role for the unorganized group. Exploiting this definition of groups, the theory describes a process that is applicable across both levels of government and the various aspects of the democratic process.

Political scientists have long recognized that intense minorities can obtain benefits disproportionate to their size (Olson 1971; Truman 1951). Less well recognized, however, is that organization alone may be sufficient but unnecessary for these benefits to accrue. For decades, scholars have simply assumed that organized groups are more intense and active than *unorganized* groups (e.g., Olson 1971; Schattschneider 1960; Truman 1951). As a consequence, scholars have all too often overlooked the influence of unorganized groups. Disproportionate benefits can accrue to unorganized groups if politicians perceive a benefit in propounding their preferences and can find issues that can be used to activate them. Of course, candidates benefit from citizens' intensity, since intense citizens are more likely to vote, volunteer, contribute, and cajole their family, friends, and neighbors to support the candidate as well. Because intense citizens are more knowledgeable, appealing to them and getting them to participate is less costly for politicians than is appealing to the largely uninterested and generally unknowledgeable masses.

The power of unorganized groups demonstrated here suggests that the standard critiques of pluralism—that groups lacking resources are disadvantaged and less able to participate or to be heard—is in need of refinement. While there are doubtless contexts in which resources are helpful, if not essential, this research shows that they are not necessary for unorganized groups to attain their policy objectives.

The evidence used to test the subconstituency politics theory produces convincing results partly because it shows that, despite their lack of formal organization, groups such as African Americans, The Faithful, Super-Educated Women, and new Cubans repeatedly gain representation when their views diverge from that of their districts as a whole. In a sense, it would be much less surprising if politicians appealed only to formal groups. The fact that they appeal to informal ones, as well, provides a more stringent test of the subconstituency politics theory.

The Importance of Group Size

These findings also raise questions about whether a minimum size is required for groups to gain representation. It could be that the absolute size of a group is the critical factor in determining whether a candidate or legislator chooses to advocate on its behalf. A large literature examines the importance of group size as applied to African Americans and trade politics. Work examining the resources needed for informal groups to gain representation does not yet exist. Alternatively, one might imagine, for instance, that a consideration influencing who gets represented might pertain to the size of the smaller group relative to the size of the larger group. Perhaps the ratio of group sizes dictates whether a candidate advocates on one's behalf. It seems obvious that if a district has only one group, then the size necessary for it to gain representation is likely smaller than the size required by a larger minority group that faces a dominant group in a district.

Evidence presented here tends to support the latter view. We see numerous examples of districts with very small groups of farmers or Armenians, for instance, who seem to gain representation on the issues important to them, if only because opposition in the district does not seem to exist. Moreover, the message from these cases highlights the importance of intensity. Across every issue examined, we observe that politicians repeatedly advocate minority-preferred positions when that minority's preferences are held with disproportionate intensity.

The understanding of groups offered by the subconstituency politics theory more completely describes the democratic process. Evaluations of the degree to which a society is democratic ought to evaluate the system as a whole (e.g., Pitkin 1967). Developing a simple theory of representation that uses psychology to explain candidates' behavior in campaigns and in Congress offers a broad explanation that should be widely applicable across levels and types of government and countries. Recent work, for example, documents the role of subconstituencies in influencing party platforms in western European democracies (Adams et al. 2008). While such claims require further testing, the existence of social identities across polities suggests that vote-seeking politicians everywhere should appeal to them.

Overall, then, the subconstituency politics theory explains how politicians mobilize an uninterested and uninformed public; the inconsistencies in the findings of past studies of representation; why candidates do not converge to the center of the distribution of voters; and the curious finding that legislators from diverse states are less responsive to their constituents. It also undermines the mechanism that underlies most contemporary accounts of responsiveness, the issue visibility thesis, by showing that those with greater exposure to news are not more knowledgeable and that politicians are no more likely to appeal to majority opinion on more visible issues than on less visible issues. And it suggests that empirical scholars need to be more rigorous and thoughtful in our evaluation of the meaning of democratic responsiveness.

Remedies?

It is hardly surprising that a system of government designed in large part to protect the property rights of the landholders from the masses also lends itself to exploitation by intense minorities (Dahl 2006). While counter-majoritarian, in a diverse polity such a system is not without benefits. Providing numerical minorities the opportunity to gain victory provides legitimacy and enhances stability. The fact that unorganized minorities, even when opposed by a majority, can both be heard and obtain policy gives them less need to opt out of the system because they have viable avenues for redress.

A problem does occur, however, when the majority's preferences are defeated by intense minorities on issues about which the people's preference is meaningful, or when the minority's preference injures the majority in some way. In these cases, one might inquire as to how a system that seems to accrue so many benefits to the intense minority might be conditioned to respond to the preferences of the majority.

The prescription for solving inequities of this sort frequently seems to require the education of the populace to provide a check on the elected who implement these minority views. To be sure, knowledge is thought to have many benefits that make for not only better citizens but also an increased ability to identify one's own self-interest (Delli Carpini and Keeter 1996). Unfortunately, proposals to increase the education of the populace seem unfeasible and may not do much to overcome the apathy that is characteristic of citizens' participation. From this perspective, the problem may be less one of public knowledgeability than of educating the public on the importance of civic activism.

The research and discussion developed here suggests an alternative solution, one that in recent times has become less frequently emphasized: transparency. While transparency is undoubtedly insufficient to reduce minority tyranny, it seems to be a necessary precondition if the Madisonian solution of countering ambition with ambition is to have any chance of success. Recall, for example, that in the period studied here, while several Senate votes were held on liberalizing ties with Cuba, none of these votes had been recorded using a roll call. Instead, all had been taken by voice. Obviously, taking voice votes makes it impossible for constituents to hold their elected officials accountable. Lack of transparency favors the interests of the minority at the majority's expense precisely because those who propound majority-preferred positions would seem to have little need to obfuscate.

Notes

CHAPTER 1

1. For an extensive account of Orlando Bosch's activities, see Bragg and Font 1991. Bosch had violated parole in the bazooka incident by fleeing the United States. He later returned illegally, at which time the Immigration and Naturalization Service tried to deport him. However, thirty-one countries refused him entry.

2. For instance, one judge described Bosch as "a leader of the Coordination of United Revolutionary Organizations (CORU), which was linked to more than 50 possible bombings and some possible assassinations" (Bragg and Font 1991).

3. Hardliners' positions are characterized by opposition to liberalizing travel, trade, and other economic ties with Cuba. Many also favor American invasion of the island to overthrow Castro.

4. State-level polling data on Cuba are scarce. The wording of the question conflates travel to Cuba with doing business there and is consequently a very conservative estimate of opposition to the travel restrictions. For instance, the same poll found that 53 percent of Hispanic Floridians (about half of whom were Cuban) opposed the travel restrictions.

5. The focus on Cuba was credited with having made an uncompetitive race competitive, at least for a short time. Polls showed that Betancourt closed to within 10 points of Diaz-Balart in early October.

6. A breakdown of the demographics of Florida's congressional districts is available online at http://www.flsenate.gov/data/legislators/senate/DistrictData/CD/CD_Stats.pdf.

7. Betancourt supported liberalization on Cuba, which relates to four distinct policy areas: dialogue, travel, sending money, and the trade embargo. According to a variety of opinion polls, Betancourt's platform reflected the majority-held preference on all but the trade embargo. Even on this issue, however, a solid majority (52–34 percent) thought the policy was ineffective and needed to be replaced: Cuba Study Group 2002.

8. On Santorum, see "Gay Issue Causes Little Pain for Santorum, Quinnipiac Poll Finds" 2003, which shows that voters think homosexual relations between consenting results should be legal (45–35 percent).

9. On Jeb Bush's order to the state police, see "Sources Say Police Nearly Faced Off over Schiavo" 2005. Poll results show that 63 percent oppose intervention in the Terri Schiavo case: see "Poll" 2005.

10. The importance of considering everyone's views reflects the normative value of liberalism where all are citizens are considered equally.

11. Alternative explanations challenge the demand input model by suggesting, for instance, that legislators shape citizens' attitudes and help them to develop their preferences (e.g., Eulau and Karps 1977; Hill and Hurley 1999).

12. Michael Bailey (2001) articulates a model of representation on trade issues that accounts for legislators who both anticipate and respond to constituents' likely views. David Mayhew (1974) explains the safety of incumbents as due at least partly to their considering and resolving issues before citizens ever have to become aware of them.

13. This issue may also be partially addressed by the fact that most studies of representation assess constituents' preferences using measures of district ideology, which legislators are also likely to use to make estimates when citizens lack meaningful preferences on an issue. Ideological preferences may be valuable in part because in the aggregate they tend to be stable over time.

14. Averages are calculated by weighting all views equally. Average district characteristics are poor proxies for the majority preference because they may not accurately reflect either the view of the majority or variation in the majority view across districts or time. Nonetheless, they are commonly used.

15. Robert Weissberg (1979, 612) notes, however, that showing that a legislator's votes systematically co-vary according to the size of some group in his district is not saying that majorities are faithfully represented.

16. Many studies fail to explicitly articulate a theoretical motivation underlying whose views legislators are expected to represent. Since these studies all rely on district average data, however, they account for the views of all citizens in the district.

17. Other forms include service responsiveness, allocation responsiveness, and symbolic responsiveness (e.g., Eulau and Karps 1977).

18. Weissberg (1978) reports that representation levels are likely to be much higher in collective terms than in dyadic terms. A number of policies supported by a majority of the public are prevented from becoming law, however, a fact that suggests slippage in both collective and dyadic representation.

19. This debate is focused on the House of Representatives rather than the Senate, because House rules concentrate power in the hands of party leaders. While party members still tend to vote together in the Senate, party leaders' ability to coerce them is much weaker (Smith 2000).

20. Many studies that attempt to parse the relative effects of party versus preferences are oblivious to the influence of constituencies on legislators' behavior (e.g., Ansolabehere et al. 2001).

21. An entire literature on shirking has developed in response: see Uslaner 1999 for a review.

22. Take, for instance, the following admonition from the website of the editors of the *American Journal of Political Science* (www.ajps.org): "After two years of managing the jour-

nal, the editors recognize that many submissions have no prospects of surviving the peer review process successfully. As examples, some submissions . . . reach mixed or inconclusive findings that do not contribute to existing knowledge. . . . Because of the very large number of papers submitted to the journal, the resultant demand on the reviewer pool, and the high expectations for what is required to earn even a revise-and-resubmit invitation, papers that the editors judge to have such limitations will not be sent out for peer review."

23. Moreover, since confidence in a result increases with the number of trials, studies that are never published provide no information about the uncertainty surrounding the null result, even if they use widely different methods and measures to search for one.

24. It also implies that politicians often behave in a manner inconsistent with popular sovereignty and liberalism.

25. Other studies implicitly employ measures of preference based on groups rather than on the average citizen when studying representation. For instance, studies compare voters' opinions on referenda or constitutional amendments with state legislators' behavior (e.g., Arneson 1927; Crane 1960; Erikson et al. 1975). Others, for instance, examine the influence of the size of the African American population on legislators' roll-call votes (e.g., Hutchings 1998; Whitby 1997).

26. Vincent Hutchings (1998), for instance, finds that the black population is a significant predictor of votes on the Civil Rights Act of 1990 but not on an important amendment to that bill.

27. That is, they frequently violate the norm of popular sovereignty.

28. This is the name that Stanley Greenberg gives this group, and it appears designed to express the shared anger toward government.

CHAPTER 2

1. E. E. Schattschneider (1960, 29) limits his study of groups to formal organizations and avers that "organized special interest groups are the most self-conscious, best developed, most intense and active groups."

2. Despite their overwhelming similarities, social psychologists draw important distinctions between social identity theory and identity theory, which differ on whether the "group" or the "role" provides the basis for an individual's identity (e.g., Brewer 2001; Stets and Burke 2000). Such questions lie beyond the scope of this project.

3. The definition of "group" advanced here does not disqualify those whose members interact or are interdependent.

4. Issue publics differentiate those citizens who hold meaningful issue positions (both pro and con) from the masses who lack meaningful preferences on most issues (Converse 1964). In particular, Phillip Converse found that those who expressed concern about a particular issue had greater stability in their beliefs than did the public as a whole.

5. Donald Green and colleagues (2002) find party to be a social identity, a view that is consistent with the conception of a group developed here.

6. Indeed, these differences may have been put aside because conditions activated the cue that relates to a different group association, that of citizen of the United States, which lad to shared attitudes toward terrorist attacks on the country.

7. The term "Reagan Democrats" refers to male, white, middle- or working-class union workers in manufacturing jobs who came to see Democrats as abandoning the values of the middle class for those of African Americans and the poor.

8. The Mariel boat lift refers to the mass exodus of Cubans who left Cuba in April–October 1980 in response to Castro's temporarily permitting anyone who wanted to leave the island to do so.

9. Psychologists also describe the active identity as salient to the individual, meaning that the identity becomes the primary one.

10. Unfortunately, the report does not allow for inferences to be drawn concerning the views of those who immigrated between 1970 and 1990. Moreover, because of the contentiousness of the issue, the data are unavailable.

11. Several studies attribute these differences to year of immigration (e.g., Bendixen 2002; Corral 2004). However, because the raw data are unavailable, alternative hypotheses cannot be excluded.

12. Pluralist accounts of representation require a knowledgeable citizenry to constrain the elected. However, alternative theories suggest that citizen knowledge is unnecessary, provided that monitoring groups or individuals exist that can make political missteps salient to the people (e.g., Arnold 1990; Fiorina 1974): see Delli Carpini and Keeter 1996 for a review and rebuttal.

13. This mechanism helps explain yet another puzzle: How can unknowledgeable citizens control their legislators? The work of Hutchings (2003), in conjunction with the subconstituency politics theory, suggests that when knowledge levels are low, they do not.

14. But see Wolpert and Gimple 1997.

15. For instance, David von Drehle (2004, A1) describes America as "engaging in voluntary political segregation."

16. This is not to say that election and reelection are the only goals, merely the proximate goals on which others are predicated (e.g., Arnold 1990; Fenno 1978; Mayhew 1974).

17. Of course, a candidate with advantageous personal attributes can vary the degree to which they try to emphasize them.

18. For an overview of her travails, see Dale 2002.

19. In a way, this typology is similar to John Kingdon's (1971) consensus model, in which legislators look to see whether conflict exists before making roll-call voting decisions. Kingdon's "field of forces," however, depends only partly on constituents' preferences.

20. Sanders, however, was not vocal on the issue.

21. Nor does the typology provide cues for how politicians behave when more than two groups with differing preferences exist in the district. Since there are usually only two viable candidates in the American system, no more than two positions can be taken on any issue. As a result, the multi-group setting seems likely to reduce to the conflicting-group scenario.

CHAPTER 3

1. Recall that Chapter 1 defined the demand model as both prospective and retrospective views of an iterative representation process in which legislators respond to or anticipate citizens' preferences (Wahlke 1971). Members of this legislature are motivated by their proximate goal, which is reelection, thereby providing an imperative to reflect the preferences of the citizenry.

2. Recall from Chapter 1 that the primary difference between the subconstituency politics theory and the demand model lies in the people whose views are represented, not in

the process of representation. Consequently, the subconstituency politics theory and the demand model are consistent in their view of elections as a feedback mechanism.

3. But see Schattschneider 1960, which argues that the problem lies within our conception of, and unrealistic expectations for, democracy.

4. Moreover, representatives receive much less coverage than do senators (Arnold 2004; Hutchings 2003). This fact is disconcerting in two ways. First, visibility is arguably more important in the House than the Senate because the House rules make it easier to obscure the traceability of legislation. Second, the House was designed to be most responsive to the people, but the lack of coverage may help make it less so.

5. Though visibility may have an indirect effect by contributing to a context in which an identity becomes active.

6. This section takes Vincent Hutchings's work on salience and context as a point of departure. Hutchings (2003) shows that context conditions citizens' awareness of legislators' behavior, although those results are weaker than the results presented here.

7. For instance, African Americans and F-You Boys score 3.14 and 2.63, respectively, as compared with the average respondent, who scores 3.59, on the 7-point education scale. Category 3 corresponds to a college degree.

8. Of course, this measure becomes less effective as the size of the group increases. If all Americans share a social identity on an issue, such as the response to the September 11, 2001, terrorist attacks, we could observe a group that has a variance identical to that of the American population.

9. This statistic is calculated using the question pertaining to whether or not Clarence Thomas should be confirmed.

10. The PSES does not permit the identification of The Faithful. *Deep South* consists of whites living in ten Southern states. *Privileged Men* are white married men with a college education. *Cosmopolitan States* refers to those living in New England, as well as in New York, New Jersey, and California.

11. Unfortunately, significance tests of the variance are not easily calculable using weighted survey data. However, using unweighted data, the variance of opinion among F-You Boys is statistically significantly smaller ($p = .10$) than the opinion variance for the sample as a whole. The unweighted variance among African Americans is significant at the .10 level using a one-tailed test. No other group differences are statistically significant.

12. Group identities need not exist or be active simply because group members happen to agree. If groups exist and are active, then their members should also be more knowledgeable about issues relevant to the group identity. However, because we want to compare citizens' knowledgeability to test the subconstituency politics theory versus the demand model, it would be inappropriate to identify groups based on their knowledge levels.

13. All results are weighted. The PSES attempted to draw random samples of approximately equal size from each state. Because some groups such as African Americans are concentrated in particular states, however, they are dramatically under-represented in the national sample. The PSES contains about 7.5 percent African Americans, while the U.S. population is about 12.5 percent African American.

14. The difference between F-You Boys and the sample ($p < .03$) and African Americans and the sample are both statistically significant ($p < .08$).

15. The knowledge baseline is the proportion of each group who correctly identified two or more of the following political figures: Dan Quayle, William Rehnquist, Tom Foley, and Al Gore.

16. It is possible that at the time of the vote, the highly exposed group was equally well able to identify senators' votes but that the knowledge receded with time, as the poll was taken well after the vote. Given the finding in Wolpert and Gimple (1997), however, this seems unlikely. Even if true, this explanation is still problematic for the issue visibility thesis, because these citizens are unable to use this information in the election.

17. The results presented later are substantively unchanged if either component of this index is included separately or if both are included together.

18. I omit education because it is one of the criteria on which the *F-You Boys* variable is constructed. Nonetheless, results are substantially similar when it is included.

19. The results are much stronger when weighted, although the estimates of the key groups are still positive and reasonably large (though African American is no longer statistically significant). The results are also very robust across different estimators (e.g., ordered probit).

20. I also estimated a model with all of the groups from Table 3.6 included, and the results are virtually identical. Among groups, only African Americans and F-You Boys are significant predictors of knowledge. I also estimated models that account for interactions between exposure and group identity. These variables were never significant.

21. Since legislators act before constituents do, the prospective view does not technically require that the citizenry be knowledgeable for legislators to try to be accountable. Citizens presumably need to become knowledgeable on some issues, however, or legislators may quickly realize that they do not need to anticipate citizens' preferences at all.

22. Appropriate data also exist for the vote on the Persian Gulf War in 1991. However, there is no clear theoretical prediction about which identities might have been activated on that issue, except perhaps a national identity, which would confound any attempt to parse differences between identity and exposure.

CHAPTER 4

1. This exchange is transcribed from Cutler and Van Taylor 1996.

2. Use of case studies offers two advantages in the study of representation. First, case studies allow us to evaluate candidates' responsiveness for districts in which public-opinion data are unavailable. Second, they allow the application of a higher standard than is commonly employed in statistical studies focusing on responsiveness or congruence. The standard employed in the case study evaluates the degree to which legislators take constituents' preferred positions. In contrast, statistical studies of responsiveness on votes in Congress, for instance, tend to only ask whether more liberal (or conservative) citizens are represented by more liberal (or conservative) legislators without requiring the legislators do what constituents wish.

3. To the extent that candidates disagree on only a small handful of issues that are of great importance to the district, studies focusing on ideological positioning seem likely to overstate the degree to which candidates will adopt similar ideological positions.

4. For convenience, I refer to both districts and states as districts in the sense of their most general meaning as legislative units.

5. When examining local legislators' behavior on zoning issues, those who represent homogeneous districts are attentive to constituents, while those who represent diverse districts vary in the degree to which they are in tune with constituents' preferences (Clinger-mayer 1994). Examining Senate trade policy, Michael Bailey and David Brady (1998) find

that legislators from more homogeneous states are strongly influenced by constituents' preferences, while those from heterogeneous states are less strongly influenced by constituents. Moreover, this general result has been extended to representation in campaigns as well (Bishin et al. 2006).

6. The final condition occurs when no district groups exist. In these cases, subconstituency politics suggest that politicians will be less likely to take position in the campaign, and when they do, the position will likely be informed by ideological or party pressures.

7. The Bush administration further tightened sanctions in July 2004, making it more difficult to travel and remit money to Cuba. Sales of foodstuffs were unaffected. In May 2008, however, cell phones were added to the list of approved items.

8. However, because new Cubans tend to assimilate into existing communities, there is no evidence that a homogeneous community consisting solely of new Cuban Americans exists.

9. Candidates' positions were obtained from two newspaper databases and the Google search engine. See Appendix 4A for more information.

10. Investigating these districts may require a larger number of cases, as news coverage may not be as comprehensive in rural regions. Moreover, a basic criterion of newsworthiness is controversy. Neither media nor challengers may be inclined to spend resources publicizing a position on which both candidates agree.

11. The states were North Dakota, Idaho, Nebraska, Montana, and Iowa. According to the 2003 American Community Survey, there are 1,193 Cuban Americans in Idaho, 299 in Iowa, 56 in Montana, 283 in Nebraska, and 157 in North Dakota. I also included House seats for states with only one district.

12. According to the 2000 Census, the south Florida districts each have Cuban American populations exceeding 5 percent of the district, making them similar to New Jersey's 13th district. I use the 5 percent threshold to determine whether a group exists.

13. For instance, Castro has a long history of refusing American offers of aid.

14. District data are taken from the U.S. Census 109th Congressional District Summary File. Data for New York is taken from the 2003 American Community Survey.

15. While the district boundaries of New Jersey's 13th district remained roughly the same between 1990 and 2000, the proportion of the district that was Cuban dropped substantially (from 48,734 in 1990 to 35,541 in 2000), suggesting there had not been a large influx of recent migrants. Unfortunately, Florida's congressional districts are not comparable over the same period because the state was awarded an additional seat following the 2000 Census.

16. Significance tests on the case-study results are calculated using the binomial distribution in which the probability of k observed successes in n trials, each of which occurs by chance at probability p.

17. This suggests a possible improvement to the model. In multi-group districts, incumbents with established positions continue to represent that group while their challengers advocate the position closest to their traditional supporters.

18. Indeed, controversy is a basic criterion of newsworthiness taught to freshman journalism students (Stephens 1993).

19. A hate crime is one motivated by race, ethnicity, gender, religion, age, nationality, disability, or sexual identity. While many states have hate-crimes legislation that extends to gays, federal law does not extend to cover those attacked because of their gender, sexual orientation, or disability. Moreover, existing laws apply only when an individual is engaged in a federally protected act such as voting.

20. For semantic ease, I use the term "gay" to refer to the broader gay, lesbian, bisexual, and transgendered community.

21. I exclude districts that are more than 50 percent African American, as social-desirability bias against gay or lesbian identity likely biases estimates of the gay population downward in these districts.

22. In cases where candidates recognize that they have no chance to win, it seems clear that the assumption that politicians try to secure the votes need to win does not hold. Robert Boatright (2004) refers to these challengers as engaging in "expressive politics," as they run to make a statement and tend to follow their personal ideologies rather than appeal to the district to maximize their support. Despite these two exceptions, subconstituency politics correctly predicted a majority of candidates' positions, including that of Billy Cartwright, a Democrat who crossed party lines to oppose extending hate-crimes protections based on sexual orientation.

23. Electoral capture (Frymer 1999; Smith 2007) occurs when groups that vote overwhelmingly for one party are exploited by that party because the opposing party has no interest in competing for that group's votes. These findings may also help to provide insight to the conclusions of scholars such as Charles Smith (2007), who contends that gays constitute a captured group. Evidence against capture would be apparent in districts dominated by gays in which the Republican candidate advocated their preferred positions. While John Den Dulk, the only candidate from such a district, voted against gay preferences in that district, the dearth of one-group gay districts makes it less clear whether gays are truly captured or whether they are victims of their relatively small size and the fact that their most ardent opponents, born-again Christians, are widely dispersed across districts.

24. $N = 788$ adults nationwide; margin of error is ± 3.5: ABC News Poll, April 22, 2007, summarized online at http://www.pollingreport.com/abortion.htm.

25. While F-You Boys are only about 7 percent of voters in our sample, Secular Warriors are about 20 percent.

26. $N = 788$ adults nationwide; the margin of error is ± 3.5: ABC News Poll, April 22, 2007, summarized online at http://www.pollingreport.com/guns.htm (accessed October 9, 2008).

27. Secular Warriors never attend church, feel threatened by religion, and show high levels of tolerance for nontraditional lifestyle choices. While these voters exist in every state, they tend to be more highly concentrated in urban areas in cosmopolitan states, and they do not own guns.

28. The districts selected for examination were those with the smallest number of F-You Boys and with the largest populations of Secular Warriors, thus creating a least likely case in that the small group has to overcome the largest possible opponent.

29. One limitation, however, is that positions are missing for candidates from three of the districts. In all three cases, the missing positions seem likely to be a function of the absence of high-quality challengers. In the closest of the three races, Tom Lantos won with "only" 75 percent of the vote.

30. The smallest difference in group size among these cases is seen in Colorado, where Secular Warriors and F-You Boys constitute 23 percent and 6 percent of the population, respectively.

31. An additional problem with the case studies is that missing data on candidates' positioning is common, and we cannot be certain that the positions that are unavailable are missing at random. If systematic processes influence whether or not we observe positions,

then the conclusions drawn from the case studies may lead to mistaken inferences about the findings.

32. Positions based on roll-call votes are ignored, as we are interested in the effect of subconstituencies on campaign positioning. One additional position was collected but not used, because opinion data from Alaska and Hawaii are unavailable.

33. Many candidates made blanket statements about opposing any new gun-control laws, for instance, but did not refer to the ban specifically. Hence, they are not included.

34. The 2004 National Annenberg Election Study asked whether respondents favored the assault-weapons ban.

35. I also note that, because Rho is not statistically significant, we cannot reject the hypothesis that the errors in the two models are not correlated.

36. Evidence suggests that this framing was successful not just in aiding the congressional passage of a partial-birth–abortion ban in 1999 and again in 2003, but also in helping to change public opinion on the abortion issue more broadly (Freedman 2003).

37. I use the National Annenberg Election Study for all estimates of Evangelicals in both states and districts. At the state level, the estimates correlate with those obtained from the National Religion Data Archive at over .9.

38. One consequence of this strategy is that, for some incumbents with well-known positions—particularly those who face only token opposition—campaign positions can be hard to obtain. As with the previous cases, all positions are based on news reports of candidates' statements outside their roll-call voting behavior.

39. Uncontested elections are omitted.

40. Unlike the case studies, this framework also enhances our ability to detect probabilistic effects (e.g., Sekhon 2004).

41. Super-Educated Women are women who hold a college degree. The Faithful are those who identified themselves as white Protestants who attend church weekly.

42. Results were also estimated using opinion data on abortion obtained from pooling the National Exit Poll results between 1992 and 2004. The results are substantively identical, although they have substantially less accurate estimates of Evangelicals.

CHAPTER 5

1. Heinz Eulau and Paul Karps (1977) refer to these as service responsiveness, symbolic responsiveness, and allocative responsiveness.

2. In general, studies that account for legislators' ideology or party find that they better explain legislators' behavior then do constituency-driven explanations. Studies that ignore these factors and account only for the average constituent's interests or preferences, however, tend to find high levels of responsiveness.

3. While seldom studied, research shows that legislators disproportionately represent groups of constituents (e.g., Bishin 2000); Clinton 2006; Dexter 1957; Fenno 1978; Fiorina 1974; Huntington 1950; MacRae 1958; Wright 1989). For example, studies show that the preferences of partisans (Wright 1989) or of partisans combined with independents (e.g., Medoff et al. 1995; Shapiro et al. 1990) explain indices of roll-call voting behavior. Moreover, legislators appeal to groups rather than to the district majority across a wide range of issues (e.g., Bishin 2000).

4. One difference between behavior in the campaign and in Congress is seen in the behavior of legislators who represent districts that have no active groups. In campaigns,

candidates from such districts have no incentive to take positions on these issues. In Congress, however, the incentives differ. Failure to cast a roll-call vote is to invite future opponents to label one an absentee. Subconstituency politics holds that these positions will be based on factors other than constituencies' preferences. Unfortunately, in these cases the theory does not provide falsifiable predictions, so these results are not presented here.

5. Only voice votes were held. We can infer the preferences of some senators from agricultural districts, however, through co-sponsorship of the travel legislation.

6. Legislators from agricultural districts have an incentive to reduce trade restrictions, but the benefit of repealing travel restrictions are less clear. In contrast, some old Cubans may want reduced travel restrictions to visit relatives but support the embargo to punish and destabilize Castro.

7. Since roll-call votes were not held in the Senate, Bill Nelson was able to avoid the tough choice between his constituents and his campaign positions.

8. Recall that significance tests are performed by evaluating the binomial probability of observing N correct predictions in k trials where each outcome has a probability of occurrence of 50 percent. Since there are only three observations, a result significant at conventional levels is not possible for the responsiveness hypothesis despite its correctly predicting every outcome.

9. Recall that the demand model holds that politicians advocate the majority-preferred position.

10. Representative Steve King, who changed his position after visiting Cuba, was the only incorrect prediction.

11. Although there are too few cases to obtain a statistically significant result ($p <$ .25).

12. In 2003, H.R. 2038, a bill reauthorizing the assault-weapons ban, was introduced and co-sponsored by 111 representatives. In 2004, supporters filed and signed a discharge petition to have H.R. 2038 reported to the floor. It garnered only seventy-two signatures. In 2005, H.R. 1312, another bill reauthorizing the assault-weapons ban, garnered ninety-four co-sponsors. It never received a vote. In 2007, H.R. 1022 reauthorizing the assault-weapons ban was introduced and had sixty co-sponsors at the time of this writing.

13. Three models of legislators' behavior are estimated to test the responsiveness and consistency hypotheses. The results in column one show the effect of constituency opinion on the vote to extend the ban. The results in column two examine the same dependent variable but employ a general measure of opinion on gun control that allows us to assess whether the results are robust across different measures of constituents' preferences. The third column examines the effects of general attitudes toward guns, as in column two, while controlling for candidates' campaign positions on gun control. Examination of general attitudes is necessary because only twenty incumbents' campaign positions on the assault-weapons ban could be identified, and of these, only four opposed the bill. Campaign positions on gun control in general are widely available, however, and as assault weapons are included in the scale, they correlate highly. Many incumbents either made no comment or made comments too general to be applied to the question of banning assault weapons. Moreover, the timing of the vote in Congress makes assessing the candidates' positions problematic. Few senators elected in 2002 spoke on the issue because the ban was still in effect at the time they ran. In addition, senators elected in 2006 have not yet been forced to take a roll-call position on the issue.

14. These estimates are obtained using Clarify (King et al. 2000).

15. Importantly, the uncertainty around these estimates tends to be higher owing partly to the smaller sample on which they are based, as campaign positions were unavailable for all incumbent senators.

16. These bills are more appropriate for comparing across chambers than is the legislation on partial-birth abortion because the theory attempts to show that legislators appeal to intense groups. Super-Educated Women are much more divided on the issue of partial-birth abortion, however, than they are on *Roe*. Hence, this issue does not seem to activate a shared identity in the same way that the issue of choice does.

17. Existing surveys have insufficient numbers of respondents to estimate subconstituencies' opinions on abortion for congressional districts.

18. Barack Obama entered the Senate in 2005 after winning election in 2004 and was not a member at the time of the vote. The second missing case was that of Joe Biden, who did not cast votes on the partial-birth–abortion ban or its amendments. In 1999, however, he voted for the identical amendment to the partial-birth–abortion ban, suggesting that he would likely support the legislation.

19. These figures are from the 2004 National Annenberg Election Study and were estimated using a gender weight based on the 2004 Current Population Survey. While examination of the sources of opinion differences across issues lies beyond the scope of this work, the point can be seen by the fact that 35 percent of Super-Educated Women strongly support banning partial-birth abortion, while only 25 percent strongly support making abortion more difficult.

20. One other abortion-related bill passed in this Congress: "Laci and Conner's Law" (H.R. 1997). However, this bill combined the abortion issue with several other issues in establishing penalties for killing a pregnant woman. In general, these results are similar to the others presented except that only *Subconstituency Opinion* is statistically significant.

21. Chamber co-sponsorship rates are in parentheses.

CHAPTER 6

1. With the notable exception of Christopher Achen (1978), very few *say* that politicians reflect all constituents equally. Instead, scholars estimate constituents' preferences using average district data that equally weight all constituents' preferences or attributes equally. Studies employing such measures thus evaluate a conceptualization of representation in which all citizens have equal influence and that presumably is sensitive to the majority preference, thus embodying the democratic values of liberalism and popular sovereignty.

2. In any system with single-member electoral districts, heterogeneity induces representational bias. Politicians can represent groups of people but cannot represent everyone when citizens disagree. I argue later that, while imperfect, substantive representation occurs when legislators act on behalf of groups.

3. Perfect substantive representation refers to the idea that legislators can act on behalf of all of the citizens in their geographic constituency.

4. While responsiveness has had a privileged place among studies of representation, it is useful to consider its limitations. A system can be highly responsive while simultaneously having large proportions of legislators who act contrary to constituents' preferences on a

majority of issues, provided that the pattern of preferences among legislators corresponds to the patterns of variation among constituencies.

5. Borrowing from Achen's regression framework: where the dependent variable is a legislator's behavior and the independent variable is the constituency's preference, this would be the case where the intercept is 0 and the slope is exactly 1.

6. The concept of heterogeneity has not been ignored. Morris Fiorina's (1974) inconclusive results have led to the investigation of the effect heterogeneity has on legislators' reelection prospects (e.g., Bond 1983; Bond et al. 2001) and on the various ways in which heterogeneity should be conceptualized (Koetzle 1998). Heterogeneity is also crucial to Richard Fenno's (1978) discussion of how members see and service their districts.

7. To date, diversity has only been examined in the context of responsiveness. Examination of other measures such as proximity will lead to different conclusions. Recall, for instance, that Achen shows that legislators from diverse districts must by definition be less proximate to their constituents.

8. Researchers also find that politicians are less responsive to groups with lower socioeconomic standing, as the views of those in the bottom third of the income distribution are "utterly irrelevant" (Bartels 2005, 14). Similarly, Martin Gilens (2005) finds that when the well-off and the poor disagree, policy outcomes reflect the preferences of the well-to-do and bear little resemblance to those of the poor.

9. District- and state-level measures of salience do not exist.

10. I use the term "district" interchangeably to refer to states and congressional districts.

11. Fenno (1978) defines the legal or "geographic" constituency as consisting of those who live within the legal boundaries of a district.

12. For purposes of illustration, we need only assume that which Fiorina (1974) has already demonstrated: when groups with strongly held preferences disagree, legislators do not take the median position between the two (which is likely to anger both) but side firmly with the group that benefits them most.

13. State-level opinion on the Cuban trade embargo is unavailable, so it cannot be examined in this context.

14. Appendix 6A describes the problem with using a binary approach and describes the nature of diversity on the issues of abortion and the Cuban trade embargo.

15. Recall that being "active" results from having an activated social identity on abortion, as established in Chapter 2. I follow the criteria established in Chapter 4 for identifying whether an active group is politically relevant in a state.

16. Virtually every state is diverse on the abortion issue, as there are few states with only one active group. On Cuban trade, in contrast, only one state and three districts are diverse.

17. All groups are identified as active based on the criteria articulated in Chapter 4.

18. The logic is seen by considering a diverse state and a homogeneous state that are dominated by The Faithful. In the homogeneous case, a candidate has an easy decision by adopting the position held by The Faithful. In the two-group state, however, the views of the non-Faithful (presumably some of whom are Super-Educated Women) pull the legislator ever so slightly toward a pro-choice position.

19. Consequently, I employ two-tailed significance tests for this analysis.

20. Of course, by predicting no difference the test provides weak evidence for evaluating the theory. However, to the extent that the results are consistent across tests, we gain increased confidence about them.

21. Recall from Chapter 4 that the farming districts are Idaho's 1st and 2nd, Iowa's 4th and 5th, Montana's 1st, Nebraska's 3rd, and North Dakota's 1st, which were selected by identifying the districts with the largest number of farmers in the states with the highest per capita levels of farmers.

22. Lacking directional hypotheses, I employ two-tailed tests.

23. Moreover, to the extent that the diversity thesis holds that responsiveness should be reduced in diverse districts, these results are opposite the expectations, though it should be noted the result is based on only one aberrant case.

24. There were no roll-call votes on abortion in the 107th Senate. These bills are the same ones examined in Chapter 5.

25. The partial-birth–abortion ban passed by the 106th Congress was vetoed by President Clinton. It was passed again in the 108th Congress and signed into law by President George Bush.

26. It is not possible to evaluate the demand model in the same way, since we cannot be sure which position is favored by the majority on each bill in these states and districts. Thus, we can only test the implications of the subconstituency politics hypothesis and the diversity thesis.

27. The 108th House also saw an amendment (H.Amdt. 772) to stop funding the enforcement of the embargo, proposed to be added to a bill ending the travel ban (S. 950). However, since the farm-state legislators have no clear reason to support ending the travel ban, the model does not make clear predictions with regard to this bill, and it is omitted from the analysis.

28. Other active pro-life religious groups, such as Catholics and Mormons, are not included in this particular active group. Because other active pro-life groups are included in the opinion estimates of the remainder of the district, these subconstituency measures are biased against the subconstituency responsiveness hypothesis. Consequently, the tests employed here are conservative.

CHAPTER 7

1. During World War I, the Ottoman Empire carried out one of the largest genocides ever recorded. Estimates suggest that between 1.2 million and 1.5 million Armenians were killed, and 500,000 more fled as refugees (Dadrian 1995).

2. The term "salience" is most synonymous with prominence or visibility but is often conflated with the concepts of importance and intensity (which are themselves frequently conflated). However, these latter terms do not share the important function that visibility does in the democratic process. The distinction is crucial because, as R. Douglas Arnold (1990) shows, skilled politicians manipulate the degree to which issues may be traceable or visible through procedural tactics to either enhance or obscure the degree to which they may get credit or blame for a bill. The distinction is also central because all bills are inherently important to someone, or else their sponsors would not go through the considerable effort required to shepherd them through the legislative process.

3. While the probability of successful retribution is exceptionally low, as noted in Chapter 3, even facing a weak challenger can be costly in terms of time and money, even if the chances of losing are hardly increased. Members of Congress are products of their communities, and taking unpopular stands may be socially costly even if they are not politically costly.

4. His results (Kingdon 1971, 43, table 2-1) show that constituency was only "a minor influence" on legislators' decisions on about half (47 percent) of the issues examined. Moreover, it should be noted that his measure of salience is not objective: "So as a rough coding, I made a judgment about how much attention the issue appeared to have received in the press, among congressmen, and among other participants in the legislative system" (Kingdon 1971, 314, app. D). One problem with such a method is that issues invisible to the public but important to members of Congress might appear quite visible using such a methodology.

5. "Thus, it would appear that representational role, as a predictive concept, becomes valuable when the issues, or policies under consideration have some minimal level of saliency among the constituents" (Kuklinski and Elling 1977, 144).

6. It is important, however, for the issue to become visible for reasons outside the legislator's control to ensure that unobserved factors are not correlated with the independent and dependent variables.

7. Non-voting delegates are not included in these analyses. The delegate from Guam withdrew co-sponsorship and is thus excluded. Opinion data are not available for legislators from Alaska or Hawaii, as the National Annenberg Election Study does not poll these states.

8. This index ranges between 0 (most conservative) and 100 (most liberal).

9. This scale ranges from 1 (very liberal) to 5 (very conservative).

10. As the influences on the withdrawal of co-sponsorship are conditional on co-sponsoring the resolution, I employ a Heckman selection model with a probit estimator on the outcome equation to estimate the influences on co-sponsorship decisions.

11. We also control for the number of bills each representative sponsored or co-sponsored in 2007. All variables are defined in Appendix 7C.

12. This result, as well as all of the other findings, holds when these variables are included separately.

13. Substantively identical results are obtained when the party variable is omitted from the outcome model.

14. Responsiveness is an aggregate measure of responsiveness and thus cannot be estimated at the district level. In contrast, proximity and centrism (e.g., Achen 1977) can be calculated for a district.

15. Multiple sets of keywords were developed for each bill. In each case, counts pertaining to the keywords that appeared most frequently were used.

16. The results are estimated using regression because the dependent variable is continuous.

17. A second visibility measure assesses the change in visibility and is calculated as the difference in the number of news stories in the year before the vote and the year before that year (i.e., two years before and one year before the vote). These results are also extremely robust to alternative specifications, such as those including different transformation of the visibility variables (e.g., visibility logged). All results are substantively identical to those presented earlier.

18. Alternatively, it is possible that there is a threshold effect for salience, as suggested by Kim Quaile Hill and Patricia Hurley (2003). To examine this possibility, I re-estimated the data by creating dummy variables that broke the votes into salient "1" and non-salient "0" at several different levels of salience (the 1 percent, 5 percent, 10 percent, and 25 percent most salient votes). The results are similar to those reported in Table 7.3.

19. I employ probit to estimate this relationship as the dependent variable is binary. *Vote* is scored "1" if the senator voted for the bill and "0" if she voted against it. *Constituent Ideology* is the constituency mean response to the ideological self-placement battery in the PSES.

20. Estimates are obtained using Clarify (King et al. 2000).

CHAPTER 8

1. If we compare Betancourt's characteristics with Al Gore's, her profile is more conducive to carrying the district in every respect except one: Gore supported the hardline positions toward Cuba that Betancourt opposed.

2. Downs's work depends on assumptions about issue intensity and issue dimensionality.

References

Abrajano, Marisa. 2005. "Who Evaluates a Presidential Candidate by Using Non-policy Campaign Messages?" *Political Research Quarterly* 58(1): 55–67.

Abrams, Dominic. 1999. "Social Identity, Social Cognition, and the Self: The Flexibility and Stability of Self-categorization." In *Social Identity and Cognition*, ed. Dominic Abrams and Michael A. Hogg. Oxford: Blackwell Publishers.

Achen, Christopher H. 1977. "Measuring Representation: Perils of the Correlation Coefficient." *American Journal of Political Science* 21(4): 805–815.

———. 1978. "Measuring Representation." *American Journal of Political Science* 22(3): 475–510.

Adams, James, Benjamin G. Bishin, and Jay K. Dow. 2004. "Representation in Congressional Campaigns: Evidence for Discounting Directional Voting in U.S. Senate Elections." *Journal of Politics* 66(2): 326–347.

Adams, James, Lawrence Ezrow, and Zeynep Somer-Topcu. 2008. "Party Policy Shifts and the Dynamics of Subconstituency Support: Evidence from Twelve Postwar Democracies." Paper presented at the annual meeting of the Midwest Political Science Association, Chicago, April 3.

Adams, William C., and Paul H. Ferber. 1980. "Measuring Legislator-Constituency Congruence: Liquor, Legislators and Linkage." *Journal of Politics* 42(1): 202–208.

Almond, Gabriel A. 1950. *The American People and Foreign Policy.* New York: Harcourt Brace.

Alston, Chuck. 1991. "Political Fallout from Thomas Vote Could Cut Any Number of Ways." *Congressional Quarterly Weekly* 49(42): 3028–3029.

Ansolabehere, Stephen, James M. Snyder Jr., and Charles Stewart III. 2001. "The Effects of Party and Preferences on Congressional Roll-Call." *Legislative Studies Quarterly* 26(4): 533–572.

Arneson, Ben A. 1927. "Do Representatives Represent?" *National Municipal Review* 16(4): 751–754.

Arnold, R. Douglas. 1990. *The Logic of Congressional Action.* New Haven, Conn.: Yale University Press.

———. 1993. "Can Inattentive Citizens Control Their Elected Representatives?" In *Congress Reconsidered,* 5th ed., ed. Lawrence C. Dodd and Bruce I. Oppenheimer. Washington, D.C.: Congressional Quarterly Press.

———. 2004. *Congress, the Press, and Political Accountability.* Princeton, N.J.: Princeton University Press.

Bailey, Michael. 2001. "Quiet Influence: The Representation of Diffuse Interests on Trade Policy, 1983–1994." *Legislative Studies Quarterly* 26(1): 45–80.

Bailey, Michael, and David Brady. 1998. "Heterogeneity and Representation: The Senate and Free Trade." *American Journal of Political Science* 42(2): 524–544.

Barone, Michael, and Grant Ujifusa. 1994. *The Almanac of American Politics.* Washington, D.C.: Congressional Quarterly Press.

Bartels, Larry. 1991. "Constituency Opinion and Congressional Policymaking: The Reagan Defense Buildup." *American Political Science Review* 85(2): 457–474.

———. 2005. "Economic Inequality and Political Representation." Unpublished ms., Princeton University, Princeton, N.J.

Baum, Matthew A. 2002. "Sex, Lies, and War: How Soft News Brings Foreign Policy to the Inattentive Public." *American Political Science Review* 96(1): 91–109.

Bendixen, Sergio. 2002. "Presentation of Cuba Study Group Poll Results." Coral Gables, Fla.: Bendixen and Associates.

Berger, Bennett M. 1960. *Working-Class Suburb: A Study of Auto Workers in Suburbia.* Berkeley: University of California Press.

Bernstein, Robert. 1989. *Elections, Representation and Congressional Voting Behavior: The Myth of Constituency Control.* Englewood Cliffs, N.J.: Prentice Hall.

Bernstein, Robert A., and William W. Anthony. 1974. "The ABM Issue in the Senate, 1968–1970: The Importance of Ideology." *American Journal of Political Science* 68: 1198–1206.

Berry, Jeffrey M. 1999. *The New Liberalism: The Rising Power of Citizen Groups.* Washington, D.C.: Brookings Institution.

"Best Political Miscalculation." 2003. *Miami New Times.* Available online at http://www.miaminewtimes.com/bestof/2003/award/best-political-miscalculation-16178 (accessed October 8, 2008).

Bianco, William T. 1994. *Trust: Representatives and Constituents.* Ann Arbor: University of Michigan Press.

Bianco, William T., John B. Spence, and John D. Wilkerson. 1996. "The Electoral Connection in the Early Congress: The Case of the Compensation Act of 1816." *American Journal of Political Science* 40(1): 145–171.

Bishin, Benjamin G. 2000. "Constituency Influence in Congress: Does Subconstituency Matter?" *Legislative Studies Quarterly* 25(3): 389–415.

———. 2003. "Democracy, Heterogeneity and Representation: Explaining Representational Differences Across States." *Legislative Studies Section Newsletter,* vol. 26, no. 1.

Bishin, Benjamin G., Jay K. Dow, and James Adams. 2006. "Does Democracy Suffer from Diversity? Issue Representation and Diversity in Senate Elections." *Public Choice* 129(1): 201–215.

Bishin, Benjamin G., and Matthew B. Incantalupo. 2008. "From Bullets to Ballots? The Role of Veterans in Contemporary Elections" Typescript, University of California, Riverside.

Bishin, Benjamin G., and David K. Park. 2008. "Evaluating Representation: Responsiveness without Representation?" Paper presented at the meeting of the Midwest Political Science Association, Chicago, April 3.

Boatright, Robert G. 2004. *Expressive Politics: Issue Strategies of Congressional Challengers.* Columbus: Ohio State University Press.

Bond, Jon R. 1983. "The Influence of Constituency Diversity on Electoral Competition in Voting for Congress, 1974–1978." *Legislative Studies Quarterly* 8(2): 201–217.

Bond, Jon R., Kristin L. Campbell, and James B. Cottrill. 2001 "The Puzzle of Constituency Diversity Revisited: Conditional Effects of District Diversity on Competition in Congressional Elections." Typescript, Texas A&M University, College Station, Tex.

Bragg, Rick, and Jose Font. 1991. "The Man Who Would Save Cuba." *St. Petersburg Times,* February 24, 1F.

Brewer, Marilyn B. 2001. "The Many Faces of Social Identity: Implications for Political Psychology." *Political Psychology* 22(1): 115–126.

Brooke, James. 1998. "Gay Man Dies from Attack, Fanning Outrage and Debate." *New York Times,* October 13, sec. A.

Burden, Barry C. 2004. "Candidate Positioning in U.S. Congressional Elections." *British Journal of Political Science* 34(2): 211–227.

———. 2007. *Personal Roots of Representation.* Princeton, N.J.: Princeton University Press.

Burstein, Paul. 2003. "The Impact of Public Opinion on Policy: A Review and an Agenda." *Political Research Quarterly* 56(1): 29–40.

Campbell, Angus, Philip E. Converse, Warren E. Miller, and Donald E. Stokes. 1960. *The American Voter.* Chicago: University of Chicago Press.

Canes-Wrone, Brandice, David W. Brady, and John F. Cogan. 2003. "Out of Step, Out of Office: Electoral Accountability and House Members' Voting." *American Political Science Review* 96(1): 127–140.

Canon, David T. 1999. *Race, Redistricting, and Representation: The Unintended Consequences of Black Majority Districts.* Chicago: University of Chicago Press.

"Caving in on Hate Crimes." 2007. *New York Times,* December 10.

"A Chance to Fight Hate: Congress Left until Next Year Legislation That Would Address Bias and Crimes against Gays and Lesbians." 2007. *Los Angeles Times,* December 24, A22.

Clausen, Aage. 1973. *How Congressmen Decide: A Policy Focus.* New York: St. Martin's Press.

Clingermayer, James C. 1994. "Electoral Representation, Zoning Politics, and the Exclusion of Group Homes." *Political Research Quarterly* 47(4): 969–984.

Clinton, Joshua D. 2006. "Representation in Congress: Constituents and Roll Calls in the 106th House." *Journal of Politics* 68(2): 397–409.

Cohen, Linda R., and Roger G. Noll. 1991. "How to Vote, Whether to Vote: Strategies for Voting and Abstaining on Congressional Roll Calls." *Political Behavior* 13(2): 97–127.

Cole, Christine. 2004. "A Challenge in the First Goli Ameri: The Iranian-Born Republican Sees Her Life Story as an Asset in Her Run for Congress." *Oregonian,* October 15, A1.

Collier, Paul. 2000. "Ethnicity, Politics and Economic Performance." *Economics and Politics* 12(3): 225–245.

Connoly, Ceci. 2000. "Lieberman Brings Energy to Gore's Presidential Bid." *Washington Post,* October 2, A8.

Converse, Phillip. 1964. "The Nature of Belief Systems in Mass Publics." In *Ideology and Discontent,* ed. David Apter. New York: Free Press.

Corral, Oscar, and Lesley Clark. 2003. "Legislators Say Cuba Letter May Get Results." *Miami Herald,* August 12, 1A.

———. 2004. "Bush Hispanics Wary over Cuba." *Miami Herald,* March 19, 3B.

Cox, Gary, and Mathew McCubbins. 1993. *Legislative Leviathan: Party Government in the House.* Berkeley: University of California Press.

———. 2004. *Setting the Agenda: Responsible Party Governments in the U.S.* Cambridge: Cambridge University Press.

Crane, Wilder W., Jr. 1960. "Do Representatives Represent?" *Journal of Politics* 22(2): 295–299.

Cuba Study Group. 2002. "Public Opinion Survey of the Cuban American Community," Bendixen and Associates, Miami, April.

Cutler, R. J., and David Van Taylor, dirs. 1996. *A Perfect Candidate.* Arpie Films.

Dadrian, Vahahn N. 1995. *The History of the Armenian Genocide: Ethnic Conflict from the Balkans to Anatolia to the Caucasus.* Oxford: Berghan Books.

Dahl, Robert A. 1950. *Congress and Foreign Policy.* New York: Harcourt Brace.

———. 1956. *A Preface to Democratic Theory.* Chicago: University of Chicago Press.

———. 2006. *A Preface to Democratic Theory,* expanded ed. Chicago: University of Chicago Press.

Dale, Mary Claire. 2002. "Democratic Power Couple's Lives Unravel over Guilty Plea to $10 Million Fraud." Associated Press, September 30.

Davies, Frank. 2001. "Poll Finds Americans Support Business with, Travel to Cuba." *Miami Herald,* April 18.

Delli Carpini, Michael X., and Scott Keeter. 1996. *What Americans Know about Politics and Why It Matters.* New Haven, Conn.: Yale University Press.

Dennis, Christopher, Marshall H. Medoff, and M. N. Gagnier. 1998. "The Impact of Racially Disproportionate Outcomes on Public Policy: The U.S. Senate and the Death Penalty." *Social Science Journal* 13: 169–181.

Dexter, Anthony L. 1957. "The Representative and His District." *Human Organization* 16(1): 2–13.

Downs, Anthony. 1957. *An Economic Theory of Democracy.* New York: Harper and Row.

Elling, Richard C. 1982. "Ideological Change in the U.S. Senate: Time and Electoral Responsiveness." *Legislative Studies Quarterly* 7(1): 75–92.

Enelow, James, and Melvin Hinich. 1984. *The Spatial Theory of Voting.* Cambridge: Cambridge University Press.

Epstein, Lee, and Jeffrey A. Segal. 2000. "Measuring Issue Salience." *American Journal of Political Science* 44(1): 66–83.

Erikson, Robert S. 1978. "Constituency Opinion and Congressional Behavior: A Reexamination of the Miller-Stokes Representation Data." *American Journal of Political Science* 22(3): 511–535.

Erikson, Robert S., Norman R. Luttbeg, and William V. Holloway. 1975. "Knowing One's District: How Legislators Predict Referendum Voting." *American Journal of Political Science* 19(2): 231–246.

Erikson, Robert S., Gerald C. Wright, and John P. McIver. 1993. *State House Democracy: Public Policy and Policy in the American States.* Cambridge: Cambridge University Press.

Eulau, Heinz, William Buchanan, Leroy Ferguson, and John C. Wahlke. 1959. "The Political Socialization of American State Legislators." *Midwest Journal of Political Science* 3(2): 188–206.

Eulau, Heinz, and Paul D. Karps. 1977. "The Puzzle of Representation: Specifying Components of Responsiveness." *Legislative Studies Quarterly* 2(3): 233–254.

"FDA Places Vitamins under Regulations to Limit Health Claims." 1993. *Los Angeles Times,* December 26, H10.

Fenno, Richard F. 1978. *Home Style: Representation in Their Districts.* Boston: Little Brown.

———. 1996. *Senators on the Campaign Trail: The Politics of Representation.* Norman: University of Oklahoma Press.

Finifter, Ada. 1974. "The Friendship Group as a Protective Environment for Political Deviants." *American Political Science Review* 68(2): 607–625.

Fiorina, Morris P. 1974. *Representatives, Roll Calls, and Constituencies.* Lexington, Mass.: Lexington Books.

Firestone, David. 2000. "46,000 March on South Carolina to Bring Down Confederate Flag." *New York Times,* January 18, A14.

Florio, Gwen. 2004. "Boycott Revived: Candidate's Stance Has Gays Protesting Brewery." *Rocky Mountain News,* June 7, 5A.

Freedman, Paul. 2003. "Partial Victory: The Power of an Unenforced Abortion Ban." Available online at http://www.slate.com (accessed December 9, 2003).

Froman, Lewis A. 1963. *Congressmen and Their Constituencies.* Chicago: Rand McNally.

Frymer, Paul. 1999. *Uneasy Alliances: Race and Party Competition in America.* Princeton, N.J.: Princeton University Press.

Gates, Gary J. 2006. *Same-Sex Couples and the Gay, Lesbian, Bisexual Population: New Estimates from the American Community Survey.* Los Angeles: Williams Institute Press.

"Gay Issue Causes Little Pain for Santorum, Quinnipiac Poll Finds." 2003. September 24. Available online at http:// www.quinnipiac.edu/x6163.xml (accessed July 7, 2008).

Geertz, Clifford. 1973. *The Interpretation of Cultures: Selected Essays.* New York: Basic Books.

Gerber, Alan, and Neil Malhotra. 2008. "Can Political Science Literatures Be Believed? A Study of Publication Bias in the *APSR* and *AJPS.*" Available online at http://polmeth.wustl.edu/retrieve.php?id=640 (accessed March 3, 2008).

Gilens, Martin. 2005. "Inequality and Democratic Responsiveness." *Public Opinion Quarterly* 69(5): 778–896.

Gizzy, John. 2006. "John Den Dulk versus Barbara Lee." Available online at www.humanevents.com (accessed March 8, 2008).

Gleek, L. E. 1947. "Ninety-Six Congressmen Make Up Their Minds." *Public Opinion Quarterly* 4(1): 3–24.

Goff, Brian L., and Kevin B. Grier. 1993. "On the (Mis)measurement of Legislator Ideology and Shirking." *Public Choice* 76(1–2): 5–20.

Green, Donald, Bradley Palmquist, and Eric Schickler. 2002. *Partisan Hearts and Minds: Political Parties and the Social Identities of Voters.* New Haven, Conn.: Yale University Press.

Greenberg, Stanley. 2004. *The Two Americas: Our Current Political Deadlock and How to Break It.* New York: Thomas Dunne Books.

Griffin, John D., and Brian Newman. 2005. "Are Voters Better Represented?" *Journal of Politics* 67(4): 1206–1227.

Gronke, Paul. 2001. *The Electorate, the Campaign, and the Office: A Unified Approach to Senate and House Elections.* Ann Arbor: University of Michigan Press.

Groseclose, Tim. 2001. "A Model of Candidate Location When One Candidate Has a Valence Advantage." *American Journal of Political Science* 45(4): 862–886.

Gulati, Girish J. 2004. "Revisiting the Link Between Electoral Competition and Policy Extremism in the U.S. Congress." *American Politics Research* 32(5): 495–520.

Hall, Richard L. 1996. *Participation in Congress.* New Haven, Conn.: Yale University Press.

Hamburger, Tom, and Peter Wallsten. 2006. "GOP Mines Data for Every Tiny Block." *Los Angeles Times,* September 24, A1.

Hamilton, Alexander, James Madison, and John Jay. 2003. *The Federalist Papers,* ed. Clinton Rossiter. New York: Penguin Group.

Hansen, John Mark. 1991. *Gaining Access: Congress and the Farm Lobby, 1919–1981.* Chicago: University of Chicago Press.

Hayes, Danny. 2005. "Candidate Qualities through a Partisan Lens: A Theory of Trait Ownership." *American Journal of Political Science* 49(4): 908–923.

Hero, Rodney E., and Caroline J. Tolbert. 1995a. "Dealing with Diversity: Racial/Ethnic Context and Social Policy Change." *Political Research Quarterly* 54(3): 571–604.

———. 1995b. "Latinos and Substantive Representation in the U.S. House of Representatives: Direct, Indirect, or Nonexistent?" *American Journal of Political Science* 39(3): 640–652.

Higgs, Robert. 1989. "Do Legislators' Votes Reflect Constituency Preference? A Simple Way to Evaluate the Senate." *Public Choice* 63(2): 175–181.

Hill, Kim Quaile, and Patricia Hurley. 1999. "Dyadic Representation Reappraised." *American Journal of Political Science* 7(1): 109–137.

Hinich, Melvin J., and Michael C. Munger. 1997. *Ideology and the Theory of Political Choice.* Ann Arbor: University of Michigan Press.

Hogg, Michael A. 2006. "Social Identity Theory." In *Contemporary Social Psychological Theories,* ed. Peter J. Burke. Stanford, Calif.: Stanford University Press.

Holian, David B., Timothy B. Krebs, and Michael H. Walsh. 1997. "Constituency Opinion, Ross Perot, and Roll-Call Behavior in the U.S. House: The Case of the NAFTA." *Legislative Studies Quarterly* 22(3): 369–392.

Huddy, Leonie. 2001. "From Social to Political Identity: A Critical Examination of Social Identity Theory." *Political Psychology* 22(1): 127–156.

Huddy, Leonie, Stanley Feldman, Charles Taber, and Gallya Lahav. 2002. "The Politics of Threat: Cognitive and Affective Reactions to 9/11." Paper presented at the annual meeting of the American Political Science Association, Boston, August 30.

———. 2005. "Threat, Anxiety, and Support of Antiterrorism Policies." *American Journal of Political Science* 4(3): 593–608.

Huntington, Samuel P. 1950. "A Revised Theory of American Party Politics." *American Political Science Review* 44(3): 669–677.

Hurley, Patricia A., and Kim Quaile Hill. 2003. "Beyond the Demand-Input Model: A Theory of Representational Linkages." *Journal of Politics* 65(2): 304–326.

Huse, Carl. 2007. "U.S. and Turkey Thwart Armenian Genocide Bill." *New York Times,* October 26. Available online at http://www.nytimes.com/2007/10/26/washington/26cong.html?_r=1&scp=1&sq=U.S%20and%20Turkey%20Thwart%20Armenian%20Genocide%20Bill.&st=cse&oref=slogin (accessed October 8, 2008).

Hutchings, Vincent L. 1998. "Issue Salience and Support for Civil Rights Legislation among Southern Democrats." *Legislative Studies Quarterly* 23(4): 521–544.

———. 2001. "Political Context, Issue Salience, and Selective Attentiveness: Constituent Knowledge of the Clarence Thomas Confirmation Vote." *Journal of Politics* 63(3): 846–868.

———. 2003. *Public Opinion and Democratic Accountability: How Citizens Learn about Politics.* Princeton, N.J.: Princeton University Press.

Hutchings, Vincent L., Harwood McKlerking, and Guy Uriel Charles. 2004. "Congressional Representation of Black Interests: Recognizing the Importance of Stability." *Journal of Politics* 66(2): 450–468.

Iyengar, Shanto, and Adam Simon. 2000. "New Perspectives and Evidence on Political Communication and Campaign Effects." *Annual Review of Psychology* 51(1): 149–169.

Iyengar, Shanto, and Nicholas A. Valentino. 2000. "Who Says What? Source Credibility as a Mediator of Campaign Advertising." In *Elements of Reason: Cognition, Choice, and the Bounds of Rationality,* ed. Arthur Lupia, Mathew D. McCubbins, and Samuel L. Popkin. New York: Cambridge University Press.

Jackson, John E. 1971. "Statistical Models of Senate Roll Call Voting." *American Political Science Review* 65(2): 451–470.

Jackson, John E., and David C. King. 1989. "Public Goods, Private Interests, and Representation." *American Political Science Review* 83(4): 1143–1164.

Jacobson, Gary C. 1983. *The Politics of Congressional Elections.* Washington, D.C.: Congressional Quarterly Press.

Jelen, Ted G., and Clyde Wilcox. 2003. "Causes and Consequences of Public Attitudes toward Abortion: A Review and Research Agenda." *Political Research Quarterly* 56(4): 489–500.

Jones, Bryan D. 1973. "Competitiveness, Role Orientations, and Legislative Responsiveness." *Journal of Politics* 35(4): 924–947.

Jones, David R. 2003. "Position-Taking and Position Avoidance in the U.S. Senate." *Journal of Politics* 65(3): 851–863.

Kahn, Kim Fridkin, and Patrick J. Kenney. 1999. *The Spectacle of U.S. Senate Campaigns.* Princeton, N.J.: Princeton University Press.

Kalt, Joseph P., and Mark A. Zupan. 1984. "Capture and Ideology in the Economic Theory of Politics." *American Economic Review* 74(3): 279–300.

Katz, Daniel. 1960. "The Functional Approach to the Study of Attitudes." *Public Opinion Quarterly* 24(2): 163–204.

Kau, James B., and Paul H. Rubin. 1979. "Self-Interest, Ideology, and Logrolling in Congressional Voting." *Journal of Law and Economics* 22: 365–384.

———. 1993. "Ideology, Voting, and Shirking." *Public Choice* 76: 151–172.

Keith, Bruce E., Candice J. Nelson, Elizabeth Orr, Mark C. Westlye, and Raymond E. Wolfinger. 1992. *The Myth of the Independent Voter.* Los Angeles: University of California Press.

Kenworthy, Tom. 1998. "Hundreds Gather to Remember Slain Man as 'Light to the World.'" *Washington Post,* October 17, A3.

Key, V. O. 1963. *Public Opinion and American Democracy.* New York: Alfred A. Knopf.

"Key Votes: Economy, Events Overseas Drive '91 Confrontations." 1991. *Congressional Quarterly Weekly* 49(52): 3763.

Keyes, William. 1989. "Blacks the GOP Can 'Micro-Target.'" *Chicago Tribune,* March 30, A23.

Kinder, Donald R., and D. Roderick Kiewiet. 1979. "Economic Discontent and Political Behavior: The Role of Personal Grievances and Collective Economic Judgments in Congressional Voting." *American Journal of Political Science* 23(3): 495–527.

King, Gary, Michael Tomz, and Jason Wittenberg. 2000. "Making the Most of Statistical Analyses: Improving Interpretation and Presentation." *American Journal of Political Science* 44(2): 347–361.

Kingdon, John W. 1971. *Congressmen's Voting Decisions.* Ann Arbor: University of Michigan Press.

Koetzle, William. 1998. "The Impact of Constituency Diversity upon the Competitiveness of U.S. House Elections, 1962–96." *Legislative Studies Quarterly* 23(4): 561–573.

Koger, Gregory. 2003. "Position Taking and Cosponsorship in the U.S. House." *Legislative Studies Quarterly* 28(2): 225–246.

Kramer, Jeff. 1992. "Elections: 29th Congressional District Waxman Takes Flak." *Los Angeles Times,* October 22, J1.

Krehbiel, Keith. 1991. "Constituency Characteristics and Legislative Preferences." *Public Choice* 76(1–2): 21–37.

———. 1993. "Where's the Party?" *British Journal of Political Science* 23(4): 235–266.

———. 1999. "The Party Effect from A to Z and Beyond." *Journal of Politics* 61(3): 832–840.

Kuklinski, James H. 1978. "Representativeness and Elections: A Policy Analysis." *American Political Science Review* 72(1): 165–177.

———. 2007. "The Limits of Facts in Citizen Decision-Making." *Extensions* 15(2): 5–8.

Kuklinski, James H., and Richard C. Elling. 1977. "Representational Role, Constituency Opinion, and Legislative Roll-Call Behavior." *American Journal of Political Science* 21(1): 135–147.

Lacy, Dean, and Philip Paolino. 1998. "Downsian Voting and the Separation of Powers." *American Journal of Political Science* 42(4): 1180–1199.

———. 1999. "Downsian Voting and the Separation of Powers in the 1998 Ohio and Texas Gubernatorial Elections." Paper presented at the annual meeting of the Midwest Political Science Association, Chicago, April 15–17.

Langer, Gary. 2004. "A Question of Values." *New York Times,* November 6, A19.

Lasswell, Harold D. 1936. *Politics: Who Gets What, When, How.* Cleveland: Meridian Books.

Lau, Richard R., and David P. Redlawsk. 2006. *How Voters Decide: Information Processing during Election Campaigns.* Cambridge: Cambridge University Press.

Lavine, Howard, John L. Sullivan, Eugene Borgida, and Cynthia J. Thomsen. 1996. "The Relationship of National and Personal Issue Salience to Attitude Accessibility on Foreign and Domestic Policy Issues." *Political Psychology* 17(2): 293–316.

Lebo, Mathew J., Adam J. McGlynn, and Gregory Koger. 2006. "Strategic Party Government: Party Influence in Congress." *American Journal of Political Science* 51(3): 464–481.

Lewis, Jeffrey B., and Gary King. 2000. "No Evidence on Directional versus Proximity Voting." *Political Analysis* 8(1): 21–34.

Lindsay, James M. 1990. "Parochialism, Policy, and Constituency Constraints: Congressional Voting on Strategic Weapons Systems." *American Journal of Political Science* 34: 936–960.

Lindsay, James M., and Randall B. Ripley. 1992. "Foreign and Defense Policy in Congress: A Research Agenda for the 1990s." *Legislative Studies Quarterly* 17(3): 417–449.

Lowell, A. Lawrence. 1902. "The Influence of Party on Legislation in England and America." *Annual Report of the American Historical Association, 1901* 1(3): 321–542.

Lublin, David. 1997. *The Paradox of Representation: Racial Interests and Minority Representation in Congress.* Princeton, N.J.: Princeton University Press.

———. 1999. "Racial Redistricting and African-American Representation: A Critique of 'Do Majority-Minority Districts Maximize Substantive Black Representation in Congress?'" *American Political Science Review* 93(1): 183–186.

Ly, Phuong, and Hamil R. Harris. 2004. "Blacks, Gays in Struggle of Values." *Washington Post,* March 15, B01.

MacRae, Duncan. 1958. *Dimensions of Congressional Voting: A Statistical Study of the House of Representatives in the 81st Congress.* Berkeley: University of California Press.

Mansbridge, Jane. 2003. "Rethinking Representation." *American Political Science Review* 97(4): 515–528.

March, William. 2002. "Cubans Remain Potent Political Force." *Tampa Tribune,* August 4, Nation/World sec., 1.

Mayhew, David. 1974. *Congress: The Electoral Connection.* New Haven, Conn.: Yale University Press.

———. 1991. *Divided We Govern.* New Haven, Conn.: Yale University Press.

McCrone, Donald J., and James H. Kuklinski. 1979. "The Delegate Theory of Representation." *American Journal of Political Science* 23(2): 278–300.

McDermott, Monika L. 1997. "Voting Cues in Low-Information Elections: Candidate Gender as a Social Information Variable in Contemporary United States Elections." *American Journal of Political Science* 41(1): 270–283.

McKelvey, Richard D., and Peter C. Ordeshook. 1976. "Symmetric Spatial Games without Majority Rule Equilibria." *American Political Science Review* 70(4): 1172–1184.

McManus, Doyle, and Maura Reynolds. 2004. "GOP Focus Is Already Fixed on Endgame; Strategists' Grass-Roots Plans to Reelect Bush Are Well Ahead of Schedule. The Emphasis Is Not on Swing Voters, but Loyal Republicans." *Los Angeles Times,* February 1, A1.

Medoff, Marshall H. 1989. "Constituency, Ideologies and the Demand for Abortion Legislation." *Public Choice* 60(2): 185–191.

Medoff, Marshall H., Christopher Dennis, and Benjamin G. Bishin. 1995. "The Impact of Legislator and Constituency: Ideology on Voting." *Journal of Socio-Economics* 24(4): 585–592.

Merrill, Samuel, III, and Bernard Grofman. 1999. *A Unified Theory of Voting: Directional and Proximity Models.* Cambridge: Cambridge University Press.

Milbank, Dana. 2007. "Belatedly, the House's History Lesson." *Washington Post.* October 11, A2.

Miller, Warren, and Donald E. Stokes. 1963. "Constituency Influence in Congress." *American Political Science Review* 57(1): 45–56.

Mullin, Jim. 2000. "The Burden of a Violent History." *Miami New Times,* April 20. Available online at http://www.miaminewtimes.com/2000-04-20/news/mullin (accessed October 12, 2008).

National Annenberg Election Study. 2004. Annenberg School for Communication, Annenberg Public Policy Center, University of Pennsylvania.

Nielsen, Kirk. 2002. "Politics and Parties and Power: How to Campaign in the New House District 25? There Is Always Cuba." *Miami New Times,* October 31. Available online at http://www.miaminewtimes.com/2002-10-31/news/politics-parties-power (accessed October 12, 2008).

Nusbaumer, Stuart. 2003. "Bush Opposes Cheaper Drugs for Americans." *Intervention Magazine,* June 21. Available online at http://www.interventionmag.com/cms/index .php?name=News&file=article&sid=424 (accessed October 12, 2008).

Olson, Mancur. 1971. *The Logic of Collective Action.* Cambridge, Mass.: Harvard University Press.

Oppenheimer, Andres. 2002. "Poll Says Cuban Exiles Shifting from Hard-Line Positions." *Miami Herald,* May 17, 1A.

Overby, L. Marvin. 1991. "Assessing Constituency Influence: Congressional Voting on the Nuclear Freeze, 1982–83." *Legislative Studies Quarterly* 16(2): 297–312.

Page, Benjamin I., and Robert Y. Shapiro. 1993. *The Rational Public: Fifty Years of Trends in Americans' Policy Preferences.* Chicago: University of Chicago Press.

Page, Benjamin I., Robert Y. Shapiro, Paul W. Gronke, and Robert M. Rosenberg. 1984. "Constituency, Party and Representation in Congress." *Public Opinion Quarterly* 48(4): 741–756.

Peltzman, Sam. 1984. "Constituent Interest and Congressional Voting." *Journal of Law and Economics* 27(1): 181–210.

Petrocik, John R. 1974. "An Analysis of Intransitivities in the Index of Party Identification." *Political Methodology* 1(3): 31–47.

———. 1996. "Issue Ownership in Presidential Elections, with a 1980 Case Study." *American Journal of Political Science* 40(3): 825–850.

Pianan, Eric, and Karen DeYoung. 2000. "Easing of Cuba Embargo Likely." *Washington Post,* June 21, A1.

Pianan, Eric, and Dan Morgan. 2000. "Deal Reached to Allow Food Sales to Cuba." *Washington Post,* October 6, A1.

Pinney, Neil, and George Serra. 1999. "The Congressional Black Caucus and Vote Cohesion: Placing the Caucus within House Voting Patterns." *Political Research Quarterly* 52(3): 583–608.

Pitkin, Hannah Fenichel. 1967. *The Concept of Representation.* Berkeley: University of California Press.

"Poll: 63 Percent in Florida Oppose Intervention in Schiavo Case." 2005. Associated Press State and Local Wire, March 25.

Poole, Keith T., and Howard Rosenthal. 1997. *Congress: A Political History of Roll Call Voting.* New York: Oxford University Press.

Rabinowitz, George, and Stuart Elaine MacDonald. 1989. "A Directional Theory of Issue Voting." *American Political Science Review* 89(1): 93–121.

Rabushka, Alvin, and Kenneth A. Shepsle. 1972. *Politics in Plural Societies: A Theory of Democratic Instability.* Stanford, Calif.: Stanford University Press.

Rice, Stuart. 1928. *Quantitative Methods in Politics.* New York: Alfred A. Knopf.

Rohde, David W. 1991. *Parties and Leaders in the Post-reform House.* Chicago: University of Chicago Press.

Rosenstone, Steven J., and John Mark Hansen. 2003. *Mobilization, Participation, and Democracy in America.* New York: Longman Publishers.

Rufty, Bill. 1998. "Ease Sanctions on Cuba, Poll Shows." *Ledger* (Lakeland, Fla.), March 21, A1.

Schaffner, Brian F. 2005. "Priming Gender: Campaigning on Women's Issues in U.S. Senate Elections." *American Journal of Political Science* 49(4): 803–817.

Schattschneider, E. E. 1960. *The Semisovereign People: A Realist's View of Democracy in America.* New York: Wadsworth Press.

Schiller, Wendy J. 2000. *Partners and Rivals: Representation in U.S. Senate Delegations.* Princeton, N.J.: Princeton University Press.

Schwartz, John. 1993. "Lawmakers Get Avalanche of Letters about Agency's Regulation of Dietary Supplements." *Washington Post,* December 7, A23.

Sears, David O., Carl P. Hensler, and Leslie K. Speer. 1979. "Whites' Opposition to Busing: Self-Interest or Symbolic Politics?" *American Political Science Review* 73(2): 369–384.

Sears, David O., and Richard R. Lau. 1983. "Inducing Apparently Self-interested Preferences." *American Journal of Political Science* 27(2): 223–252.

Sebnem, Arsu, and Brian Knowlton. 2007. "Planned House Vote on Armenian Massacre Angers Turks." *New York Times,* March 29. Available online at http://www.nytimes.com/2007/03/30/washington/30turkey.html (accessed October 12, 2008).

Sekhon, Jasjeet S. 2004. "Quality Meets Quantity: Case Studies, Conditional Probability, and Counterfactuals." *Perspectives on Politics* 2(2): 281–293.

Shannon, W. Wayne. 1968. *Party, Constituency and Congressional Voting.* Baton Rouge: Louisiana State University Press.

Shapiro, Catherine R., David W. Brady, Richard A. Brody, and John A. Ferejohn. 1990. "Linking Constituency Opinion and Senate Voting Scores: A Hybrid Explanation." *Legislative Studies Quarterly* 15(4): 599–621.

Sheinn, Aaron Gould. 2004. "Beasley's Past Dogs Him in Runoff." *The State* (Columbia, S.C.), June 20, D1.

Shepsle, Kenneth. 1978. *The Giant Jigsaw Puzzle.* Chicago: University of Chicago Press.

Sherif, Muzafer, and Hadley Cantril. 1947. *The Psychology of Ego-Involvements: Social Attitudes and Identifications.* New York: John Wiley and Sons.

Sherif, Mufazer, and Carl I. Hovland. 1961. *Social Judgment.* New Haven, Conn.: Yale University Press.

Shotts, Kenneth W. 2003. "Does Racial Redistricting Cause Conservative Policy Outcomes? Policy Preferences of Southern Representatives in the 1980s and 1990s." *Journal of Politics* 65(1): 216–226.

Singh, B. Krishna, and Peter J. Leahy. 1978. "Contextual and Ideological Dimensions of Attitudes toward Discretionary Abortion." *Demography* 15(3): 381–388.

Smith, Charles A. 2007. "The Electoral Capture of Gay and Lesbian Americans: Advice and Implications from the 2004 Elections" *Studies in Law, Politics, and Society* 40: 103–121.

Smith, Steven S. 2000. "Positive Theories of Congressional Parties." *Legislative Studies Quarterly* 25(2): 193–215.

"Sources Say Police Nearly Faced Off over Schiavo." 2004. Associated Press State and Local Wire, March 25.

Stephens, Mitchell. 1993. *Broadcast News,* 3rd ed. New York: Harcourt Brace.

Stets, Jan E., and Peter J. Burke. 2000. "Identity Theory and Social Identity Theory." *Social Psychology Quarterly* 63(3): 224–237.

Stimson, James A., Michael B. MacKuen, and Robert S. Erikson. 1995. "Dynamic Representation." *American Political Science Review* 89(3): 543–565.

Sulkin, Tracy. 2005. *Issue Politics in Congress.* New York: Cambridge University Press.

Sullivan, John L. 1973. "Political Correlates of Social, Economic, and Religious Diversity in the American States." *Journal of Politics* 35(1): 70–84.

Sunstein, Cass R. 2003. *Why Societies Need Dissent.* Cambridge: Harvard University Press.

Tajfel, Henri, and John C. Turner. 1986. "The Social Identity Theory of Inter-Group Behavior." In *Psychology of Intergroup Relations,* ed. S. Worchel and L. W. Austin. Chicago: Nelson-Hall.

Terry, Deborah J., Michael A. Hogg, and Julie M. Duck. 1999. "Group Membership, Social Identity and Attitudes." In *Social Identity and Cognition,* ed. Dominic Abrams and Michael A. Hogg. Oxford: Blackwell Publishers.

Theriault, Sean M. 2005. *The Power of the People: Congressional Competition, Public Attention, and Voter Retribution.* Columbus: Ohio State University Press.

Truman, David B. 1951. *The Governmental Process: Political Interests and Public Opinion.* New York: Alfred A. Knopf.

Turner, Jon C., Michael A. Hogg, Penelope J. Oakes, Stephen D. Reicher, and Margaret S. Wetherell. 1987. *Rediscovering the Social Group: A Self-Categorization Theory.* Oxford: Basil Blackwell.

Uslaner, Eric M. 1999. *The Movers and the Shirkers.* Ann Arbor: University of Michigan Press.

van Knippenberg, Daan. 1999. "Social Identity and Persuasion: Reconsidering the Role of Group Membership." In *Social Identity and Cognition,* ed. Dominic Abrams and Michael A. Hogg. Oxford: Blackwell Publishers.

Veiga, Alex. 2000. "Poll: South Florida Cubans Favor Travel to Homeland, Dialogue." Associated Press, November 26.

Von Drehle, David. 2000. "Get Out the Vote Drive Goes into High Gear as Campaign Ends." *Washington Post,* November 7. Available online at http://community.seattle times.nwsource.com/archive/?date=20001107&slug=4051686 (accessed October 12, 2008).

———. 2004. "Political Split Is Pervasive." *Washington Post,* April 25, A1.

Wahlke, John C. 1971 "Policy Demands and System Support: The Role of the Represented." *British Journal of Political Science* 1(3): 271–290.

Wallsten, Peter. 2003. "Kerry Calls for Maintenance of Current Cuba Sanctions." *Miami Herald,* September 1, 1A.

Weissberg, Robert. 1978. "Collective versus Dyadic Representation in Congress." *American Political Science Review* 72(2): 535–547.

———. 1979. "Assessing Legislator–Constituency Policy Agreement." *Legislative Studies Quarterly* 4(4): 605–622.

Whitby, Kenny H. 1997. *The Color of Representation: Congressional Behavior and Black Interests.* Ann Arbor: University of Michigan Press.

White, William S. 1956. *Citadel: The Story of the U.S. Senate.* New York: Harper and Brothers.

Wilkerson, John D. 1990. "Reelection and Representation in Conflict: The Case of Agenda Manipulation." *Legislative Studies Quarterly* 15(2): 263–282.

Williams, Lena August. 1992. "A Correction: No Plan to Curb High Potency Vitamins as Drugs." *New York Times,* August 16. Available online at http://query.nytimes.com/gst/fullpage.html?res=9F0CEFDA103EF935A2575BC0A964958260&sec=&spon=&page wanted=1 (accessed October 12, 2008).

Wilson, William J. 1987. *The Truly Disadvantaged: The Inner City, the Underclass, and Public Policy.* Chicago: University of Chicago Press.

Wlezien, Christopher. 1995. "The Public as Thermostat: Dynamics of Preferences for Spending." *American Journal of Political Science* 39(4): 981–1000.

———. 1996. "Dynamics of Representation: The Case of U.S. Spending on Defence." *British Journal of Political Science* 26(1): 81–103.

Wolpert, Robin, and James M. Gimpel. 1997. "Information, Recall, and Accountability: The Electorate's Response to the Clarence Thomas Nomination." *Legislative Studies Quarterly* 22(4): 535–550.

Wright, Gerald R. 1989. "Policy Voting in the U.S. Senate: Who Is Represented?" *Legislative Studies Quarterly* 24(4): 465–486.

Zollo, Cathy. 2002. "Election 2002: Mario Diaz-Balart Claims District 25 House Seat." *Naples Daily News,* November 6. Available online at http://www.naplesnews.com/02/11/naples/d853331a.htm (accessed September 12, 2003).

Index

Benjamin G. Bishin is Associate Professor of Political Science at the University of California, Riverside.